Nikon F4

and F3

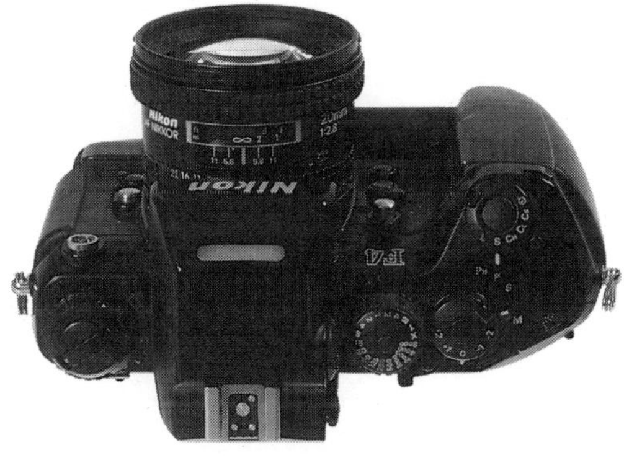

Heiner Henniges

HOVE~FOUNTAIN BOOKS

Nikon F4 and F3

First English Edition October 1989
English Translation: Rols Kruger, Nikon, Germany
Translation Editor: Georgina Fuller
Technical Editor: George Wakefield
Sub-editing & Design: Shirley Kilpatrick
Typeset by Icon Publications Limited, Kelso, Scotland
Printed in Germany by Kösel GmbH, Kempten

ISBN 0-86343-235-2

Published by
HOVE FOUNTAIN BOOKS
the joint imprint of

Fountain Press Ltd
45 The Broadway, Tolworth
Surrey KT6 7DW

&

Hove Foto Books
34 Church Road, Hove
Sussex BN3 2GJ

UK Trade Distribution by
Fountain Press Ltd

Contents

contd over/

CONTENTS

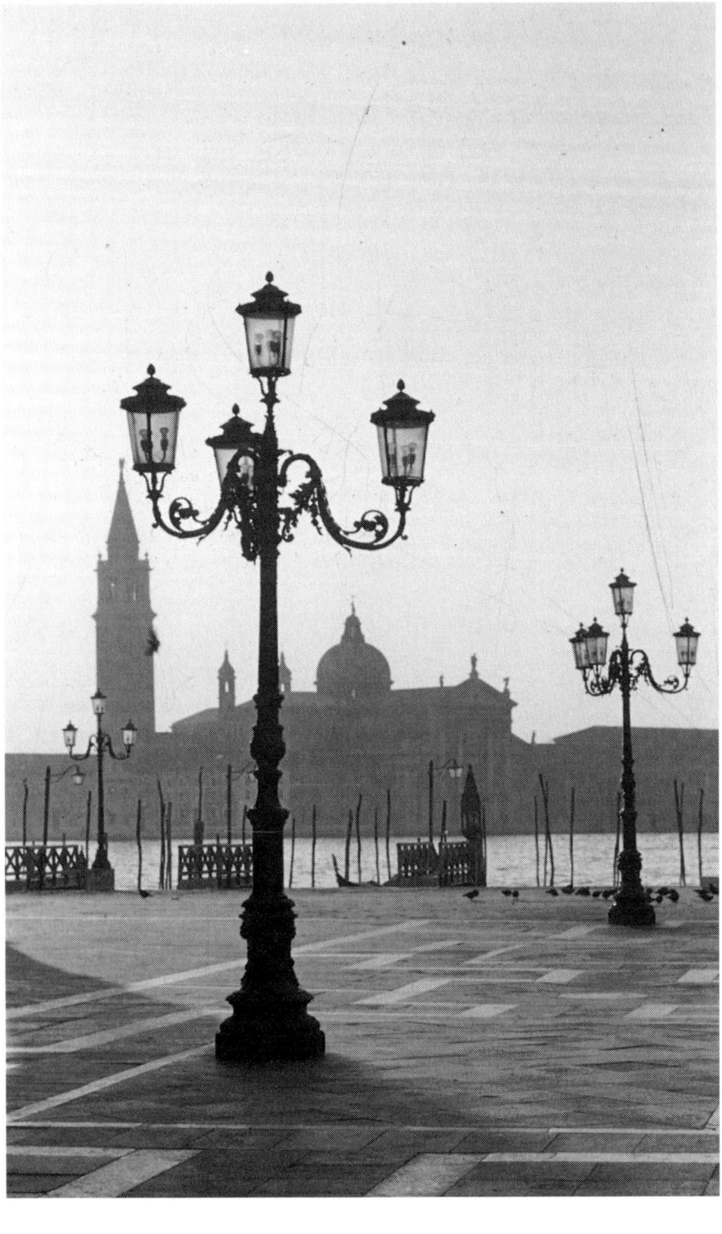

The Professional

Ever since the first Nikon F was introduced in 1959, Nikon cameras have been the equipment preferred by professionals. For the past thirty years photographers have recorded events all over the world using Nikon cameras. They were at all major sporting events. Whenever important leaders met, the camera was a witness. They accompanied astronauts into outer space as well as explorers on expeditions to the last frontiers of the earth. They documented wars and catastrophes, but they also brought many beautiful aspects of the world to our attention. They supported scientists in recording the results of their research and satisfied the constant hunger of magazines for ever more spectacular photographs. Whether it was fashion, advertisement or photojournalism – the pictures made by Nikon photographers brought the world events closer. It is not an exaggeration to say that pictures supplied by Nikon photographers have contributed decisively to the way we see the world today.

Thirty years of experience in producing professional cameras as well as the experience of the world's best photographers are built into the latest top model by Nikon. The Nikon engineers created the most modern autofocus single lens reflex camera of all – the Nikon F4. This achievement becomes even more admirable considering the fact they managed to retain the compatibility with the existing F system. The Nikon F4 bayonet mount allows the use of almost all of the manual focusing Nikkor lenses ever produced. Tens of thousands of Nikon photographers can continue to use their array of lenses when they decide to switch over to the F4. This is not just a financial advantage. In many situations autofocus is faster, more accurate and safer. There are cases though, where manual focusing is necessary. In addition, special lenses such as shift lenses for perspective correction, PC Nikkors, or macro equipment are only available in a manual focus version. They can all be used with the Nikon F4. It is not an autofocus camera – it is a professional camera system with the built-in option of a fast and reliable autofocus mode. It is up to the photographer to decide which method he prefers.

Nikon autofocus lenses are also designed to allow for easy manual focusing. The Nikon F4 is not a special-purpose camera but a piece of equipment without compromise for specialists. It is a camera which can

An against-the-light shot like this view of Venice presents no problems for the Nikon F4. Matrix light-metering copes with the high contrast without losing the atmosphere of the lighting.

Nikon F4s with AF-Nikkor f1.4 50mm lens and High Speed Battery Pack MB-21

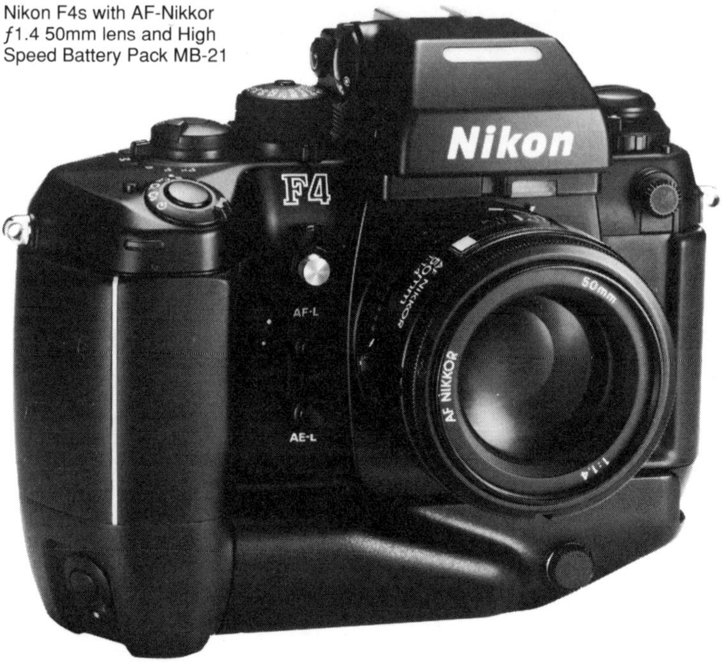

be universally adapted to all sorts of photographic demands. Even though it is an all-purpose camera it is not a camera for everybody. Quite the contrary, if you intend to make use of all the possibilities built into this camera, photographic knowledge and experience are required. The F4's high degree of automation and the many computerised functions will only supply better pictures to those who understand how and when to employ them. Even if the Nikon F4 offers the professionals more solutions to picture-taking problems than any camera before, in the end it can only be as good as its operator.

The Professional Characteristics of the Nikon F4

Durability: the body of the Nikon F4 is die-cast with a special anti-corrosive aluminium alloy of extraordinary strength. This material has already proven its reliability in the F3 and it can be manufactured to extremely exact tolerances compared to other alloys because it is much less susceptible to blowholes during casting.

The basic body consists of front and rear parts, the hand grip and the finder mounting sections. The average thickness of the casting walls is

Nikon F4 with AF-Nikkor *f*1.4 50mm lens and Battery Pack MB-20

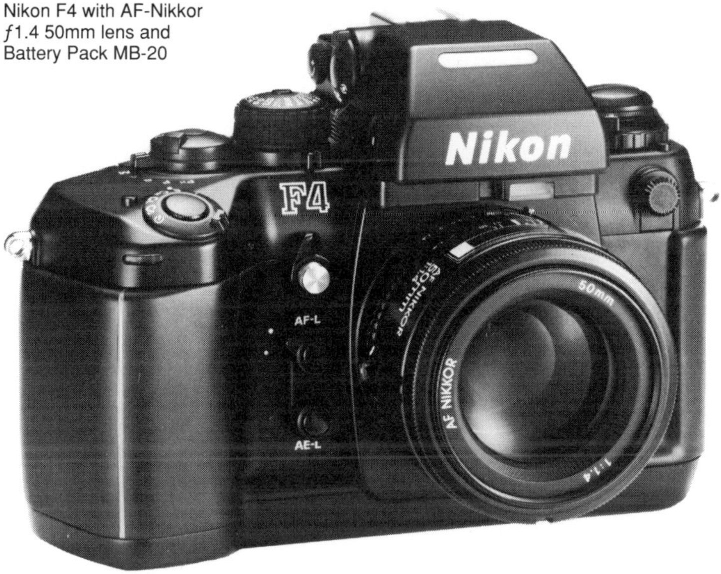

1.3mm for the front part and 1.2mm for the rear part. The box-shaped construction with bridges and the hollowed-wall design increase strength against shocks. On the outside, the body is protected by a shock-absorbing rubber compound which further reduces internal shocks. The microelectronics of the standard Multi-Meter Finder's pentaprism are protected by special double-reinforced plastic covers. The levers and dials are fitted with rings or rubber bellows in order to resist the intrusion of moisture or dust.

Size: it will remain the Nikon engineers' secret of how they managed to pack so much high-tech into such a relatively compact body. All in all they crammed about 1,750 parts into the Nikon F4, in addition to the four motors and batteries. If they had tried to include all these parts in conventional technology the Nikon F4 would have turned out at least 50% larger than the F3. Even so, no compromises were made just for the sake of compactness. Everything a professional camera should have is incorporated into the body of the Nikon F4. In spite of autofocus and the built-in motordrive the F4 is smaller and weighs less than the F3 (along with the additional motor).

Compatibility: the Nikon F4's bayonet mount, the interface between lens and body, accepts three different communication systems, one for Nikkor lenses with built-in microcomputers (AF and AI-P Nikkors), one for Nikkor lenses with built-in motors (Nikon F3 AF lenses) and one for lenses without electrical contacts (AI-S, AI, non-AI, modified AI and Series E lenses). As a result the Nikon F4 will fit into any existing range of Nikon equipment.

Focusing: the Nikon F4 offers the photographer a choice of several focusing modes. The electronic rangefinder working in all modes is sensitive enough to register light all the way down to EV-1, the equivalent of less than the light of one candle. Beyond this the standard B-type screen offers focusing with the clear matte surface. In autofocus mode the photographer can choose between Single or Continuous Servo Autofocus. Depending on the circumstances the latter mode can include the Focus Tracking Function. Combined with the Nikon Multi-Control Backs MF-23 or MF-24, the F4 also offers "Freeze-Focus" function. Nikon Speedlites incorporating AF-Illuminators even allow for autofocus function in complete darkness.

Shutter unit: the Nikon F4's electromagnetically controlled focal-plane shutter is capable of super-fast speeds of up to 1/8000th sec. and 1/250th sec. flash synchronisation. Reliability has been tested for more than 150,000 cycles. Dual multi-bladed blinds prevent even the slightest light leakage – especially critical during mirror-up shooting – and the high-quality material ensures durability.

Metering: three types of metering system are available in the Nikon F4. Matrix Metering ensures a correct exposure automatically in complex lighting conditions without the need for a manual override. Centre Weighted Metering concentrates 60% of the meter's sensitivity to the 12mm circle outlined in the middle of the screen. Spot Metering allows for the exact evaluation of tiny subjects or minute details.

Exposure control: two Program modes, Aperture Priority, Shutter Priority and Manual Mode are available. Automatic TTL flash exposure is possible in all modes. Of course, a manual override of +/–2 stops is also possible. The optional Multi-Control Backs MF-23 and MF-24 offer Automatic Exposure Bracketing.

Motors: four coreless motors are responsible for film advance, film rewind, shutter charging control and autofocus operation. Four film advance modes are selectable. The fastest mode **CH** runs up to 5.7 fps. [US version – UK is 4 fps]

Interchangeable Viewfinders: three additional viewfinders for special situations are available besides the standard Multi-Meter Finder. They are: an AE Action Finder, a 6x High Magnification Finder and a Waist-Level Finder. In addition the focusing screens are also interchangeable.

General Accessories: the Nikon F4's professionalism also shows in the extensive range of compatible accessories. It is by far the most complete system available. Next to the largest lens program of all, Nikon also offers countless special accessories for close-up or reproduction photography, multi-control camera backs, remote control equipment, and other accessories to increase further this unique camera's versatility.

The Construction

The Nikon F4 was designed literally to the photographer's hands and built to withstand his tough daily work. Of course, you should always handle a precision instrument like a camera with care, but the construction of the body is designed to function, with absolute reliability, even in extreme environmental conditions such as heat and cold or tropical humidity. Every single one of the 1,750-plus parts is subject to stringent quality control checks. The standard viewfinder and the shutter unit consist of around 200 parts each. Every part built into the F4 is manufactured in a specialist Nikon plant. The shutter, for example, comes from the Ohi plant in Tokyo, the birthplace of the legendary Nikon F2 and F3 cameras. The pentaprisms for the viewfinder are produced at the Nikon Tochigi plant where the Nikkor lenses are also built. The Nikon Sendai plant, with the latest laser trimming technology available, produces the electronics.

This modular manufacturing principle ensures that every part is made by highly skilled experts in specialist plants. Every single module is checked after completion so that only A1 parts are shipped to the Nikon Mito plant near Tokyo for the final assembly. This last stage in manufacturing consists of eight steps. The assembly line starts with the die-cast body incorporating the shutter unit, connecting parts, FPC boards and the winding unit. The first computer check is next followed by the installation of the mirror box. After that, 80% of the final assembly is complete. Another computer check follows. Front and rear body parts are then combined and the AF-module installed.

Another computer check follows and the autofocus function and accuracy are adjusted by a special system. Simultaneously the TTL and spot sensors and the shutter function are tested.

Finally the body covers and the rubber surface are mounted. The viewfinder is manufactured separately. It consists of, among other things, FPC boards and sensor units which are protected by a double-layer plastic cap. The Nikon F4 with the standard Multi-Meter Finder is complete. Before preparing for shipment the optical precision and adjustment are checked once more. Random samples of the Nikon F4 undergo further severe tests such as extreme electrical noise, high and low temperatures and humidities , very bright light and vibration.

These tests are only a few examples of the numerous quality checks imposed on the F4. Thirty years of close co-operation with professional photographers throughout the world have shown Nikon that reliability is the most important prerequisite for any professional tool.

The Bayonet

The Nikon F4's bayonet mount is a link between the past and the future. It will take almost any Nikon SLR lens ever built. That spells continuity of more than 29 years! This intelligent interface between body and lens recognises, accepts, and works with three different and independent communication systems – one for lenses with built-in microcomputers, one for the AF Nikkor lenses with incorporated motors once designed for the Nikon F3 AF, and one for lenses with mechanical couplings. Regardless of the differences the electronic rangefinder can almost always be employed to assist manual focusing. The only condition is that the lens must have a maximum *f*-stop of at least 5.6. Autofocus operation is possible with every AF-Nikkor lens including the above-mentioned ones for the former F3AF.

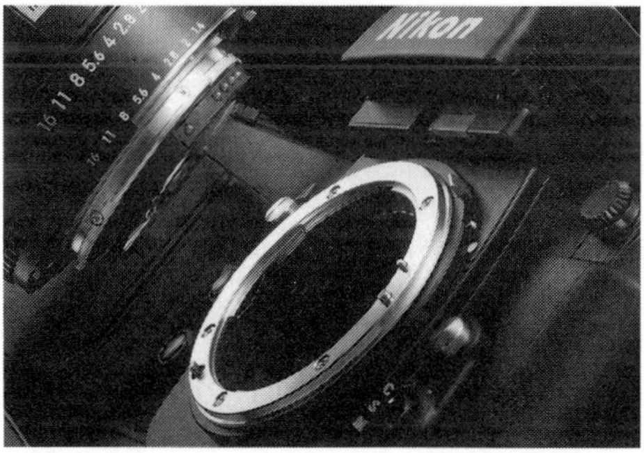

The bayonet of the Nikon F4 is an intellegent interface between the camera body and the lenses. It is capable of communicating with three different lens information systems.

In addition, quite a number of the normal Nikon lenses can be used as AF lenses, with the help of the Autofocus Teleconverter TC-16A, as long as their maximum *f*-stop is at least 3.5.

Matrix Metering for difficult lighting situations is available for all AI and AI-S standard lenses as well as for all lenses with integrated microcomputers. Every lens of at least AI standard allows for Aperture Direct Readout in the viewfinder.

The Information Exchange between Camera and Lens

Since 1959 constant innovation in the design of Nikon lenses has improved the transmission of information to the camera body. Since the introduction of the AI-S standard Nikkor lenses in 1981, additional data such as the focal length, the lens type (AF or AI-S), and the lens speed are also relayed via mechanical contacts, pins, and levers. AI standard lenses had already incorporated Automatic Aperture Indexing and thus made automatic full-aperture metering possible by means of the AI coupling ridge. AI-S standard lenses are easily identified by their orange-coloured minimum *f*-stop. E series Nikon lenses are identical to the AI-S Nikkor lenses in terms of the body/lens interface. The first AF-Nikkor lenses for the Nikon F3AF were introduced after the former and are equipped with additional electrical contacts for the control of the AF-motors incorporated in those lenses. The latest lenses of the AF Nikkor type were introduced along with the first camera of the present AF series with the autofocus motor built into the body, the F-501. These lenses are equipped with a microcomputer and further electrical contacts. Please refer to the chart in Appendix I as to the compatibility and function range of the different lens types.

The Shutter Unit

The electromagnetically controlled Nikon Pro-Tech, vertical-travel, focal plane shutter is another masterpiece by the Nikon engineers. It is capable of an awesome speed of 1/8000th sec. as well as a 1/250th sec. syncronisation speed. Dual multi-bladed blinds prevent any light leakage whatsoever, even during mirror-up operation.

Four of the shutter blades consist of special epoxy material reinforced with carbon fibres, the other four are made of an especially durable aluminium alloy. The use of these extremely light-weight and strong materials allowed a higher travelling speed without sacrificing reliability.

The faster a shutter is supposed to be able to operate, the thinner and lighter the blinds must be. In cameras without the possibility of locking the mirror in the up position, this does not represent any danger, as the mirror always assists the shutter blinds in the prevention of any light-leakage. In the Nikon F4 the shutter has to manage alone because of the mirror lock-up option. This called for a unique dual-blind concept, i.e. before the shutter of the F4 is released both blinds are situated in front of the film plane. So when operated some of the blades are forced to travel much further than in conventional shutters. With this in mind Nikon chose carbon-reinforced epoxy material for these blades since it is lighter in weight than aluminium yet stronger. These blades are only 0.09mm thick, have a low density and a very small moment of inertia. As a result they can travel a longer distance, including a change of direction, compared to the alloy-blades, without being excessively strained.

The special technique employed in the shutter blinds allowed for a very high travelling speed without durability being reduced at all. The width of the slit between the two blinds is kept consistently accurate and provides precise exposures even with the top speed of 1/8000th sec. In order to prevent vibration during the shutter blind travel a special tungsten-alloy balancer is incorporated. This is necessary since even a camera mounted on a tripod is subject to vibrations, especially when shutter speeds from 1/15th to 1/250th sec. are used. Faster and slower

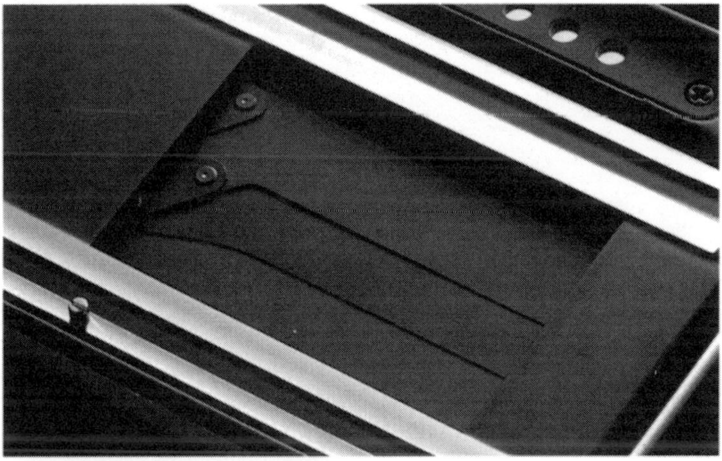

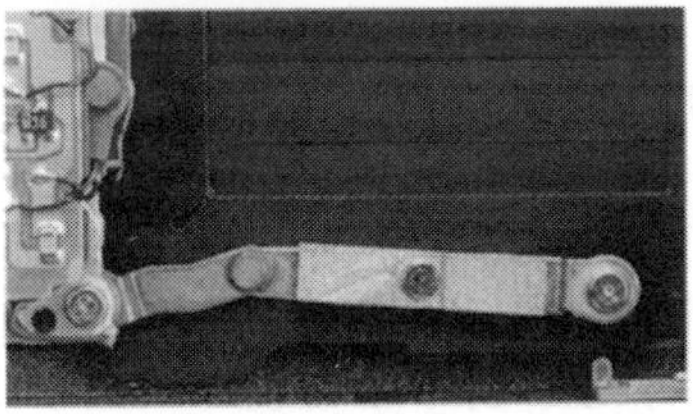

One of Nikon's engineering masterpieces is the superfast Pro Tech Shutter of the F4. The special tungsten-alloy shutter balancer absorbs vibration due to the shutter curtain travel.

speeds are hardly affected by such vibrations.

Nikon chose tungsten for this mechanism because of its high density of about 18.5. Therefore, the balancer only needs to move slightly during exposure. The contra-movement of the balancer compensates for the shutter movement and cuts vibrations. Additionally, an ingenious braking system prevents any shutter bounce. Nikon tests have proven reliability for at least 150,000 cycles.

How the Shutter Blinds Move

Normally, the film plane is covered by the dual multi-blade shutter blinds. This system prevents any light leaking past the blades. The moment the shutter release button is fully pressed, the mirror moves upwards and the rear blind does so simultaneously. The instant the mirror is in the upper position, the front blind starts travelling downwards and the film is exposed to the light coming directly from the lens. The rear blind follows the front blind on its way down until the film plane is completely covered. When the shutter speed is very fast, e.g. 1/8000th sec, the rear blind starts immediately after the front blind, i.e. with only a narrow slit between them. When the film is automatically advanced to the next frame after the exposure, the shutter resumes its original dual-blind formation.

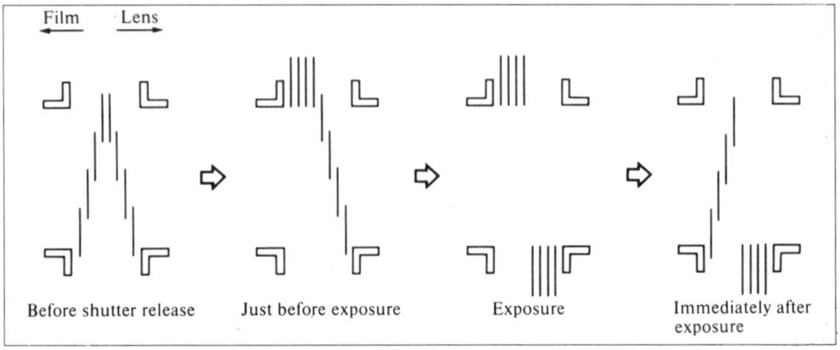

For extra protection against light leakage, especially with the mirror locked up, the F4 uses two rows of blades. As the film advances the other curtain closes.

The Motors

Four coreless motors are built into every Nikon F4: one for film advance, one for shutter charging, one for film rewinding and one for autofocus operation. Unlike conventional types, Nikon's coreless motors have less inertia resulting in a quick response for efficient drive. Despite the autofocus motor's compact size it is powerful enough to drive even long telephoto lenses with ease.

The shutter-charging motor, situated beside the sprocket, takes care of the mirror operation. Only about 1/5th of a rotation suffices for the mirror and aperture control and the resetting of both the shutter magnets the rest is used to charge the shutter blinds.

The Spool Motor is located inside the film spool. It advances the film. Unlike other cameras the sprockets function as a perforation counter not as the actual means of film advance. However, when the 250-exposure Multi Function Back MF-24 is used, the sprockets do help drive the film.

Four film-advance modes are selectable (with the High-Speed Battery Pack MB-21), single frame advance, continuous high-speed at a max. 5.7 fps, continuous low speed at 3.4 fps, and continuous silent film advance (achieved by motor-stepping at changing speeds allowing an amazingly quiet 1 fps).

The Rewind Motor (located next to the film cassette chamber) also changes the filters of the autofocus module. The shutter charging and the spool motor work simultaneously to achieve high-speed film advance. In continuous low mode they are driven sequentially.

This exposure was spot-metered, aiming at the doll's face, and compensated by –1/2 *f*-stop to retain the backlit impression.

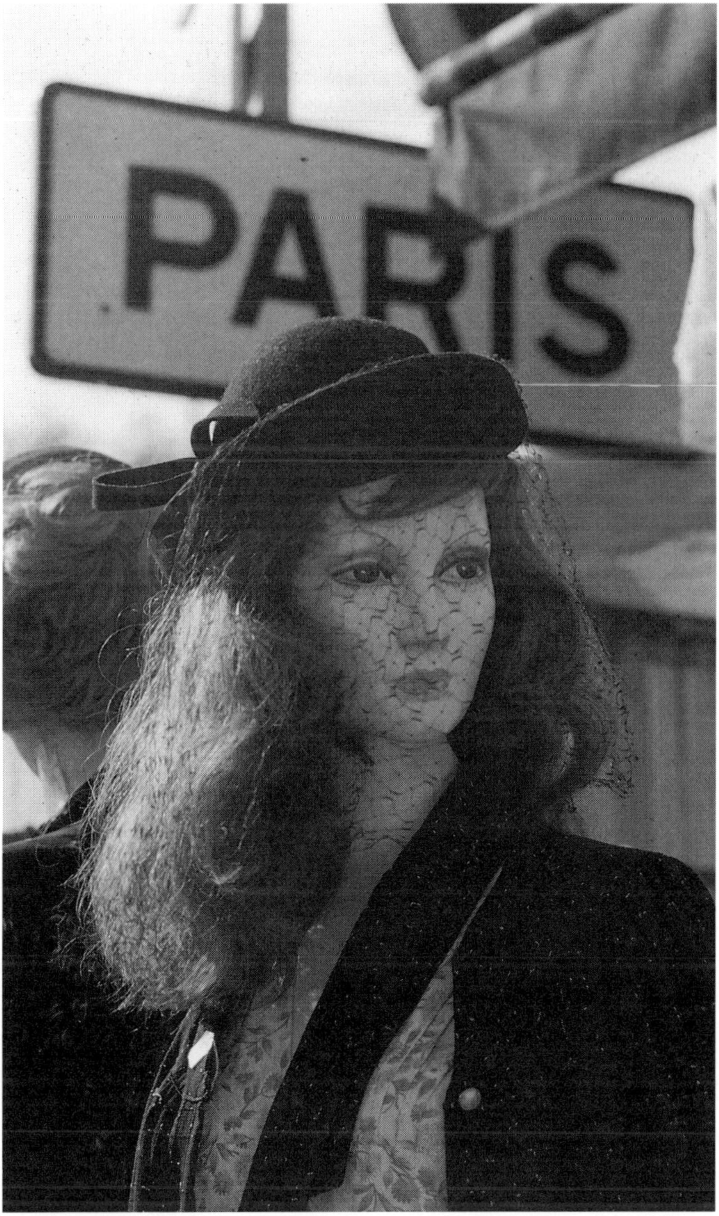
PARIS

The Microelectronics

The Nikon F4 has the largest computer system ever built into a 35mm camera. This includes nine ICs in the F4's body, two of which are 8-bit microcomputers and one with a 4-bit capacity. A hard circuit board consisting of several layers of epoxy resin is located under the mirror box. Printed circuits are sandwiched between these layers. Circuit boards of this kind are routinely used in computers but the F4 marks the first time they have been incorporated into a 35mm camera.

The viewfinder itself is equipped with four ICs including one 8-bit microcomputer. 200 high-sensitivity CCD's are responsible for electronic rangefinding and a pair of Multi-Meter sensors detect scene brightness. These sensors register the scene in five segments.

Each of the two groups of sensors located on both sides of the viewfinder eyepiece consists of three silicon photo diodes so the segment in the middle is monitored by both groups. In Matrix Metering, data obtained from all five segments is computated, whereas in Centre Weighted Metering only the data from the central segment comes to bear. A spot sensor and a TTL sensor for automatic flash exposure control are also part of the electronic array in the F4.

The different microcomputers belong to a network controlled by software developed over several years which is the professional know-how built into the F4.

The Design

The F4's design is based on recommendations of professional photographers all around the world and blended into its present shape by the man who had also created the F3, the Italian Georgio Giugiaro, known best for his automobile designs. His credo has always been: form follows function. No wonder the camera is well balanced and it fits perfectly in your hands. Every single dial or lever was designed so that they can be operated without taking the camera from your eye and also so that professionals accustomed to earlier Nikon models will immediately feel at home. The big shutter speed dial is located exactly where it has always been and has a ribbed rubber surface. The speed settings clearly click into position and the **X** position, for flash synchronisation, locks in order to prevent accidental resetting. When you take the camera into your hands, your index finger will almost automatically land on the shutter release button. The tapered lower left edge of the High-Speed Battery Pack MB-21, which turns the F4 into an F4s also enhances the camera's natural handling.

Numerous accessories enable you to employ the Nikon F4 for close-up photography. The AF Micro Nikkor 55mm *f*2.8 will even allow you to achieve a reproduction ratio of 1:1 without the need for any additional accessories.

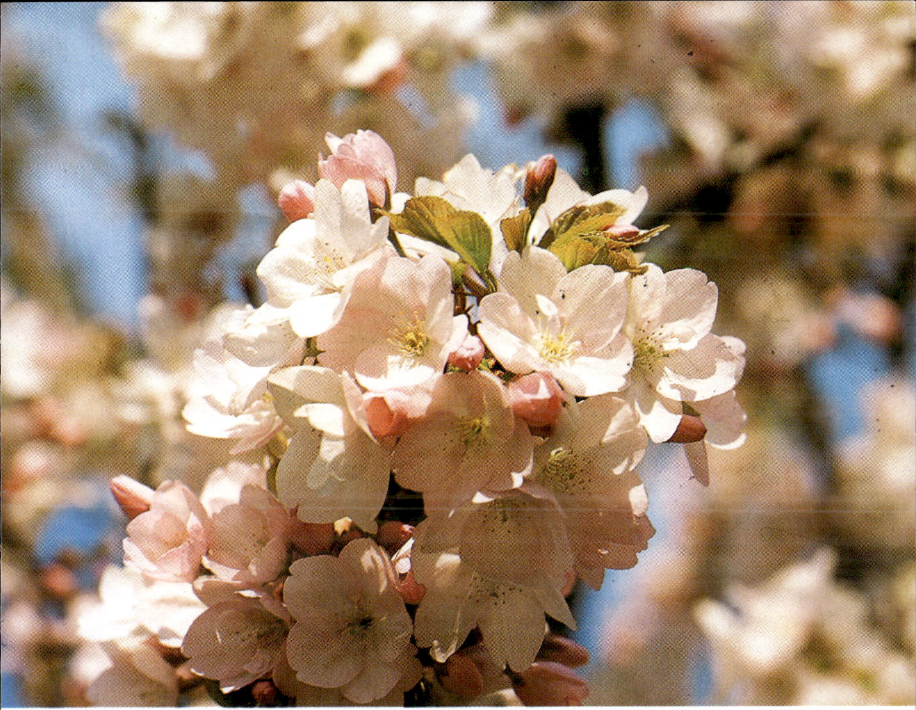

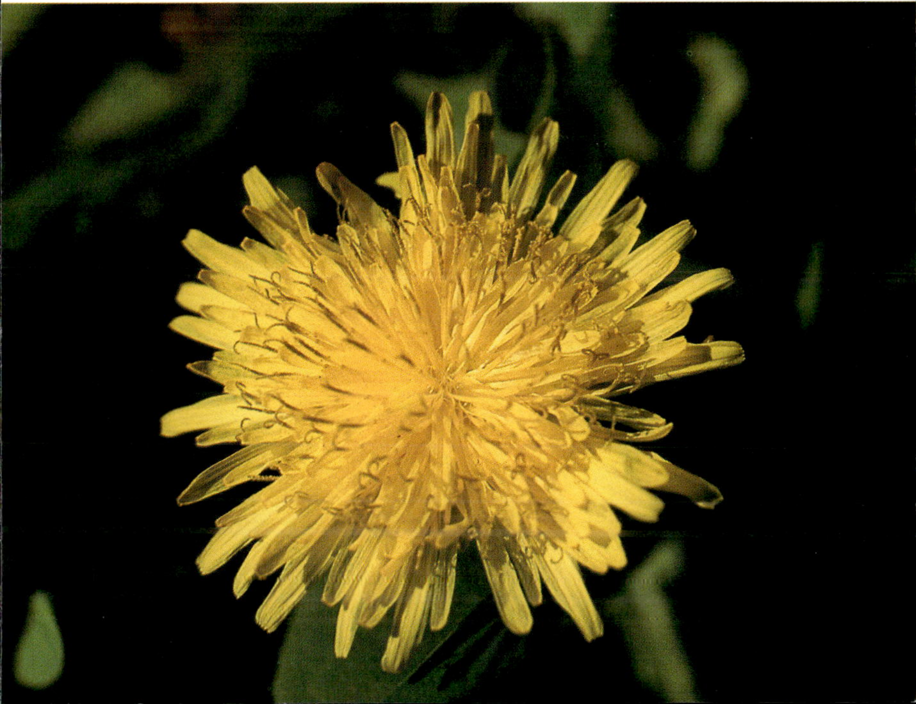

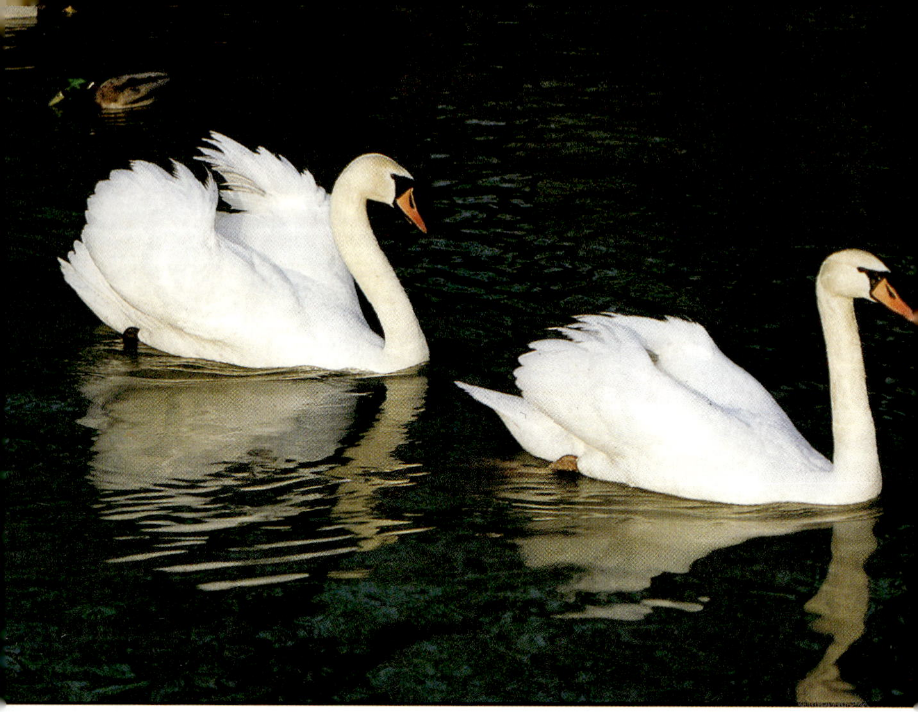

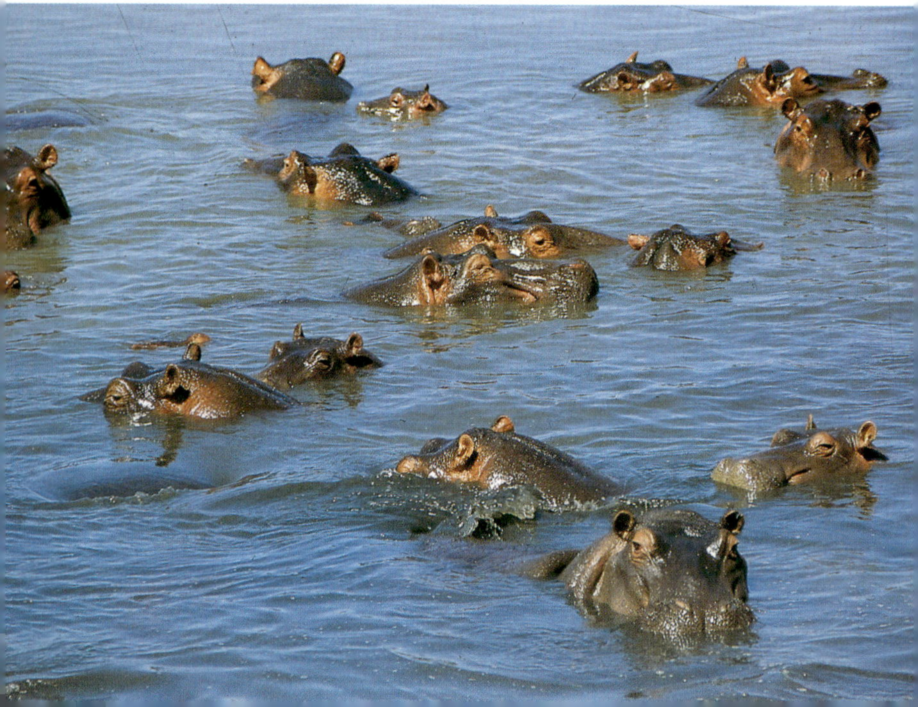

Operating the Camera

More than in other cameras, the Nikon F4's countless possibilities call for complete command of every single dial, lever, and button and their functions. If you do not fully understand their significance you will not be able to take advantage of all the operational modes of this unique camera to bring out your creativity. So, to begin with, we will explain the main controls very thoroughly. We will also point out their specific importance for everyday use. The Nikon F4 is available in two versions, differing solely in their battery packs. Normally the camera is equipped with the Battery Pack MB-20 and called F4. If you choose the F4s it comes with the High-Speed Battery Pack MB-21. In the following we will also explain the additional controls of the MB-21.

The Controls on the Top of the Camera

Film-advance mode selector: this is designed as a ring around the shutter release button and located on the slightly tapered top of the grip section. Six settings are available including the power-off function in the **L** (Lock) position. When the camera is not in use it should always be set to **L** to prevent unnecessary battery drain. The other settings are **S** for single frame shooting, **CH** for continuous high speed advance mode of up to either 4 fps or 5.7 fps, depending on the battery pack in use, **CL** for a lower speed of either 3.4 fps or 3 fps respectively, **CS** (continuous silent) for an extremely quiet film advance at a rate of either 1 fps or 0.8 fps, and finally the position for the self-timer function.

The self-timer runs for 10 seconds and is electronically controlled. A red LED located slightly to the right and just below the shutter release button on the front of the grip section blinks while the self-timer is activated. During the final 2 seconds the LED blinks noticeably faster, warning you to get ready. The self-timer operation can be cancelled at any time by turning the film advance mode selector to another position. A number of professionals use the self-timer not only to get into the picture but also as a handy alternative to a cable-release or remote control accessory. In case of long exposures from a tripod this reduces camera shake when pressing the shutter release button.

The film advance mode selector is locked in every position to prevent accidental setting. The little button to the right of the selector must be pressed to unlock the dial. This can be done very easily without having

The matrix metering system proves to be especially handy and reliable by coping with high-contrast scenes without the need for manual exposure compensation.

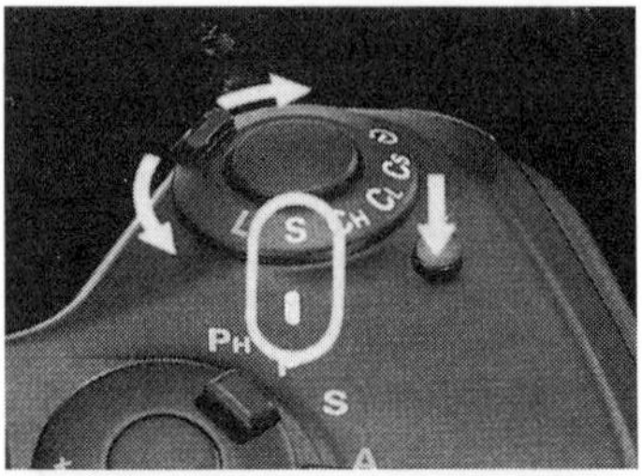

The selector switch surrounding the shutter release has six different click-stop positions; L (main on/off switch and shutter release lock), four film-advance modes, and the self-timer. It can not be rotated unless the lock button is pressed (left). The modes, below, are **S** (single frame); **CH** (5/5.7 fps); **CL** (3/3.4 fps) and the special ultra-quiet film advance **CS** which is a unique feature of the camera.

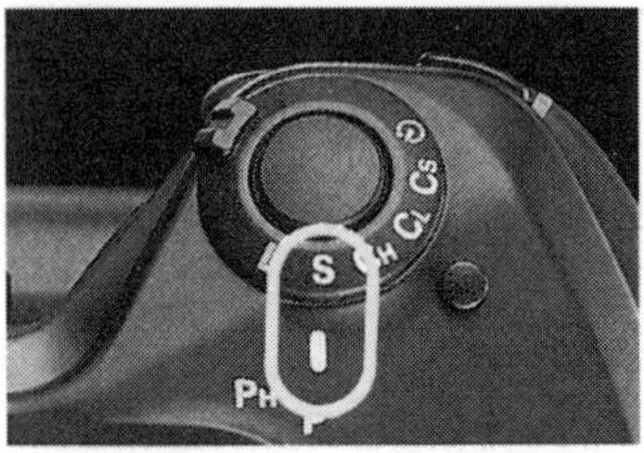

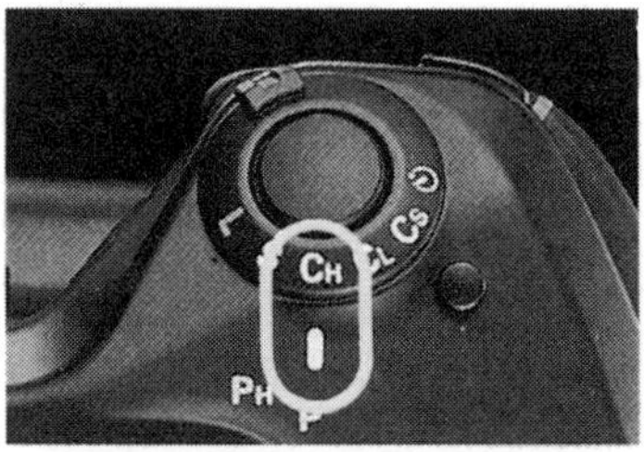

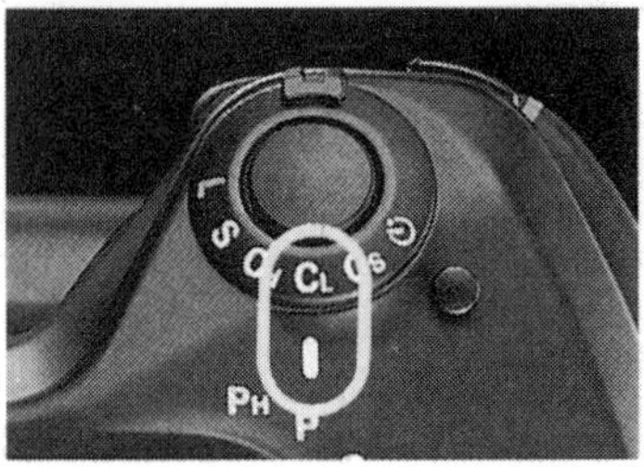

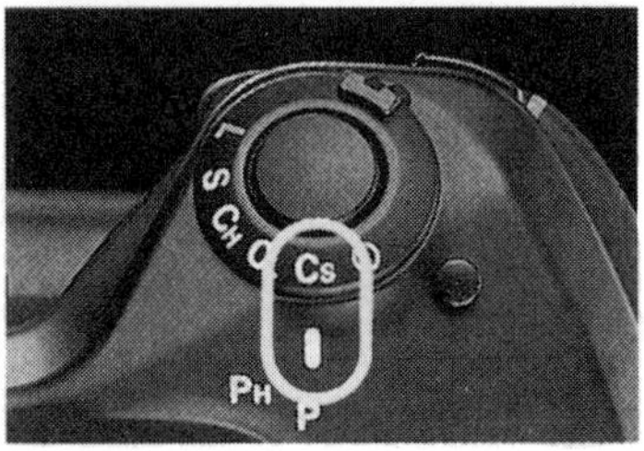

to take your eye from the viewfinder. A bit of practice is all it takes to unlock the dial with your index finger while your middle finger can easily do the setting by holding the knob on top of the dial. As mentioned before the dial locks noticeably in every position but you can dial continuously by keeping the lock button pressed, although the moment you let go the dial will again lock in the next position.

Shutter Release Button: the Nikon F4's electromagnetic shutter release button is located in the centre of the film advance mode selector and has two positions. When the selector is set to **L** the button is locked. In every other position of the selector, slightly pressing the button activates the camera's electronics, and the lens is automatically focused to the correct distance of the subject framed by the brackets in the viewfinder. When using the Battery Pack MB-20 the shutter release

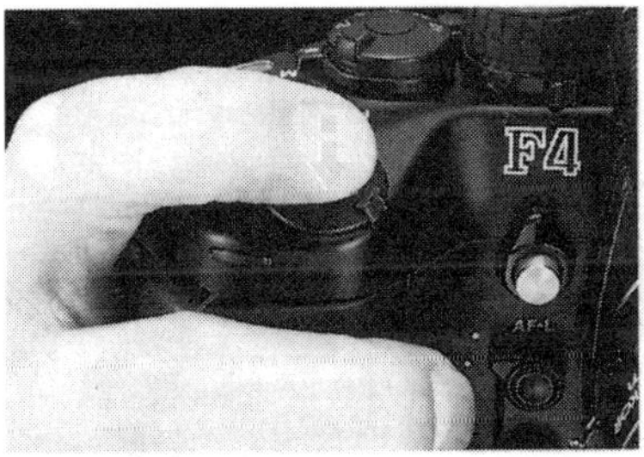

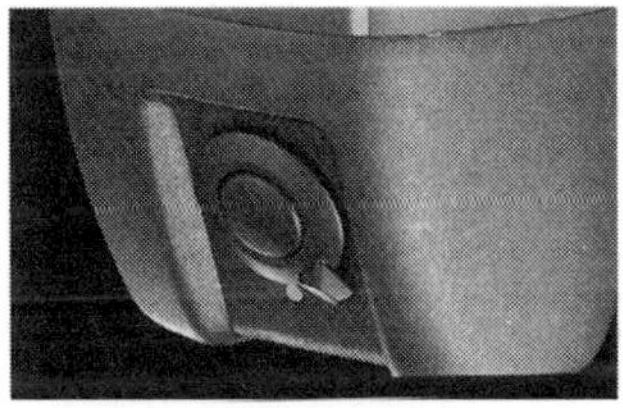

The F4s has an additional shutter releas button for vertical format shooting.

button also serves as a battery tester. If the batteries are in order the LCD in the viewfinder will remain on for 16 seconds after slightly pressing the button, but the LED focus indicators in the viewfinder disappear immediately after you let go and focus operation also stops. The aperture set on the lens can be seen through the ADR (Aperture Direct Readout) window.

The High Speed Battery Pack MB-21 has an additional shutter release button on the lower right side of the grip section. This button is convenient when holding the camera vertically. A switch concentric to the button allows it to be locked separately to prevent any accidental release. A red index mark shows when the button is unlocked.

Exposure Mode Selector: the Nikon F4 offers a choice of five different exposure modes which are selected by a lever protruding to the right from underneath the exposure compensation dial. **M** stands for manual mode, **A** for Aperture Priority, **S** for Shutter Priority, **P** for Normal Program Mode, and **PH** for the High Speed Program Mode.

Exposure Compensation Dial: this dial allows for intentional over- and underexposure settings and is also locked against accidental use. In order to set the compensation value the lock must first be released by pressing the knob towards the centre of the dial. As long as the lock release is held the compensation values can be set to within a range of +/– 2 EV in 1/3 EV increments. Since the exposure compensation

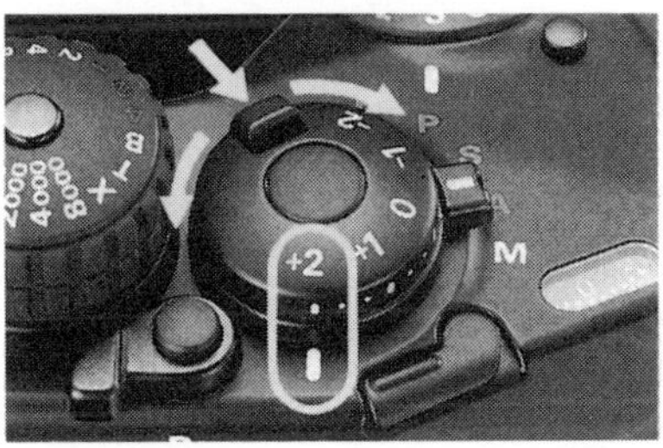

The exposure compensation dial allows manual override of up to +/– 2 *f*-stops.

symbol and value appear in the viewfinder, you could also compensate by manually setting a film speed other than that on the film cassette, but if you do it this way you might forget to reset it, because you will not find any warning symbol in the viewfinder.

Multiple Exposure Lever: in order to take multiple exposures on the same frame this lever, located between the compensation dial and the frame counter on the top of the camera, must first be pulled slightly outwards and then release the shutter. When the camera is set to single frame advance and the multiple exposure lever has been activated, the film will not advance after the shutter has been released, but the lever will return to its original position. When you release the shutter a second time the same frame will be exposed once again and this time the film will be automatically advanced. If you intend to expose the same frame more than twice the multiple exposure lever must be activated again before every additional exposure.

When the camera is set to one of the continuous shooting modes the same frame will be exposed again and again as long as you keep the shutter release button pressed. But you do have to hold the multiple exposure lever so that it does not resume its original position automatically, otherwise the film would be advanced again. After the final exposure you should push the lever back into the normal position. Then you should cover the lens, preferably with the appropriate cap, and expose once again. The film will be advanced after this final exposure and an unexposed frame will be ready. In case you accidently pull the lever all you have to do to prevent any multiple exposure is to push it back before you release the shutter so the camera can advance the film in the normal manner. Note that in multiple exposure operation compensation is necessary depending on subject and background brightness and number of exposures. It has proved to be easiest to place your brighter subjects in front of a distinctly darker background.

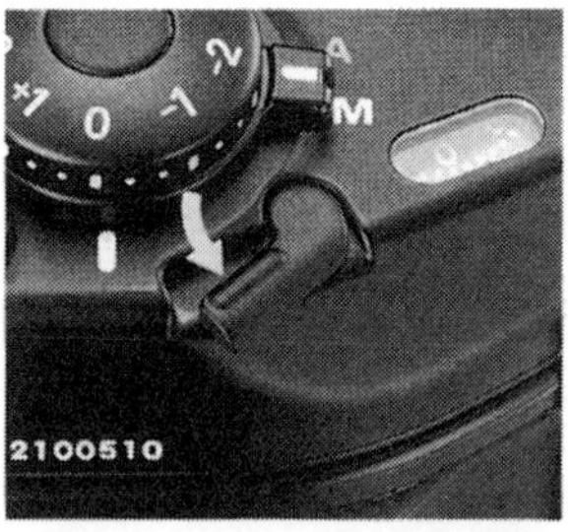

The small lever between the exposure compensation dial and the film counter window must be pulled outwards in order to facilitate multiple exposures

Shutter Speed Dial: in either manual or shutter speed priority mode you can set any one of 16 different speeds from 4 to 1/8000th sec. with the shutter speed dial immediately to the right of the viewfinder.

Intermediate settings are not possible. In addition you also have **B**, **T**, and **X** positions.

When the shutter speed dial is set to **B** (below, upper left) the shutter will remain open as long as you keep the release button pressed. This function is only possible in manual mode.

The **T** position (below, upper right) is ideal for lengthy exposures. Once you have released the shutter it will remain open until you rotate the shutter speed dial to any other position. After the shutter has been released in this position the camera will not need any further battery power regardless of how long the exposure takes. Depending on whether or not the exposure is longer or shorter than 32 sec. it must be completed in different ways. If the exposure is shorter than 32 sec. all you have to do is to rotate the dial to a different position. If the exposure has taken longer than 32 sec. the shutter release button must also be slightly pressed so that the mirror returns to its original position and the film will be advanced.

The **X** setting (lower left), which locks into position, makes sure that you do not accidently set any faster speed than the top flash sync speed of 1/250th sec. when using the specially adapted flash units. So, just for safety's sake, why not make a habit of always using the **X** position for flash. Like the **B** and **T** settings, **X** can only be unlocked by pressing the button in the middle of the shutter speed dial (lower right). Any manually-set shutter speed of up to 1/250th sec., which is marked in red for easy identification on the dial, will be correctly synchronised.

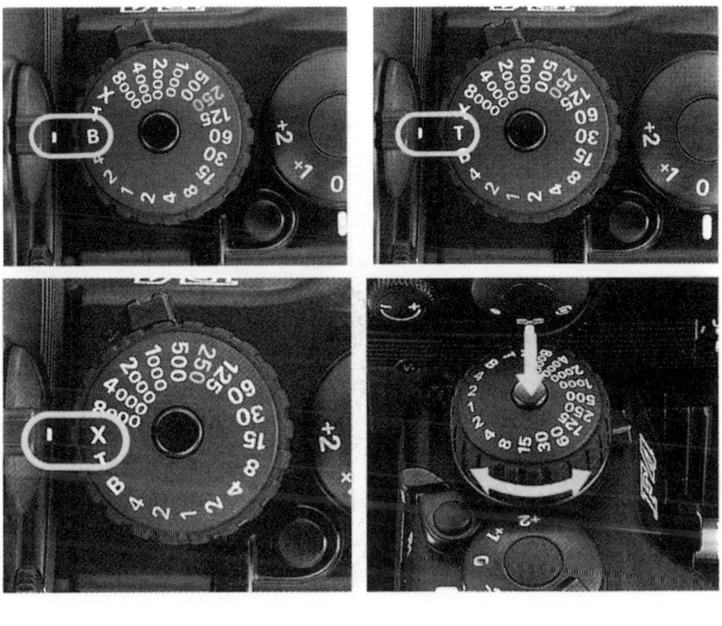

Viewfinder Illumination Switch: the Nikon F4 has an additional viewfinder illuminator so you can read all the information even in the dark, including the ADR window. The illumination is activated by pushing the switch located directly underneath the shutter speed dial, on the front edge of the camera, to the right so that a red dot becomes visible. As soon as you slightly press the shutter release button the viewfinder information will be floodlit in a light green tone. It is automatically switched off either 16 sec. after the shutter has been released or by switching the camera off. Although the illumination is switched off automatically the lever should be returned to its original position in order to conserve battery power.

The viewfinder illumination switch is located under the shutter speed dial.

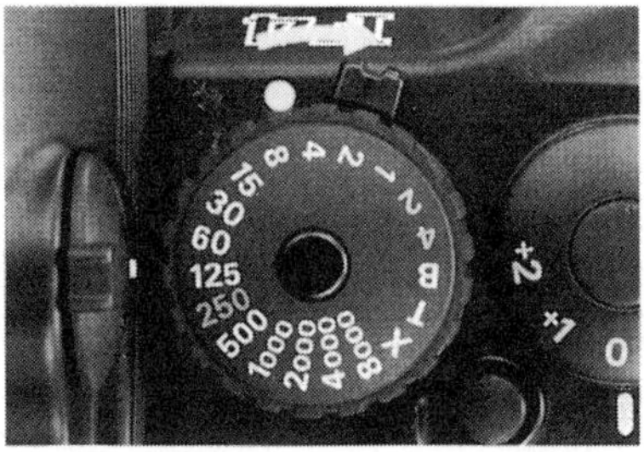

Film Rewind Switch R1: this little lever fits in snugly immediately behind the shutter speed and compensation dials. In order to rewind manually you first have to unlock this lever by pressing the button on top of it and then push it out, at an angle from the camera, which prevents any accidental disengagement of the film advance mechanism. As soon as you have done this you can lift up the film rewind crank located immediately to the left of the viewfinder and commence winding the film back into the cassette. This rewind switch will return to its original position immediately after the next shutter release operation.

To rewind manually, first disengage the transport by pressing the centre of lever R1 and moving it outwards.

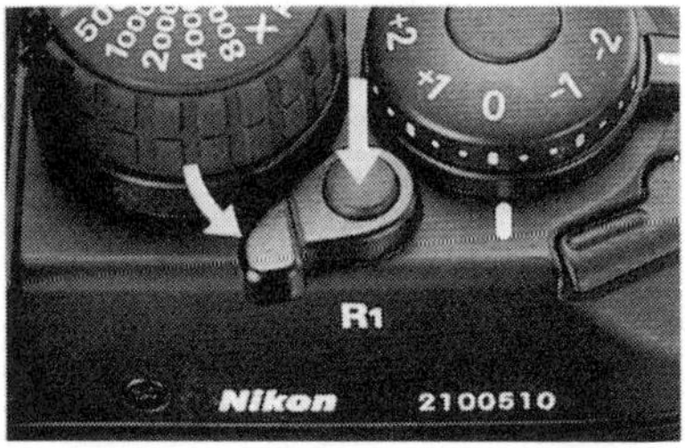

Film Rewind Switch R2: in order to activate the power rewind function you also have to use this lever, located directly beneath the film speed dial on the back of the camera. First press its lock release button and then push the lever to the left. As soon as the film has been wound completely into the cassette the red LED, next to the film speed dial, which blinks during the rewind operation lights up continuously. When the camera back is opened the rewind switch R2 returns to its normal position automatically.

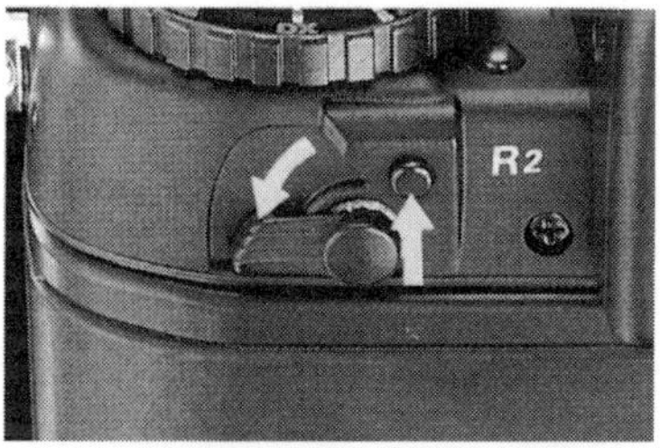

For the power rewind function you must first use rewind switch R1 then operate lever R2.

Film Rewind Crank: the folding crank for manual rewind operation is located immediately above the film speed dial on the top left-hand part of the camera. A little arrow which can be seen when the crank is unfolded indicates the direction of the rewinding operation. Professionals will not do without this additional facility. First they can rewind the film even if the batteries are exhausted, and secondly because the noise caused by power rewind can be highly undesirable in certain situations.

The rewind crank is also used to open the camera back. First you have to press the camera back lock lever in the direction indicated by the arrow and then you can pull the film crank upwards until the camera opens.

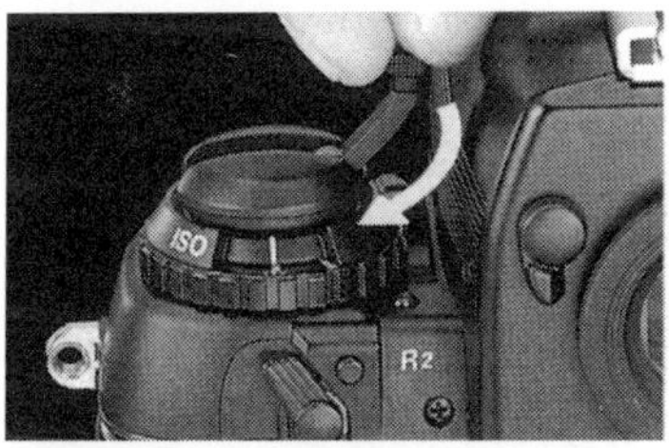

The rewind crank is also used to open the camera back. A lock prevents any accidental opening.

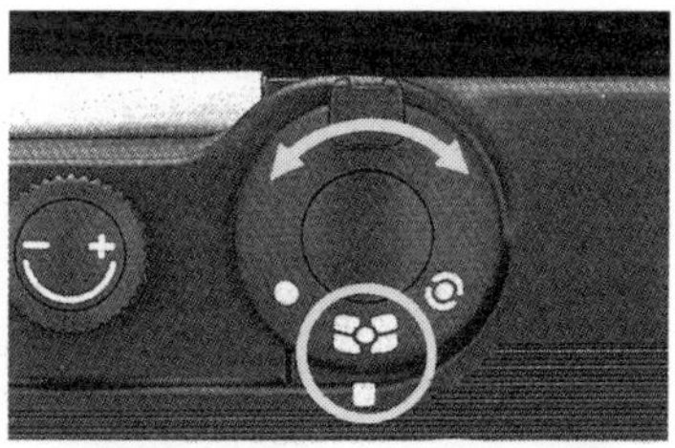

The DP-20 metering mode selector has three positions for spot, centre-weighted and matrix metering modes.

Metering System Selector: three metering systems are available in the Nikon F4. Matrix Metering, Centre Weighted Metering, and Spot Metering. The selector dial is located on the right-hand side of the standard Multi-Meter Finder. Although this dial does click into position very distinctly it has no lock function, so it could happen that it is set accidently while transporting the camera, so you should check the viewfinder information for the symbol of the selected metering mode before you make your shot to be on the safe side.

Dioptre Adjustment Knob: this small knob is right behind the metering mode selector. Photographers who normally wear spectacles can set the viewfinder from –3 to +1 dioptres. In order to do so you have to pull out the knob and turn in the + or – direction until you see the lines in the viewfinder image very clearly, then push the knob back in and the setting will remain locked until you wish to reset. In case the built-in range is not sufficient the additionally available viewfinder correction eyepieces for the F3HP can be used.

Eyesight correction settings between +1 and –3 dioptres allow individual adaptation and are possible without additional correction lenses.

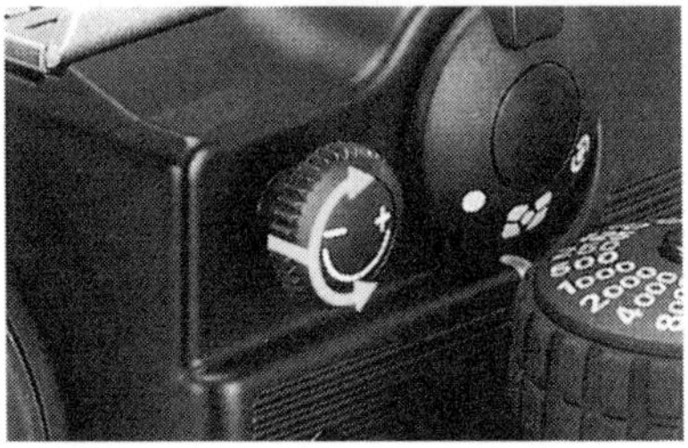

Exposure Compensation for Different Focusing Screens: since two of the metering systems are located within the viewfinder, slight compensation may be necessary when you use screens other than the advanced type B Brite View screen provided. This can be done with the little screw-like dial on the bottom of the viewfinder after removing it from the camera body. The compensation which is possible within the range of –2 to +0.5 EV in steps of 0.5 EV can be seen in the scale window on the right side of the viewfinder. Leaflets included with the interchangeable screens inform about the amount of necessary compensation. The screwdriver is provided with the camera.

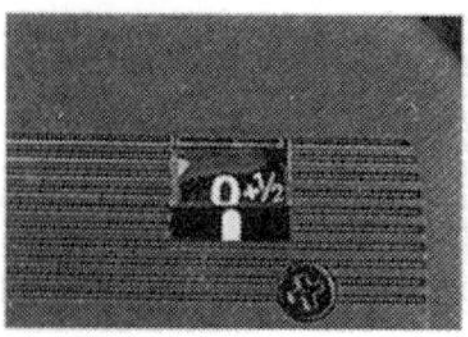

After changing finder screens, exposure compensation for the metering systems is adjusted beneath the viewfinder. It can be controlled by the window at its side.

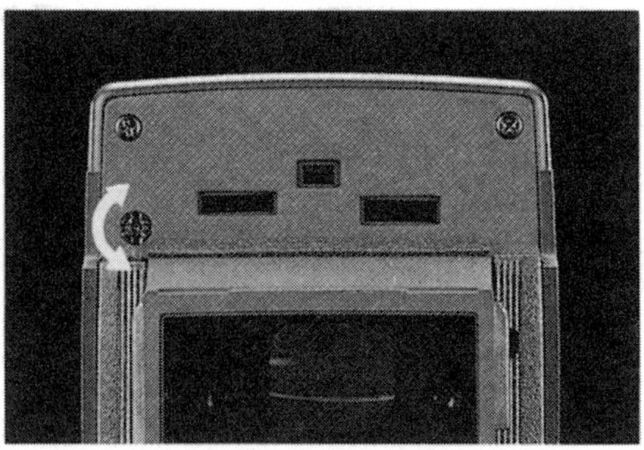

How to Unlock and Remove the Viewfinder: first push the release lever, located between the finder and the film speed dial, to the right then slide the viewfinder out away from the lens. To attach it, slide forward until it clicks into place. Before attaching or detaching the DP-20 finder make sure the film advance motor selector is set to **L** to prevent short circuiting.

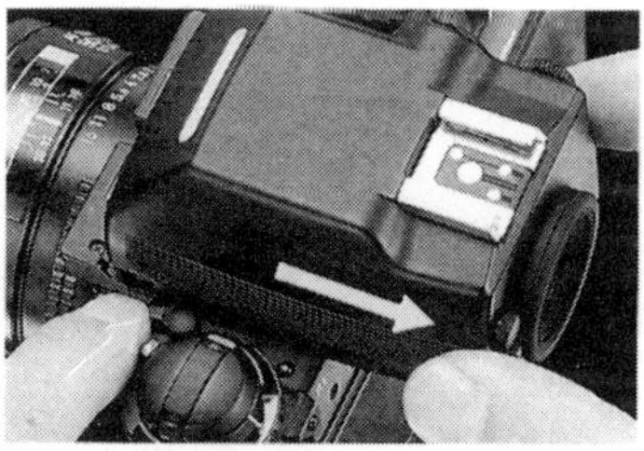

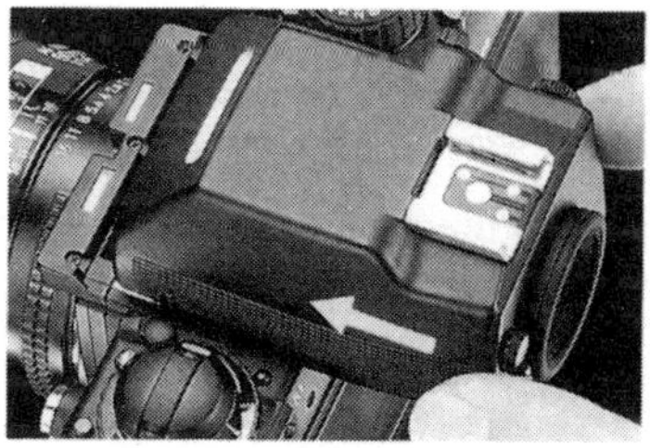

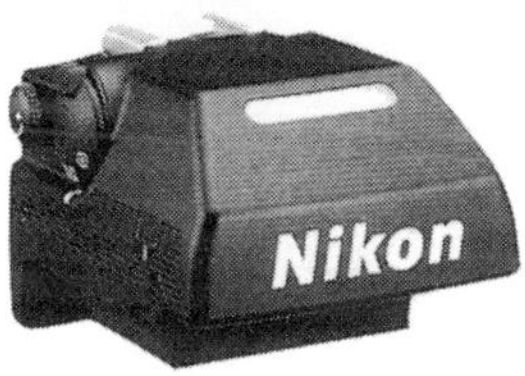

In order to remove the viewfinder, the lock lever must be first pushed to the left before the finder can be pulled backwards off the camera.

Accessory Shoe: the ISO-standard hot shoe on top of the Multi-Meter Finder allows direct mounting of a wide range of dedicated electronic Nikon Speedlites including SB-24, SB-23, SB-22, SB-20, SB-18, SB-16B, and SB-15. Other Nikon Speedlites may be mounted with a compatible Nikon flash unit coupler. Four electrical contacts in the shoe provide the following when used with a compatible Nikon Speedlite: proper synchronisation of the flash unit, automatic flash output stop, identification of a TTL flash unit, viewfinder flash-ready symbol and automatic switching to the proper sync speed with Nikon dedicated Speedlite units.

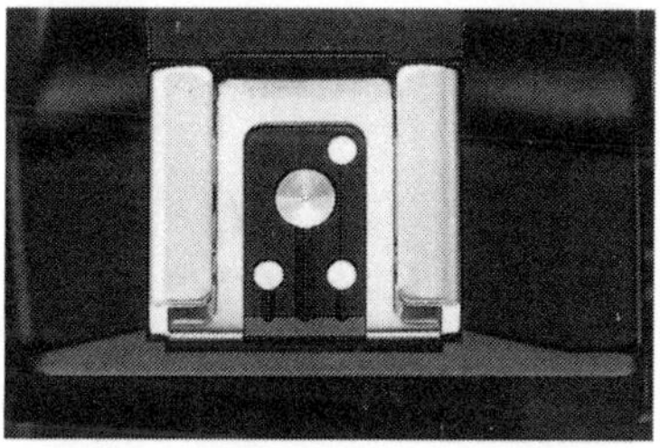

The accessory shoe has four electrical contacts for data exchange between the camera and the flash unit.

Eyepiece Shutter Lever: during self-timer operation in automatic exposure modes it is advisable to use the eyepiece shutter which prevents light from entering the eyepiece and adversely affecting the automatic exposure meter reading. Just turn the lever to the left to close the shutter. The eyepiece shutter is coloured red to provide a visual reminder that it is in use.

The eyepiece shutter prevents stray light affecting the metering system in the case of long exposure from a tripod.

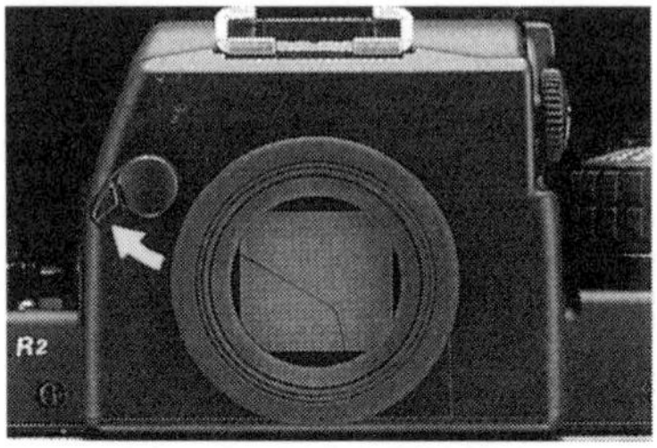

Film Speed Dial: the F4 offers two ways to set the film speed: either manually or automatically by sensing DX-coded film. To set the film speed automatically turn the dial to **DX** and use only coded films. The film speed range for automatic setting is from ISO 25 to 5000. If a non-DX-coded film or one with a defective DX-code is loaded, or no film is loaded, lightly pressing the shutter release button causes the red alert LED to blink and the shutter locks. Even if DX-coded film is loaded a manual setting always has priority. The manual film speed setting is possible in 1/3rd EV steps from ISO 6 to ISO 6400. The scale on the dial has number settings and the two dots between each pair of ISO numbers stand for intermediate settings. The film speed dial is also lockable against accidental setting. It can only be rotated when the lock release button located immediately above the dial is pressed at the same time.

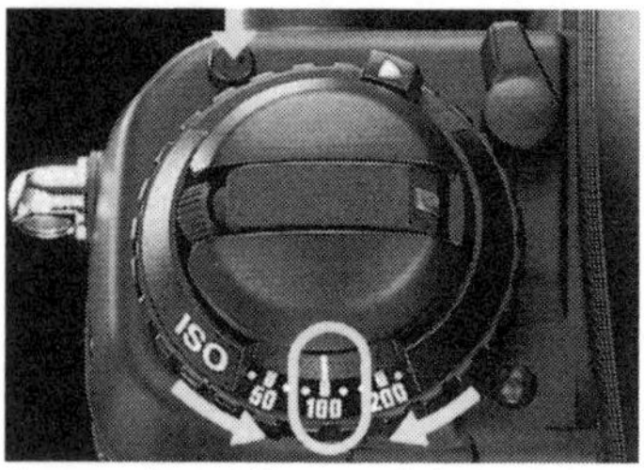

A manually-set film speed always has priority. So, in order to take advantage of the DX-code reading facility, the dial must be set to **DX**.

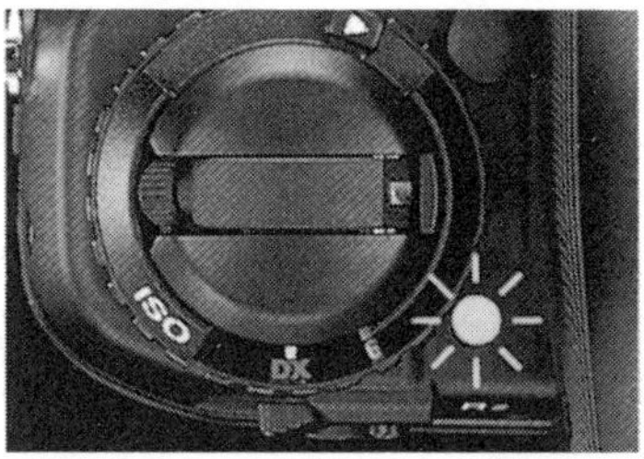

If the film speed dial is set to **DX** but an uncoded film is loaded, the shutter release button will lock. The warning light on top of the camera will blink.

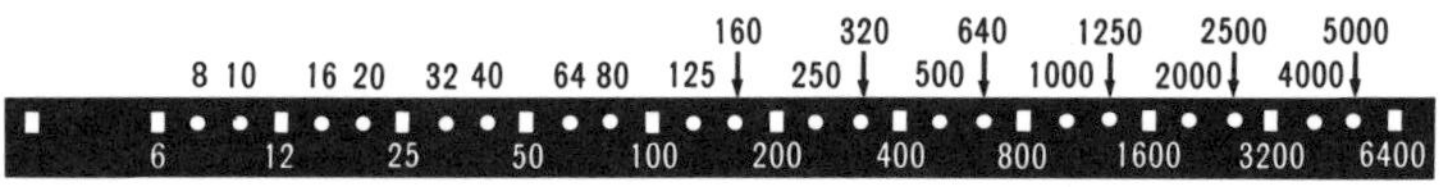

The black scale shows the increments on the ISO scale. The numbers above the scale are the ISO values of the intermediate dots.

The Controls on the Front of the Camera

Depth of Field Preview Button: this button is located to the left of the bayonet. When you use Nikon lenses with an automatic diaphragm – and almost all Nikkors are of this type – the viewfinder image is always seen at the maximum aperture, i.e. at its brightest, so that you can control your picture framing to best advantage. On the other hand this image does not correspond to the effect of the aperture you have actually preset. By pressing the depth of field preview button, the lens is stopped down to the selected aperture, enabling you to examine the depth of field before shooting. The smaller the preset aperture is, the darker the resulting viewfinder image will be. The portions of the picture that appear in focus in the viewfinder, when you press the button, will also be in focus on the film. Naturally, this technique is only possible in aperture priority and manual modes. As long as the button remains pressed, the electronic rangefinder and the autofocus will be switched off. Lenses with a meter coupling ridge, i.e. an automatic diaphragm, will not allow stop-down metering as the camera calls for metering at full aperture.

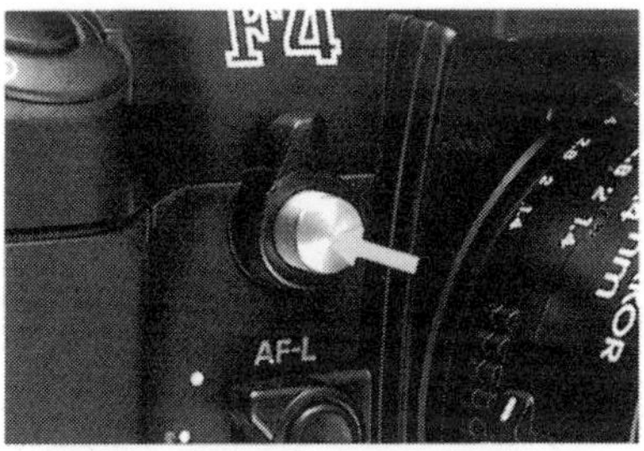

The preview button allowing depth-of-field control is a special feature for creative photography.

Mirror Lockup Lever: when you do photomicrography or use super-telephoto lenses it is advisable to lock the mirror in the up position before you shoot, in order to avoid camera vibrations due to the shutter and mirror functions affecting your picture. To lock the mirror, push the depth of field preview button and turn the mirror lockup lever anti-

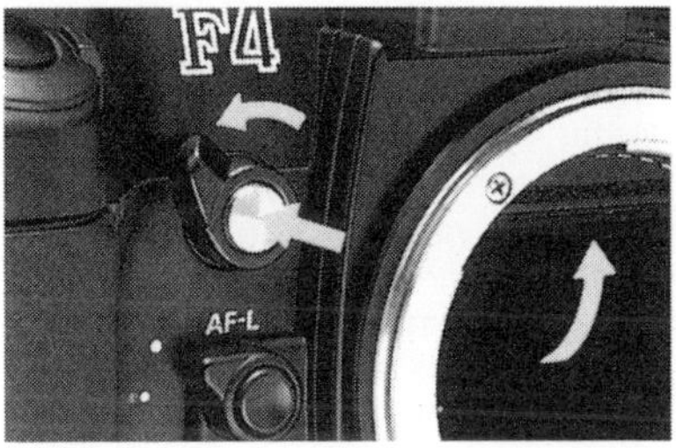

The mirror can be locked in the up position for exposures as free from vibration as possible.

clockwise until it stops. All the automatic modes including autofocus are switched off when the mirror is in the up position. Any LCD indicators in the viewfinder are due to stray light entering through the eyepiece and do not represent any valid information.

Autofocus Lock (AF-L) Button: this button, located directly below the depth of field preview button, comes in handy when you are using an autofocus mode and intend to focus on an off-centre part of your composition. If so, just aim the focus brackets in the viewfinder at this specific detail, lightly press the shutter release button and finally the AF-L button as soon as the green in-focus LED in the viewfinder lights up. As long as the AF-L button remains pressed you can continue to compose your picture and the focus setting will be locked even if you take your finger from the shutter release button. This also makes it possible to use the AF-L function in the Continuous Servo mode without having to keep the shutter release button pressed in order to lock the focus setting. The possibility of locking both the exposure and focus setting simultaneously is very practical in everyday use. This is done by turning the AF-L/AE-L simultaneous lock lever from its normal position, indicated by a white dot, to the position marked by both a white and a red dot. Whereas only the focus setting is locked when pressing the AF-L button in the first position the exposure setting will be locked additionally in the second case.

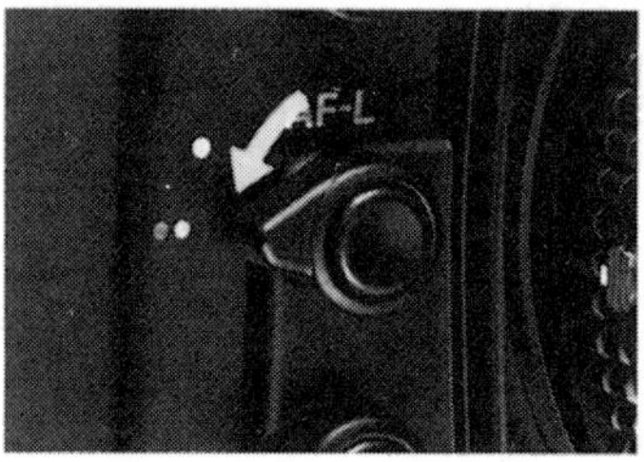

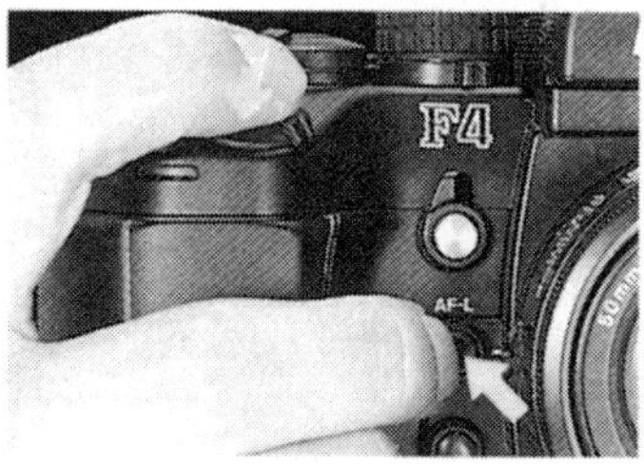

The Nikon F4 allows simultaneous locking of both AF and exposure meter readings.

Automatic Exposure Lock (AE-L) Button: if you want to concentrate the exposure meter reading on an off-centre subject too, the AE-L button lets you do so in the same way as the above-mentioned AF-L button works. First, aim the centre of the viewfinder at the subject you wish to have the metering emphazised on and, while lightly pressing the shutter release button also press and hold the AE-L button. Then you can recompose and shoot. The AE-lock function is confirmed by the **EL** signal in the viewfinder LCD. If you happen to be using Single Servo Autofocus mode you will have to refocus after recomposing your picture. To do so press the shutter release button again after taking your finger off for a moment in order to reactivate the autofocus operation. Automatic Exposure Lock is possible in both Spot and Centre Weighted Metering modes. As any exposure compensation considered necessary by the camera is done automatically in the Matrix Metering Mode no exposure lock function is possible in this case.

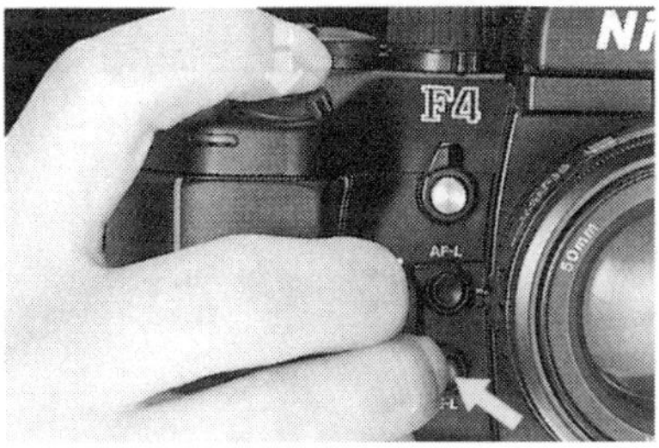

Exposure meter readings can be locked with the AE-L button whenever the system has been activated.

Sync Terminal: in addition to the ISO-standard hot shoe the Nikon F4 also has a separate screw-in type sync terminal to connect flash equipment without the usual hot shoe. The terminal is located in the top right-hand corner of the camera and takes all standard PC-type plug-in cords as well as the threaded Nikon cables. Professionals prefer the latter because the connections cannot be accidentally disengaged after being firmly screwed in, even in the heaviest action. Photographers can tell a lot of stories about how often they have hooked into something with the cable or how often it just slipped off unnoticed. Thanks to the threaded terminal Nikon sync cords are immune to this.

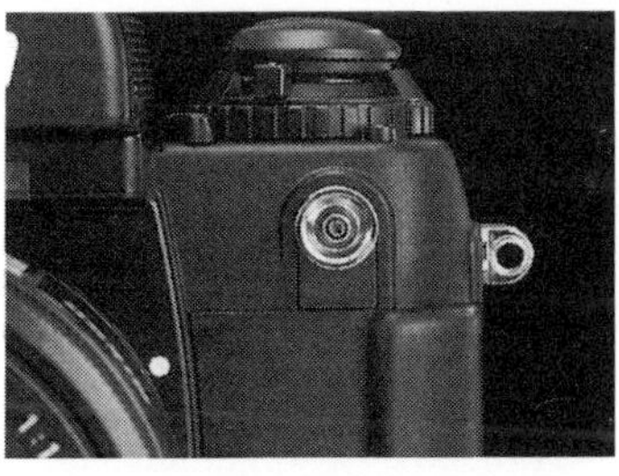

The F4 has a threaded sync. terminal for synchro cables in addition to the ISO type hot shoe.

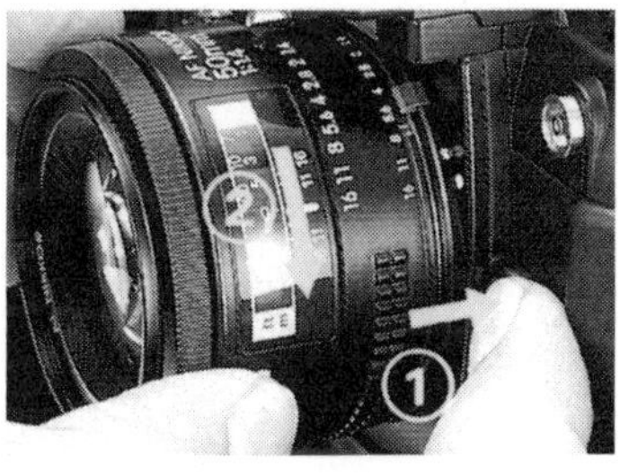

The lens release button must be pressed in order to remove a lens from a camera body.

Lens Release Button: this button to the right of the camera's bayonet must be pressed in order to remove the lens. After unlocking the lens, by pressing this button, turn it clockwise until it is free.

Focus Mode Selector: this switch is located immediately below the lens release button and has three positions. **M** for manual focusing, **S**

for Single Servo and **C** for Continuous Servo. In **S** mode the shutter cannot be released until your subject is in focus, whereas it can be released any time in **C** mode. When you set the film advance mode selector to **CL** and the focus mode selector to **C** an object moving towards or away from the camera at a steady pace will automatically activate Focus Tracking. In such cases the camera will calculate the object's speed and direction and continue to drive the lens into the proper position even after mirror operation until immediately before shutter operation.

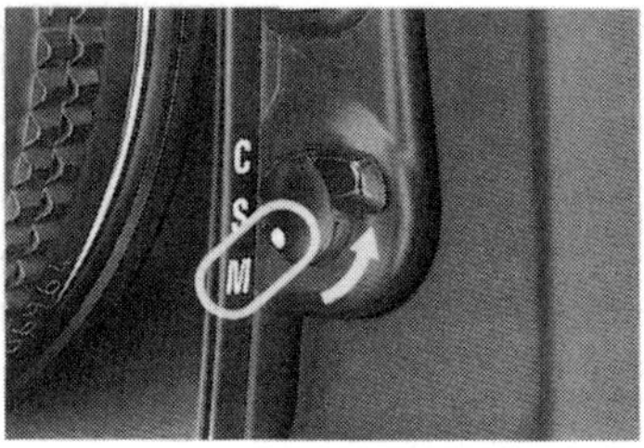

The focus mode selector switch with Manual, Single and Continuous positions

Remote Terminal: this threaded terminal with two electrical contact pins is located in the lower right-hand corner of the High-Speed Battery Pack MB-21 and enables you to use the F4 with an extensive range of remote control equipment.

Release Terminal: cable releases such as Nikon models AR-3 or the double-type AR-7 intended for the use with a bellows can be screwed into the release terminal in the bottom left-hand corner of the camera back.

Tripod Socket: both the base of the F4 and the High-Speed Battery Pack MB-21 have a standard 1/4" tripod socket which also serves as a mount for the MB-21.

Lock Screw: the bottom part of the MB-21 and MB-22 is mounted on the F4 by aligning the screw and the guide pin to the tripod socket and the guide pin hole and then tightening the lock screw clockwise. Even if this has been done correctly the lock screw will still have some play. If the lock screw is too tight you can use a coin to loosen it but normally you should be able to do it with your fingers.

Battery Check Button: you will find two LEDs and this button to the left of the lock screw on the base of the High-Speed Battery Pack MB-21. If both of the LEDs light up when you press the check button the battery power is sufficient. If only one lights up the batteries are either exhausted or not installed correctly.

Another battery check being that as long as the viewfinder LCDs remain on for 16 seconds after slightly pressing the shutter release button the batteries are OK but if the display turns off immediately afterwards they have to be replaced.

Release Lever: both the grip sections of the F4 and the F4s have a release lever on the bottom. In order to remove the grip, lift up the lever and turn it anti-clockwise – the direction indicated – to the index mark. The MB-20 and the grip section of the MB-21 have the same lock mechanisms. They are both remounted in reverse order.

Getting Started

Every single function of the Nikon F4 depends on a sufficient power supply. The four incorporated motors, the light metering system and the extensive computer controls cannot do without. Power can be supplied by AA type batteries, Nicads of the same size, or directly from the mains. The power packs are loaded with different numbers of batteries.

Power Supply

Nikon Battery Pack MB-20: together with this battery pack, designed to take four AA-type batteries, you will get the most compact version of the F4. In order to install the batteries lift up the release lever on the bottom of the pack, turn anti-clockwise to the index mark, and then remove the pack. After installing the batteries as shown inside the pack, remount it by rotating the release lever clockwise until it stops. Please be sure the batteries you buy do not have positive-terminals thicker than 5.5 mm.

Alkaline-manganese batteries will give you the highest overall performance including fast frame rates and a high number of film rolls per set. Nicads will have to be changed more often but their advantage is that they are rechargeable. The batteries are tested by lightly pressing the shutter release button. If the viewfinder LCDs stay on for 16 sec after taking your finger off again, power supply is sufficient. If they turn off immediately you will have to replace the batteries.

Nikon High-Speed Battery Pack MB-21: to install the batteries you can remove the grip section of the MB-21 in the same way as described for the MB-20 above. But, unlike the MB-20, it only takes three AA-type units, either batteries or rechargeable Nicads. The correct position for the plus and minus terminals is indicated on the inside of the pack. In addition a little switch allows for the different power sources. When you use Nicads it has to be set to **KR-AA** and if you use normal batteries, set to **LR-6**. You do not have to remove the bottom part of MB-21, which also takes three units of 1.5 V or 1.24 V in its battery holder, to install them according to the terminal markings. After that, push the holder back into MB-21B until it clicks into position and replace the grip section and secure it with the release lever.

The battery condition in the High-Speed Battery Pack can be checked the same way as with the MB-20. In addition it has a check button. If the power supply is sufficient both of the LEDs next to the button will light up when you press it. If only one lights up you should change the batteries as soon as possible. When neither of the LEDs react the energy source is either exhausted or installed incorrectly. The film mode advance selector should always be kept in the L position when the camera is not in use to conserve power.

External Power Regulator MB-22: this consists of a grip and a bottom part similar to those of the High Speed Battery Pack. The terminal allows the connection with the Nikon AC/DC Converter MA-4 via the Power Cord MC-11. A regulator inside the MB-22 reduces the 15 V current delivered by the MA-4 to 8.2 V.

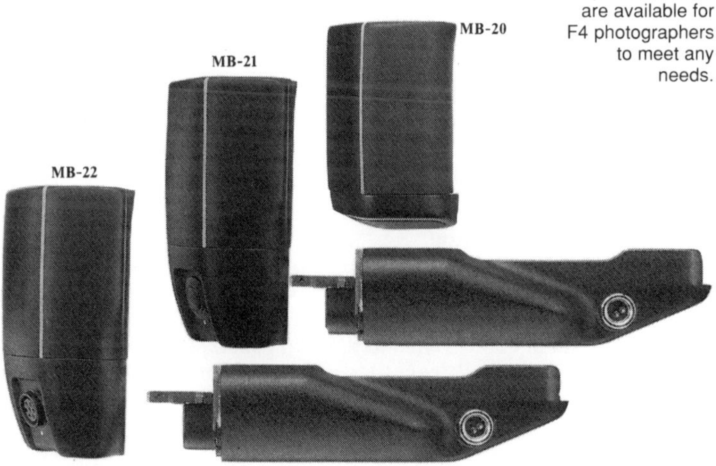

Three different power sources are available for F4 photographers to meet any needs.

Nikon AC/DC Converter MA-4 and External Power Cord MC-11: the F4 can be supplied directly from the alternating current mains through the converter MA-4 which delivers a 15 V current to the external

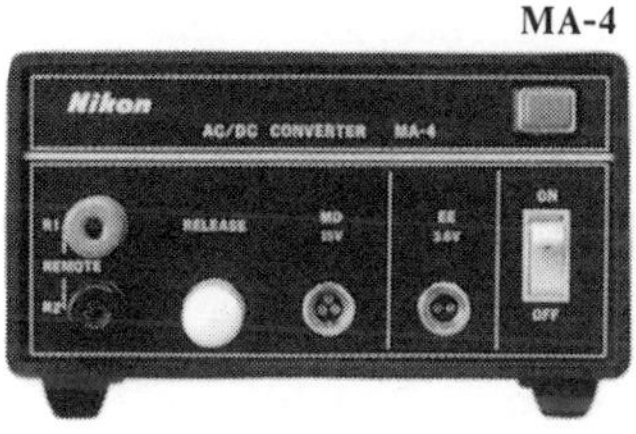

The F4 can be supplied with power from the mains with the AC/DC converter MA-4 and the connecting cable MC-11.

power regulator MB-22 through the power cord MC-11. A direct power supply from the mains allows for permanent studio use without having to change batteries.

How to Load the Film

The camera back can be opened by pushing the lock lever and pulling up the rewind knob at the same time. The film cassette can then be inserted into the chamber and the film leader pulled along the guide rails to the red index mark under the take-up spool. Be sure to avoid any film slack. Then close the camera back. As soon as you press the shutter release button the camera will automatically advance the film to frame 1. To help save battery power the shutter is not activated during the film loading operation. The Nikon F4 uses only a minimum length of the film leader to ensure correct loading so that you will always get at least 36 exposures and in many cases one or two more. Please be sure not to touch the shutter blinds with your fingers or the film leader while inserting the cassette. The camera cannot load the film if you have pulled out the leader too far but in this case the red LED next to the film speed dial will blink and the release button will be locked. To ensure correct loading you will have to rewind the film manually which can be done with the rewind crank very easily and then repeat the loading procedure. You should always load the film with your back to the sun or in shadow because bright light might find its way through the cassette slit and fog the film.

If you use an uncoded film and the film speed dial is set to **DX** the shutter release button will lock when pressed and the red warning LED on the top of the camera will blink. Automatic film loading operation will commence after you set the film speed manually within a range of ISO 6 to ISO 6400. If you are using a DX-coded film but an ISO film speed is set manually the camera will always give priority to the manual setting. The dial locks in 1/3rd EV steps but only has numbered settings for whole ISO steps from 6 to 6400. Every step represents twice the sensitivity of the former. Two dots between each pair of numbers stand for the intermediate settings. If you want automatic film speed setting you should turn the dial to **DX** and insert a DX-coded film.

The additional facility of manually setting the film speed is absolutely necessary for professional photographers. First because many of them never use certain films at their face value as they prefer certain amounts of over- or underexposure, depending on the type of film, and secondly because they are often forced to underexpose and have the films push-processed afterwards. Such cases call for settings different from the DX-code. Another reason for manual setting is the naturally uncoded type of film with variable sensitivity whose ISO speed is only determined through processing. More details in the chapter about films.

How to Mount the Lens

You can use all kinds of different Nikon lenses with the F4 but only AF-Nikkors let you take advantage of every single automatic mode. Some of the older lenses can be used in autofocus mode with the Autofocus Teleconverters TC-16 and TC-16A. Manual focusing with the help of the electronic rangefinder is possible with nearly every Nikon or Nikkor lens. The chapter about lenses will inform you what lenses allow which functions. Right now the subject is the actual mounting and dismounting of a lens.

To mount a lens, align the indexes on the camera and lens then press the lens onto the camera bayonet and turn it anti-clockwise until it clicks into place. To remove a lens, press the lens release button and turn the lens clockwise until the indexes are aligned again before disengaging.

If you want to use manual focusing Nikkors of the non-AI type on the Nikon F4 the meter coupling lever has to be unlocked, by pressing the meter coupling release button, and pushed into the up position. Metering is then done in the way described in the chapter about exposure metering – as stop-down metering. Spot metering is not possible, though. You must remember to push the meter coupling lever back to its normal position when you intend to mount an AI-standard lens, because otherwise a lens with an automatic diaphragm will either function improperly or at best only with stop-down metering. The release button for the meter coupling lever is a tiny button next to the bayonet index.

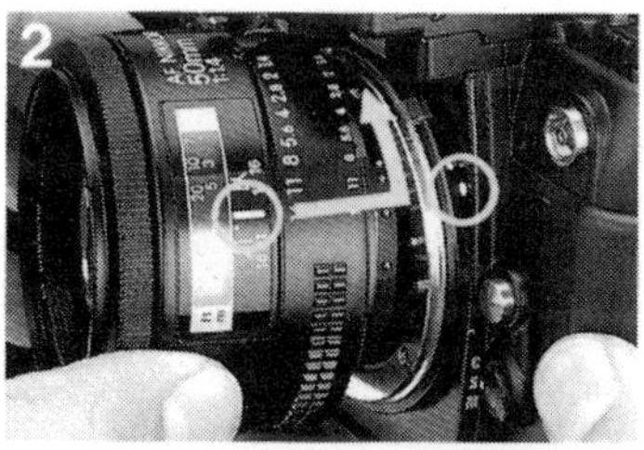

In order to remove the lens, the lens release button must first be pressed and the lens then rotated clockwise. When attaching a lens, first align the index marks on the camera body and lens before rotating.

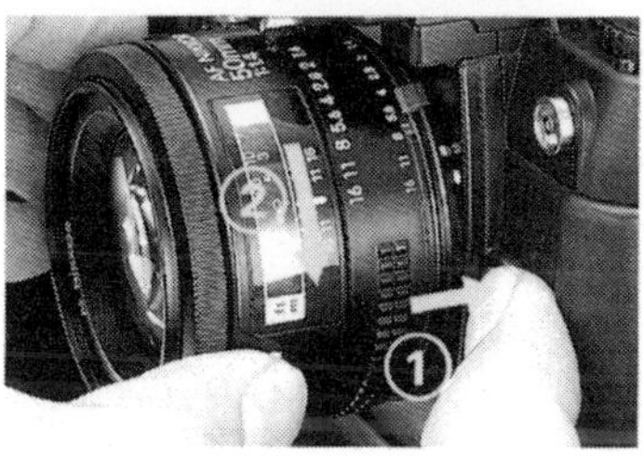

Setting the F4

Before he makes his first shot a Nikon F4 photographer has to make a number of decisions. Many of them can be left to the F4's numerous automatic modes but certain technical and creative intentions call for preliminary checks and settings.

1. Film Speed Settings: the photographer has to choose between manual or automatic DX-code setting.
2. Metering Mode: which of the three metering modes available is best suited for the prevailing lighting?
3. Exposure Metering Mode: he has to decide which of the four automatic and the manual modes he favours. Depending on his choice he will have to preset the aperture on the lens or set it to the smallest *f*-stop when he has chosen one of the program or speed priority modes. In manual mode he will have to set the aperture and shutter speed according to the electronic analog display in the viewfinder.
4. Manual Override: depending on personal taste, experience, or other circumstances the photographer may consider it necessary to override an automatic exposure. In any case he will have to decide if he wants to follow the meter reading or not.
5. Focusing: the photographer can choose between three different operating modes even in the case of focusing. He can leave it up to autofocus and choose between Single and Continuous Servo Modes. Or he can focus manually with the assistance of the optical signals of the electronic rangefinder.
6. Film Advance Mode: this is also something the photographer has to decide upon beforehand. He has to choose between single or continuous frame advance at a high or lower speed, or even very quietly.
7. Film Advance Control: the red LED next to the film speed dial lights up when the film is not being advanced correctly or the film speed dial is set to **DX** when an uncoded film or a film with an unreadable code is being used.
8. Battery Check: sufficient battery power is a prerequisite for the correct functioning of the automatic controls, so a battery check belongs to the preparatory operations.

Fast lenses are a prerequisite for pictures like this one. Autofocus and matrix metering make it easier still.

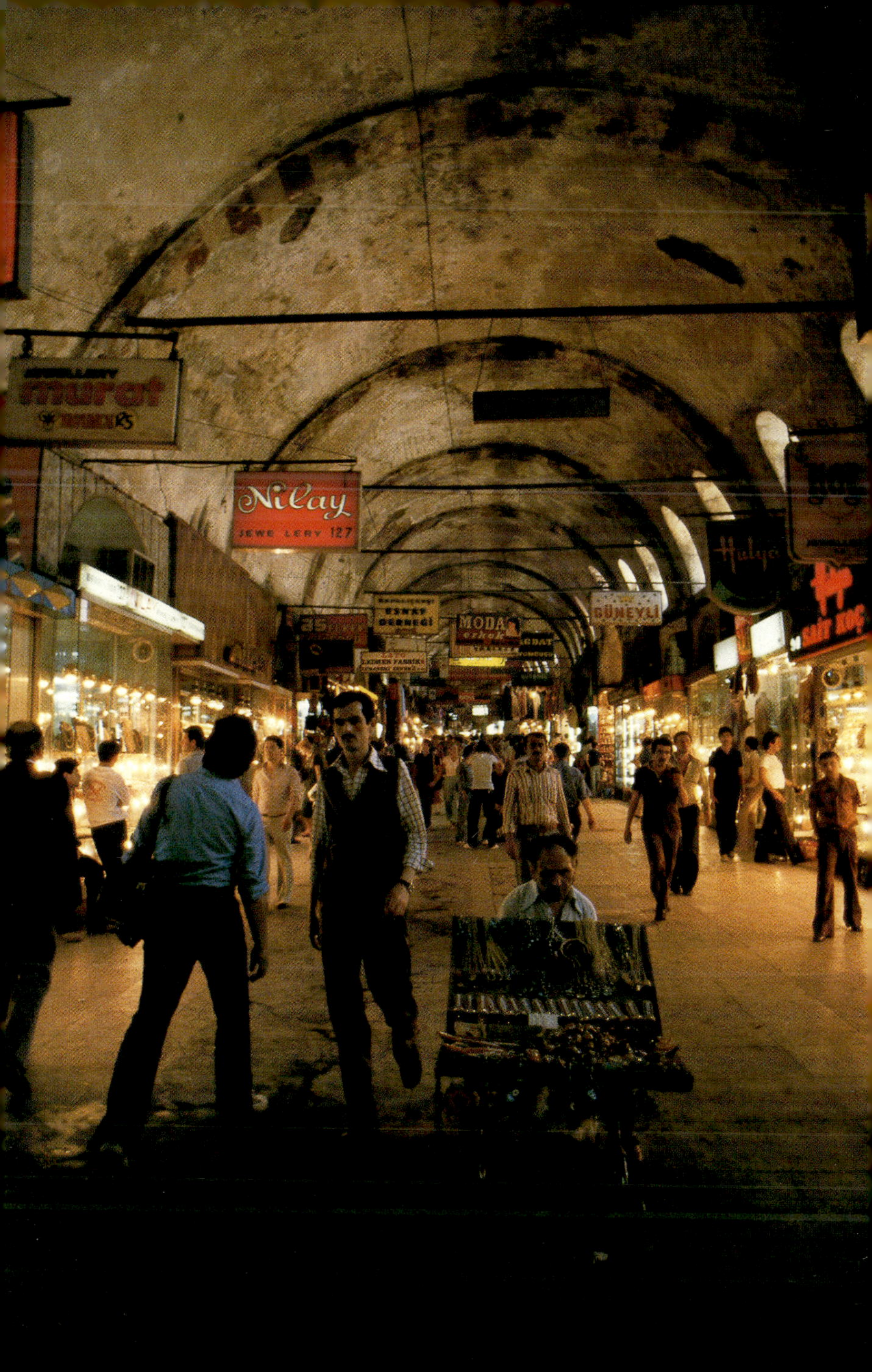
murat
Nilay
JEWE LERY 127
MODA
GÜNEYLİ

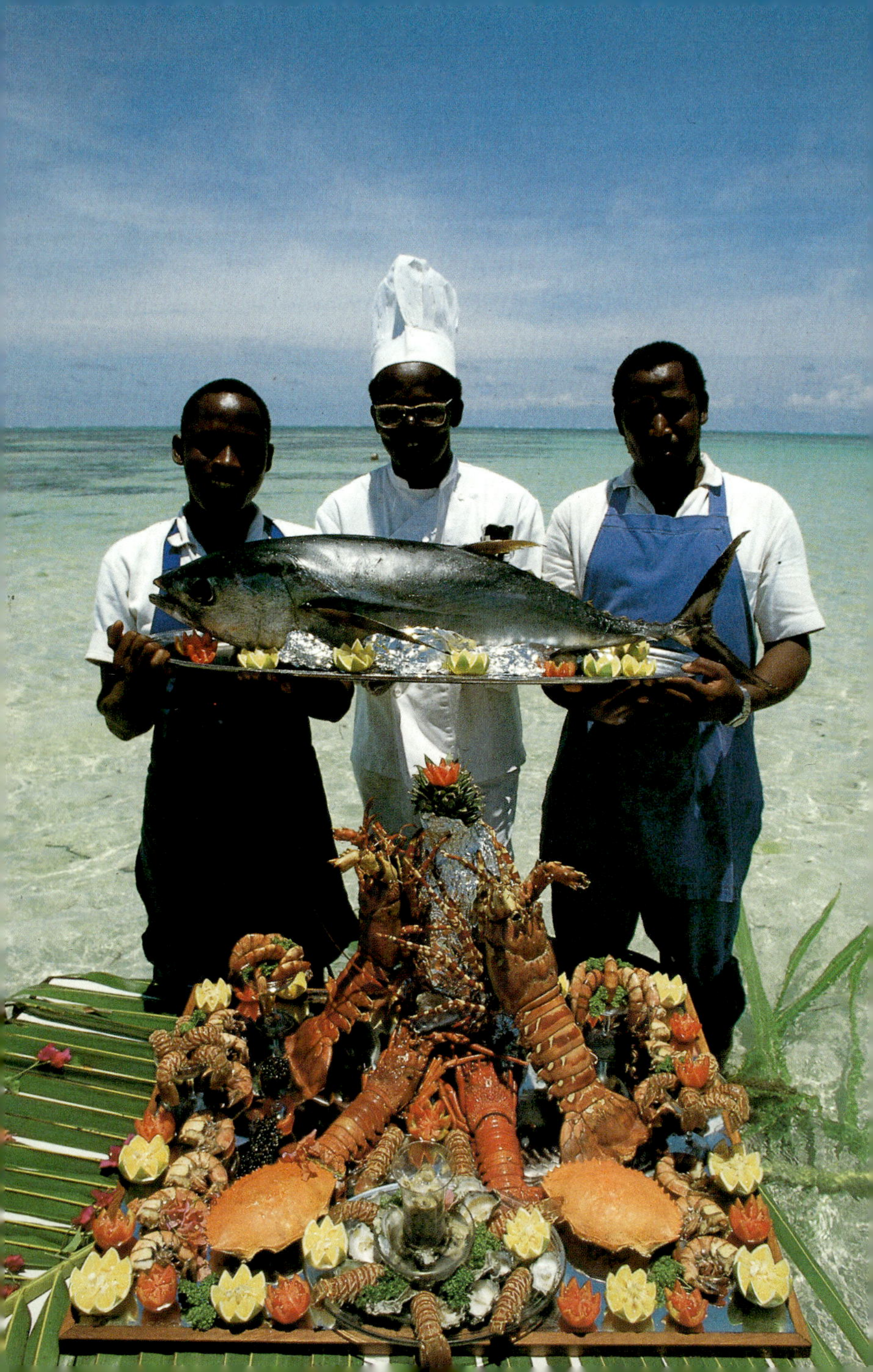

In addition to the previously mentioned preparations, which naturally are not all necessary before every shot, the photographer may have to consider further possibilities which different situations call for; depth of field control, autofocus or exposure lock when the subject is off-centre as well as self-timer, or multi-exposure operation.

The Multi-Meter Finder DP-20

Every setting can be checked by controlling the position of the dials, levers, and buttons, but the LCDs in the Nikon F4's Multi-Meter finder are the main information source during shooting. The High-Eyepoint type pentaprism finder is ideal for those who have to wear glasses since you have an overview of the complete frame from an eyepoint of 22mm. It can be adjusted to your eyesight within the range of –3 to +1 dioptres with a built-in system.

The F4's standard Multi-Meter finder offers virtually 100% frame coverage. It has approximately 0.7x magnification ratio with a 50mm lens set to infinity. Additional features include the metering mode selector, exposure compensation for interchangeable viewfinder screens, a standard hot shoe, and an eyepiece shutter. A window on top secures an adequate illumination of the LCDs which can be electrically lit when it is dark outside.

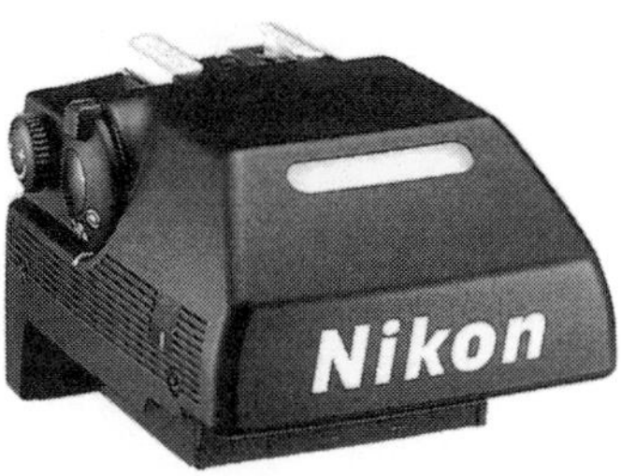

The Multi-Meter finder is a standard part of the Nikon F4 and the Nikon F4s.

The Viewfinder Information

The advanced B-type Brite-View screen is supplied as standard equipment. It has a matte/fresnel field with 5mm and 12mm diameter reference circles for Spot and Centre Weighted Metering Modes and AF-brackets.

Polarising filters can help saturate colours. It is advisable to use circular polarising filters with the Nikon F4.

The viewfinder information is located above and below the focusing screen. Not all the information possible can be seen simultaneously because it varies according to the operating mode. The top LCD, from the left, shows any exposure compensation. This enables the photographer to see how much compensation in either a plus or minus direction has been set, shown in the form of decimal ciphers like 0.3; 0.7; 1.0; 1.3; 1.7 or 2.0. A plus or minus sign also appears immediately to the right. An additional square LED signal in the right corner of the top display row generally indicates the use of exposure compensation. This seemingly redundant signal is in fact very helpful if, for example, a photographer were to shoot in the dark and switch off the viewfinder illumination to conserve power or because he thinks he knows what the displays will show. Then there is a frame counter which shows what picture number will be exposed next. This is especially important for reporters who have to know when the film in the camera has enough frames left and/or when to change films on special occasions.

The Aperture Direct Readout, in short the ADR window, is located in

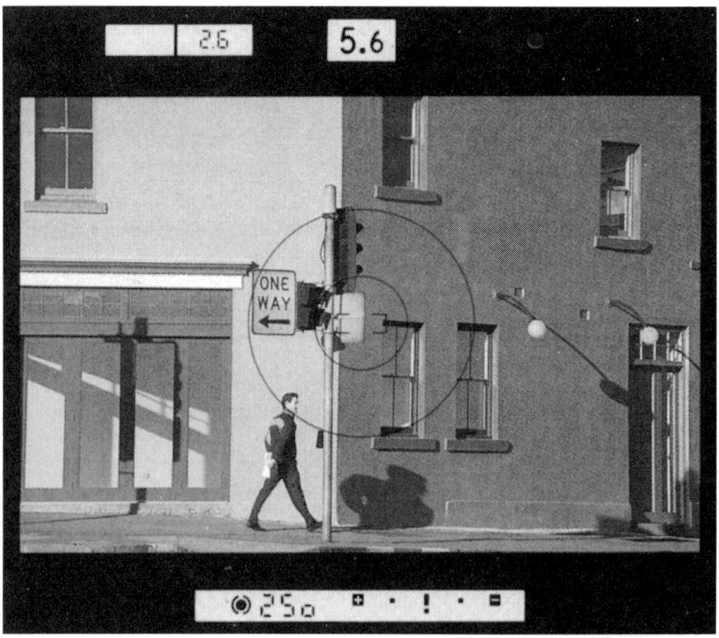

All the camera's operations appear in easily readable displays above and below the viewfinder display.

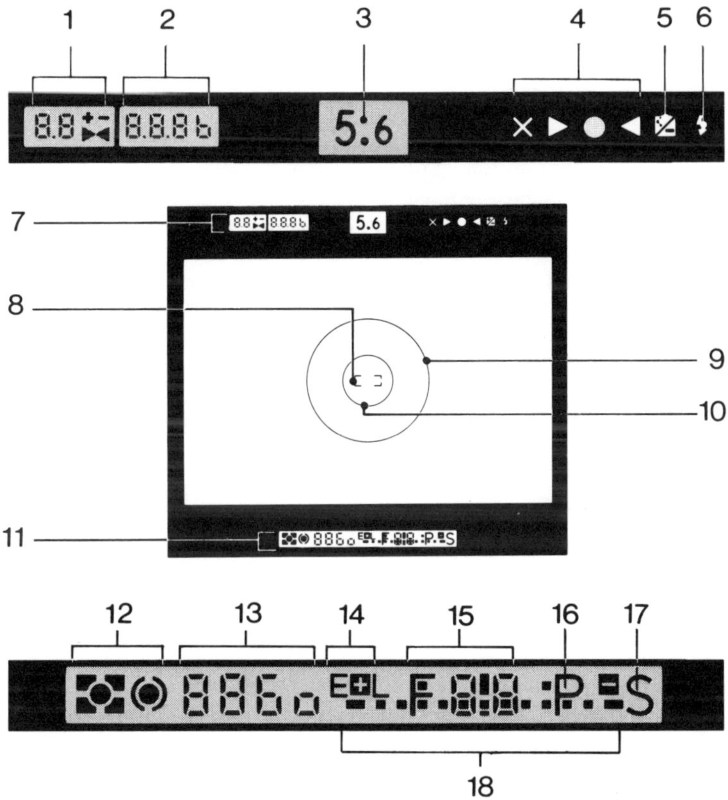

1. Exposure compensation value
2. Frame counter
3. ADR (Aperture Direct Readout)
4. Focus indicators
5. Exposure compensation indicator
6. Flash ready-light signal
7. Body side display
8. Focus brackets
9. 12mm diam. reference circle
10. 5mm diam. reference circle
11. Finder side display
12. Metering system
13. Shutter speed
14. AE-lock indicator
15. Aperture (P/S), A(A).
    No indication (M)
16. P(P). No indication (S/A/M)
17. S(S). No indication (P/A/M)
18. Electronic analog display.
    No indication (P/S/A)

the middle of the top row and allows you to read the setting through the viewfinder. A chain of LEDs is next; the red **X** lights up when electronic rangefinding is impossible due to subject conditions. Two red triangular LEDs serve as indicators for the electronic rangefinder indicating in which direction to focus the lens. The green LED in the middle indicates correct focus. The flash-ready symbol lights up when a dedicated Nikon flash unit is mounted and ready. It will blink when the unit is improperly mounted or if the flash output was insufficient.

In the lower row the metering modes – Spot, Centre Weighted, and Matrix are indicated on the extreme left. Next to this the shutter speed is shown. In exposure modes with automatic shutter control **HI** and **LO** appear when the working range of the exposure meter is exceeded. If the lens was not set to its smallest aperture, i.e. the highest number, in program and shutter speed priority modes, **FEE** will appear instead of an aperture value. When you choose a program mode **P** will appear and **S** stands for the shutter priority mode. In aperture priority mode an **A** will appear instead of an automatically-set value.

An electronic analog display will light up when manual mode is selected. The index for a correct exposure is located in the middle with plus and minus signs on the left and right indicating the maximum range of +/–2 EV steps. In between dots mark the +/–1 EV positions. A varying chain of dots below these signs indicate the deviation of the manual setting from the meter reading in increments of 1/3rd EV.

Focusing

Depending on the situation or the photographer's preferences and habits, the Nikon F4 allows a choice of either manual or automatic focusing. When using the optional Multi-Control Databacks MF-23 or MF-24, for 250 exposures, the Freeze-Focus function is also available. In this mode the F4's shutter will be automatically released the moment a subject is at the preset focus distance which can be very helpful if you intend to shoot moving subjects at a specific point. This could enable you to catch an athlete exactly over a certain hurdle or at the finish-line. Animal photography can also be improved by the automatic releasing of the camera in Freeze-Focus mode. Shy species could be "caught" automatically the moment they appear outside their nest or den. The focus mode is chosen either with the appropriate selector or – in the case of Freeze-Focus – by setting the multi-control camera backs to that mode. If you employ lenses with an autofocus manual switch this will have to be operated as well.

The photographer has a choice of two autofocus modes when he decides to use automatic focusing; Single Servo and Continuous Servo Autofocus, the latter with or without the Focus Tracking mode. With the help of a Nikon dedicated flash unit incorporating an LED illuminator the F4 can continue to focus automatically even in complete darkness. By projecting a red light pattern it provides the necessary subject illumination and contrast required by the autofocus system up to a limited distance.

Manual Focusing

If you intend to focus manually first you will have to turn the focus mode selector to the position **M**. Some lenses with an **A/M** switch need an additional preliminary setting. After these preparations you can focus as usual by turning the lens's focusing ring. When you mount non-AF lenses no such preparations are necessary and you can immediately commence focusing without any additional settings.

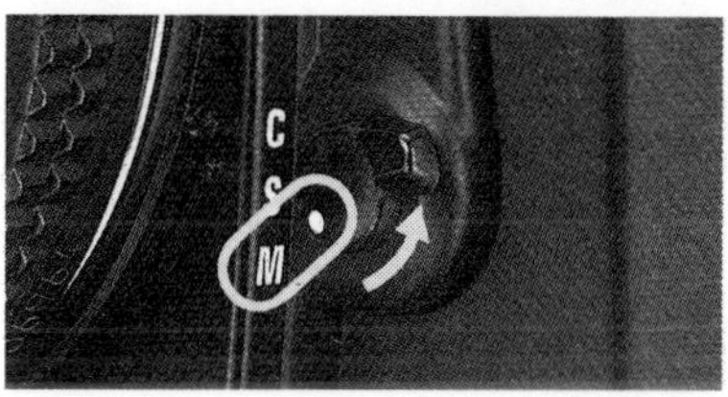

The focus mode selector must be set to **M** for manual focusing.

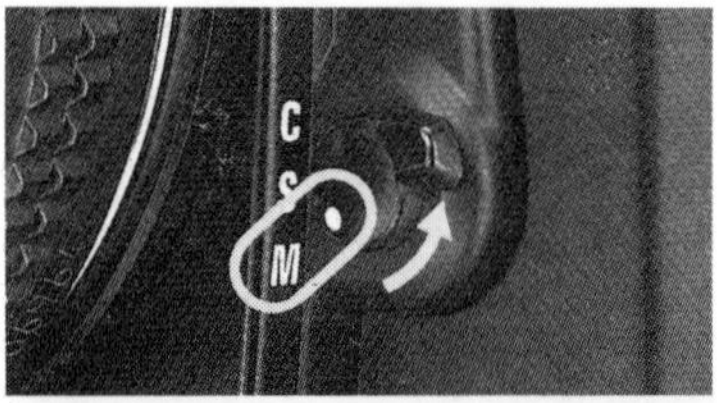

Manual focusing is a lot easier with the help of the electronic rangefinder. The triangular LEDs indicate the direction in which to focus. The green circular LED lights up when the subject is in focus.

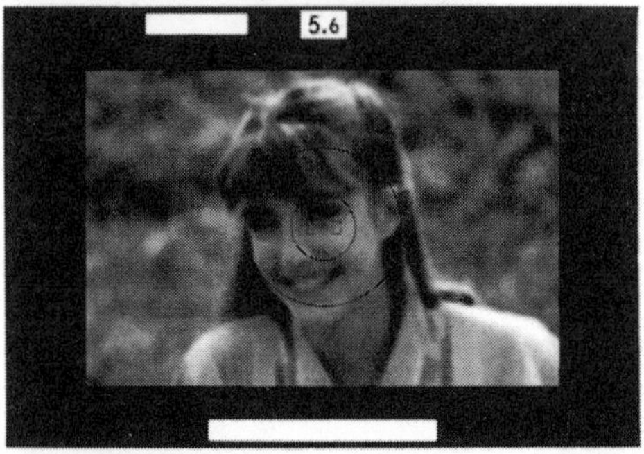

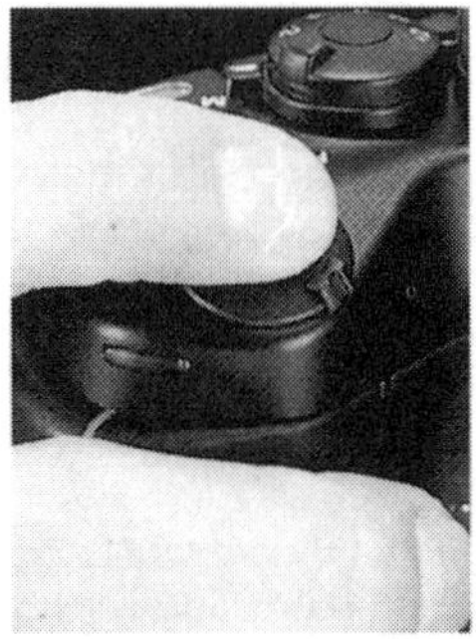

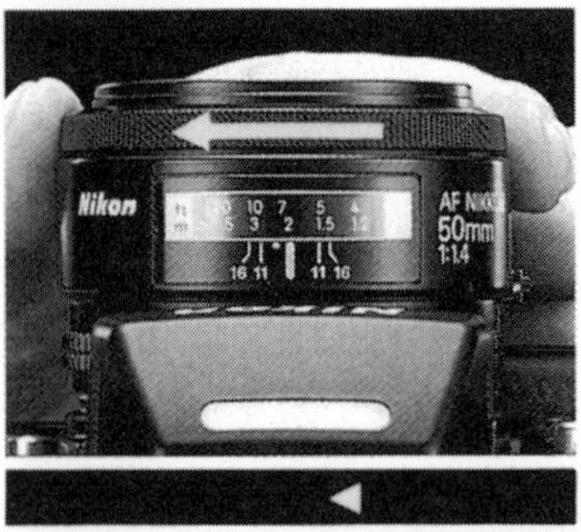

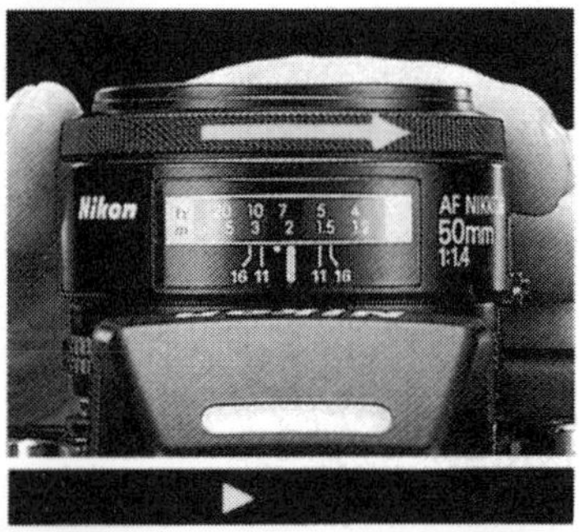

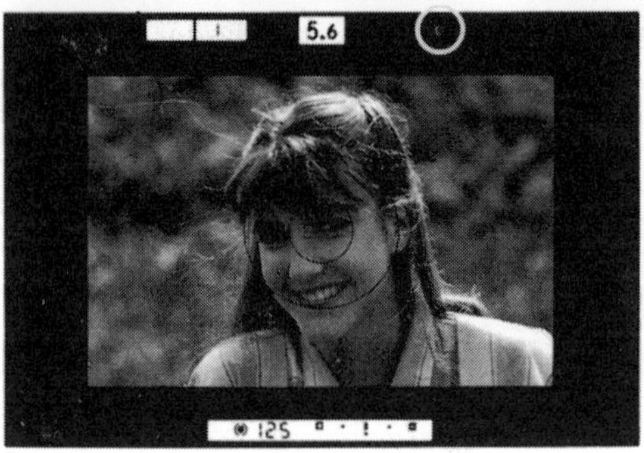

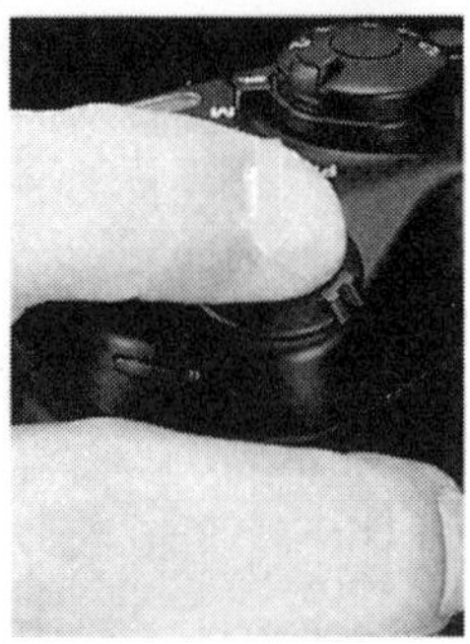

Manual Focusing with the Electronic Rangefinder: the built-in electronic rangefinding system in the F4 even works for non-AF lenses, as long as they have a minimum aperture of at least *f*5.6. Even if the focus indicators in the viewfinder light up when using lenses of lower minimum apertures, they cannot be considered reliable with such lenses.

When you want to employ the electronic rangefinder, point the focus brackets in the viewfinder at the subject detail that is supposed to be sharp, then lightly press the shutter release button and the focus indicators will light up in the viewfinder display. The two red LED triangles indicate if the lens is set to too far or too near. If the left one lights up the focus plane is in front of the subject and beyond the subject if the right one lights up. The triangles point in the direction the focus ring should be turned to obtain a sharp subject. When the focus setting is correct the red triangular LEDs will be replaced by a green in-focus LED.

If the right red LED will not disappear even if the focus ring has been turned all the way to the left, the subject must be closer to the camera than the shortest focusing distance of the attached lens will allow, so in this case the photographer will have to change his position and move further away. As soon as the green in-focus LED lights up the shutter release button can be fully depressed. Regardless of a correct focus setting the shutter can always be released in the manual focus mode.

Manual Focus Using the Clear Matte Field: there are situations in which the electronic rangefinder cannot be used, such as with lenses

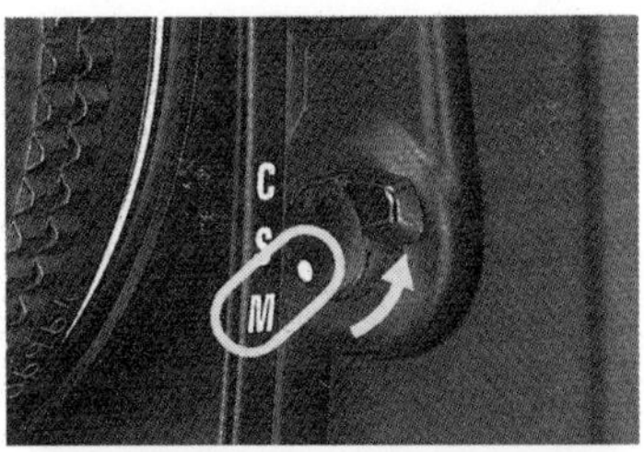

In the case of manual focusing on the clear matte screen, the focusing ring of the lens is rotated until the subject appears in focus. The focus mode selector must be set to **M**.

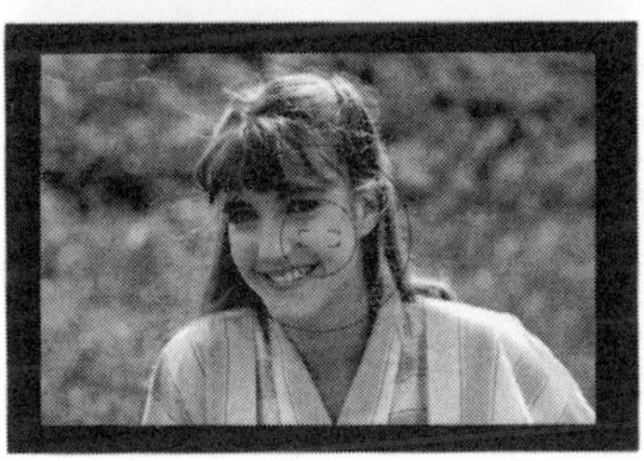

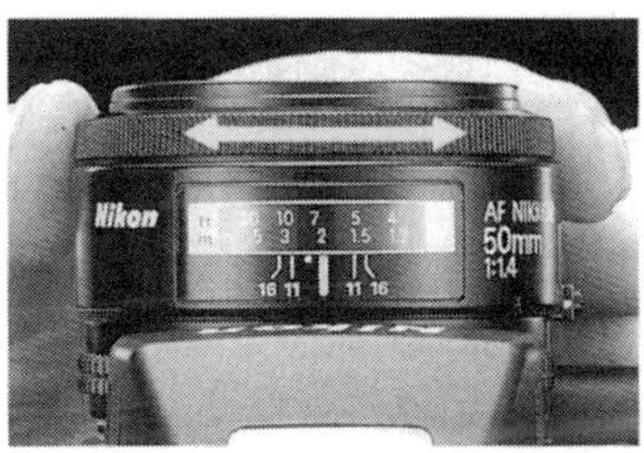

with maximum apertures of less than *f*5.6, or when the subjects have shiny surfaces, or are uniformly coloured and without any contrast and structure. A red **X** will appear in the viewfinder in those cases and indicate that focusing has to be done with the clear matte screen.

With the mode selector set to **M** the focus ring on the lens must be turned until your subject does not appear blurred but clearly in focus on the screen.

Automatic Focusing

The F4's automatic focusing works either in Single or Continuous Servo Mode. In Single Servo mode **S** the shutter can only be released after the camera has focused the lens on the subject framed in the brackets of the viewfinder. As long as you keep the shutter release button lightly pressed the setting will remain locked. In Continuous Servo mode **C** the autofocus system constantly follows every change of distance as long as the shutter release button is kept pressed. It can be released any time, even if the subject happens to be out of focus. In this case the mode selector next to the bayonet must be set to **C**. In both modes lenses with an **A/M** switch must be set to the **A** position.

In order to focus automatically, frame the detail of the subject you want to have in focus with the brackets in the centre of the viewfinder, lightly press the shutter release button until the green in-focus indicator lights up, and finally fully depress the release button. If the autofocus system is set to Single Servo mode and not able to focus due to lighting or the subject's surface conditions the red **X** focus indicator will light up

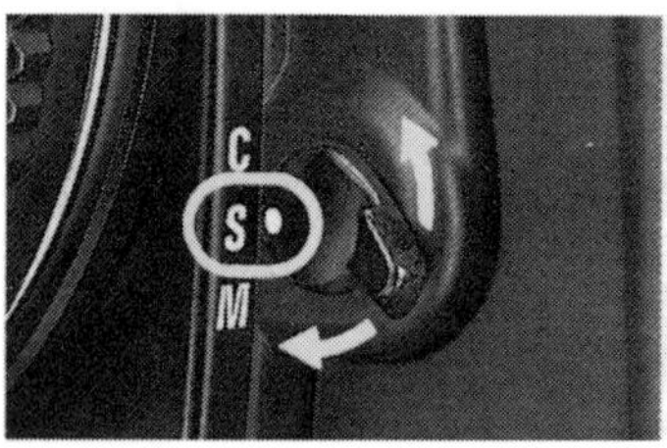

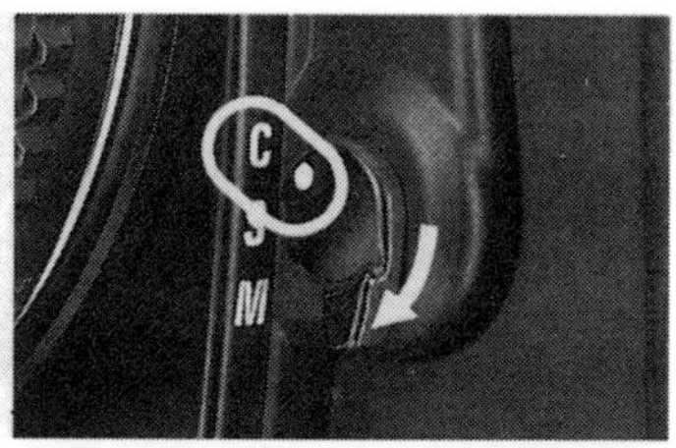

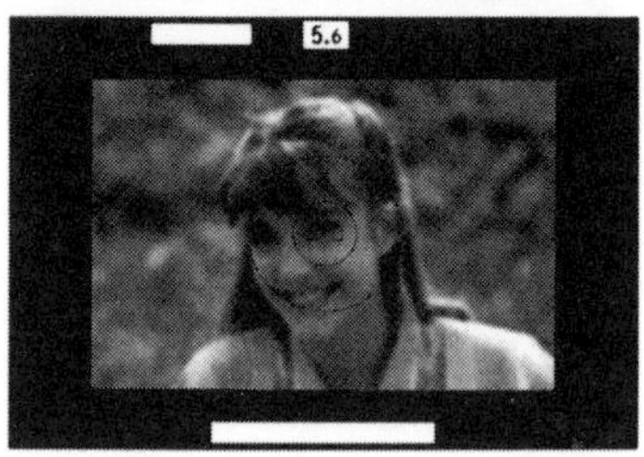

The focus mode selector must be set to either **S** or **C** for automatic focusing. The subject should be framed in the AF backets.

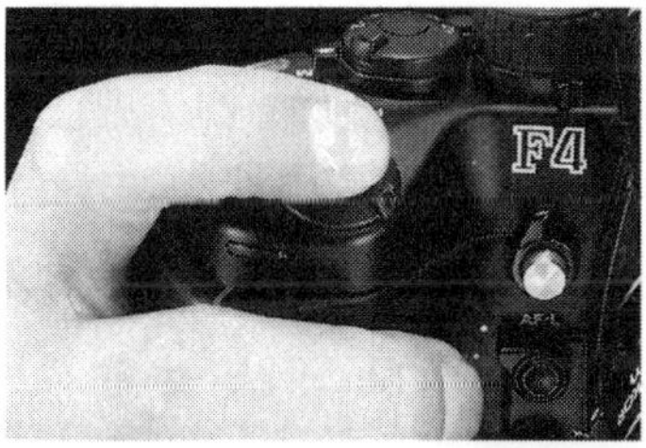

Lightly pressing the shutter release button will focus on the subject within the AF brackets. In Focus Priority, the shutter release priority will be locked until the subject is in focus.

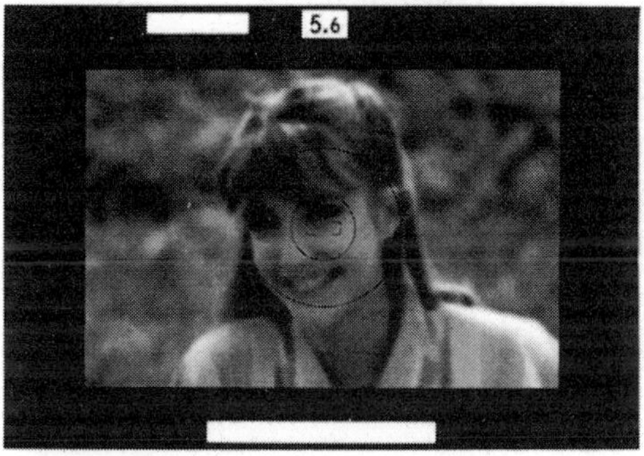

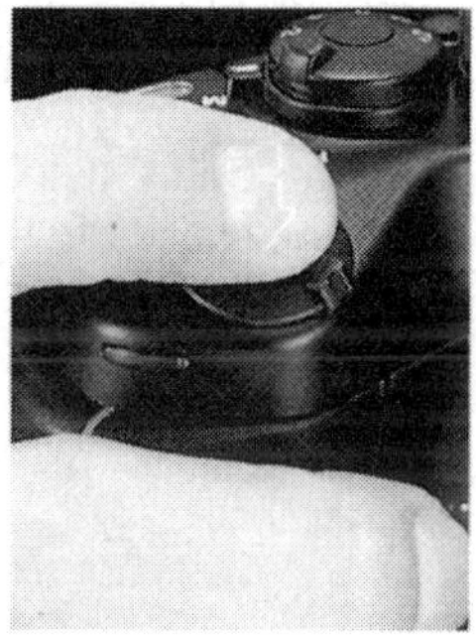

Viewfinder display for subject impossible to be focused on automatically.

and the shutter release will be locked. When you are using Continuous Servo mode the shutter can be released even in such situations, but it is advisable to switch to manual focusing on the clear matte screen in these cases to ensure a sharp picture. It is also possible to perform a substitute focusing of a subject which is located at the same distance but illuminated better, then lock the setting, frame the final composition, and finally release the shutter. The F4 offers an easy, appropriate, focusing mode for almost every conceivable photographic situation. It is important for the photographer to be familiar with them so he can find the best solution for every problem.

Situations that Cause Difficulties for any Autofocus System where Manual Focusing, with the Help of the Clear Matte Screen, should be Selected:

- subjects with bright shiny surfaces such as aluminium or silver
- backlit subjects
- subjects with details framed in the AF-brackets at different distances from the camera
- smooth uniformly-coloured surfaces

- when using red or orange filters
- when using a linear polarising filter
- when using special filters such as a soft focus filter.

Circular polarising filters do not cause any problems for autofocus or electronic rangefinder operation.

The Autofocus Lock

If an important part of the subject is off-centre you should employ the autofocus lock function. In Single Servo mode the important detail should be framed in the AF brackets in the centre of the viewfinder. As soon as you press the release button the lens will automatically be focused on just that detail and the green in-focus indicator will light up in the viewfinder. This setting will remain locked for as long as you keep the release button depressed. Then you can recompose and finally release the shutter.

When you are using Continuous Servo mode, off-centre details will have to be mastered with the help of the Autofocus Lock button. As before, aim at your main subject lightly pressing the release button, but as soon as the green in-focus indicator lights up press the AF-L button on the front of the camera. While keeping the button pressed, recompose, and finally shoot. The focus setting will remain locked as long as the AF-L button is pressed, even if you take your finger off the release button. The AF-L button can also be employed in Single Servo mode.

It is also possible to lock the autofocus and the exposure meter settings simultaneously by turning the lever downwards, then both functions will be locked whenever the AF-L button is pressed. This combination proves to be very practical since, with very few exceptions (like pictures of silhouettes or shadows) the object intended to be in focus is always the main detail and should also be exposed correctly.

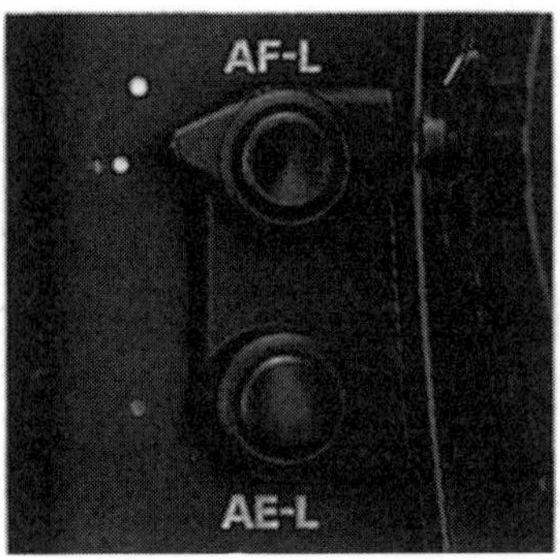

Focus and exposure meter readings can be locked with the AF-L and the AE-L buttons. It is also possible to lock both readings simultaneously with just one button.

Automatic Focus Tracking

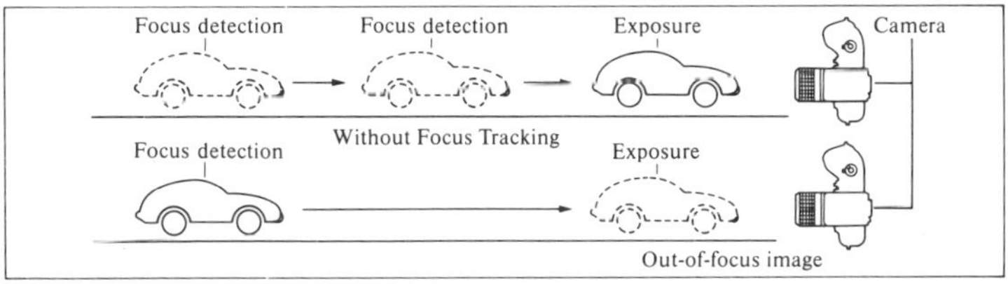

This schematic drawing illustrates the principle of Focus Tracking which is the result of new AF software enabling the system to produce in-focus photographs of moving subjects.

One of the special features of the Nikon F4 is this function which is automatically activated when the film advance mode selector is set to **CL**, the focus mode selector to **C**, and the automatic rangefinder registers a subject moving away from, or towards, the camera at an even pace. The Nikon F4 analyses the speed of the moving subject according to focus detection data and drives the autofocus lens into the position that will ensure correct focus precisely at the moment the mirror is already up and the shutter is released.

The in-focus indicator will not light up during this operation. Instead

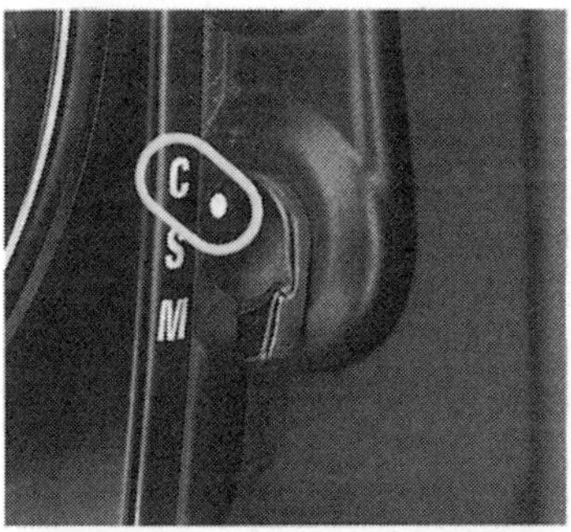

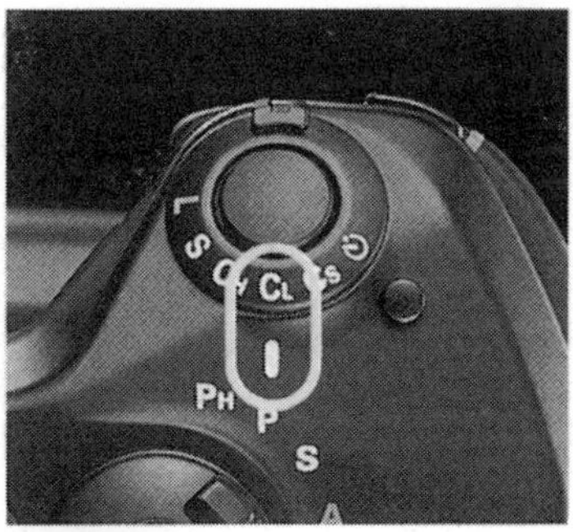

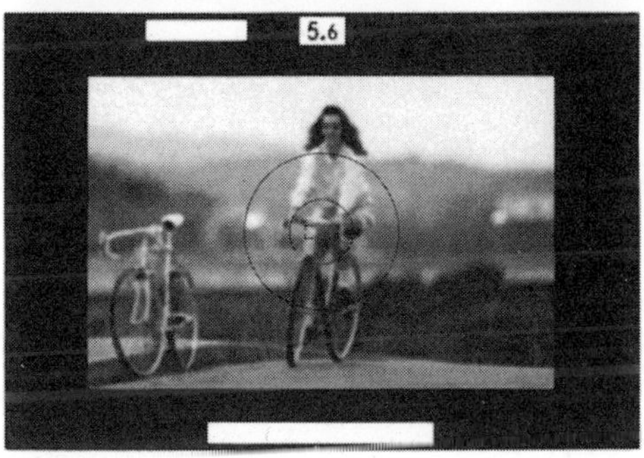

The focus mode selector must be set to **C** and the film transport dial set to **CL** in order to activate the focus tracking mode.

you should release the shutter when the two triangular LEDs in the viewfinder light up at the same time. The Nikon F4 will also recognize when the subject's movement becomes erratic and will automatically revert to the normal Continuous Servo mode. To ensure correct operation of this function the subject must be kept inside the focus brackets in the viewfinder.

In Focus Tracking Mode the main subject must be framed in the AF brackets and the shutter released when both triangular LEDs light up together.

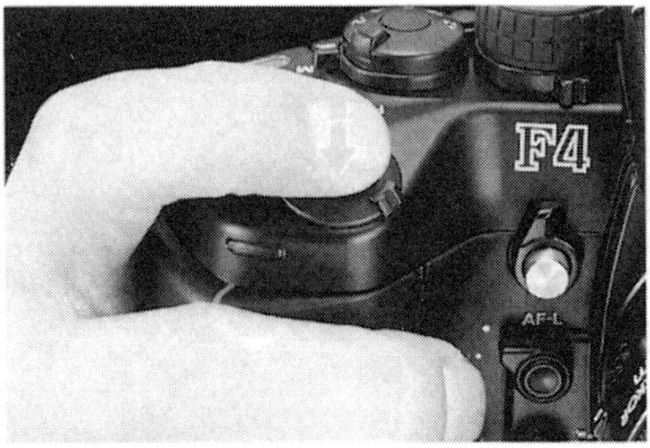

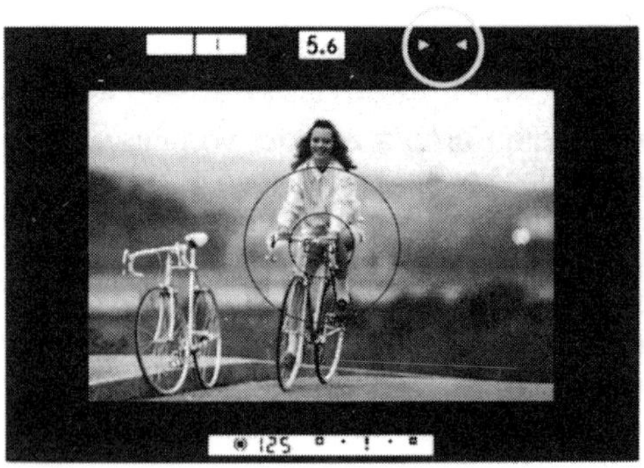

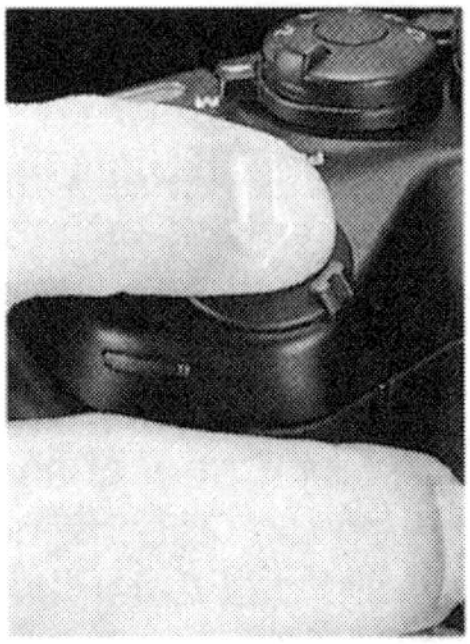

F4 Autofocus System

The advantages of this autofocus system include ultra high-speed response, reliable focus-detection capability even in light as low as EV-1, and detection of low-contrast scenes and minute subjcct details. Technically the extremely quick response is made possible by the advanced AM 200 autofocus sensor module with high-sensitivity CCD sensors, a high-speed 8-bit microcomputer, and a super-responsive coreless autofocus motor.

AM 200 Autofocus Module: approximately 30% of the light coming through the lens is necessary for focus detection and this passes through the main mirror of the F4 onto a sub-mirror which reflects it down to the AM 200 AF-unit, known from other Nikon cameras but improved for use in the F4. This module consists of an optical block with two rows of 100 highly-sensitive CCDs (Charged Coupled Devices) each. By comparing the electronic output of the two line sensors, the system detects both the amount and direction of deviation. The sensitivity characteristics of the CCD sensors can quickly store sufficient brightness data even in dim lighting conditions or in low contrast scenes for focus detection. Since these sensors offer an excellent signal-to-noise ratio and full discharge they ensure correct detection without interference from outside sources.

Computer and Software: the built-in 8-bit microcomputer unit uses software designed by Nikon. It is responsible for the ultra high-speed computation of the focus detection data obtained from the 200 CCD sensors and also for relaying the operation instructions for the autofocus operation in almost "real time". All in all three computers communicate in the Nikon AF-system. Two of them are incorporated in the body and one is built into the AF-lenses.

The new Nikon AF software enables accurate focusing of moving subjects by calculating their speed. Usually, an AF SLR, when taking a picture of a subject moving towards or away from the camera, detects the distance from camera to subject, moves the lens until correct focus is obtained, and then releases the shutter. However, this method can result in unsharp pictures because the subject may continue to move – out of the focus setting – during the period between focus detection and exposure. With the Focus Tracking function of the F4, focus is detected at least twice before the exposure and the camera calculates the difference between the two to ascertain the subject's moving speed.

Since the camera's computer knows exactly how long it takes to set the lens and how far the subject will have moved by then it will drive the lens into the proper position until exposure, to obtain correct focus. This technique allows for consecutive focused pictures of moving subjects in an AF-mode.

Autofocus Illuminator: where existing light contrast or subject detail is insufficient for AF operation, or even in complete darkness, the red illuminator incorporated in Nikon AF flash units enables a correct autofocus detection. When these units are switched on and the shutter release button is lightly pressed they project a LED-patterned beam of light onto the subject, supplying the AF system with the necessary contrast. Depending on whether focusing is done in available light or with the help of a Nikon Speedlite's AF illuminator and its infrared light, the F4 automatically switches the appropriate filters in front of the sensors. In normal shooting a filter that cuts out infrared light is employed to prevent incorrect focus detection due to the chromatic aberrations of the lens in use. The other filter transmits infrared light and is used in flash photography because of the infrared light-emitting AF illuminator in Nikon Speedlites. This feature improves autofocus accuracy in every shooting situation. Every time the filters are switched they are also cleaned by two little dust removers.

LED Focus Status

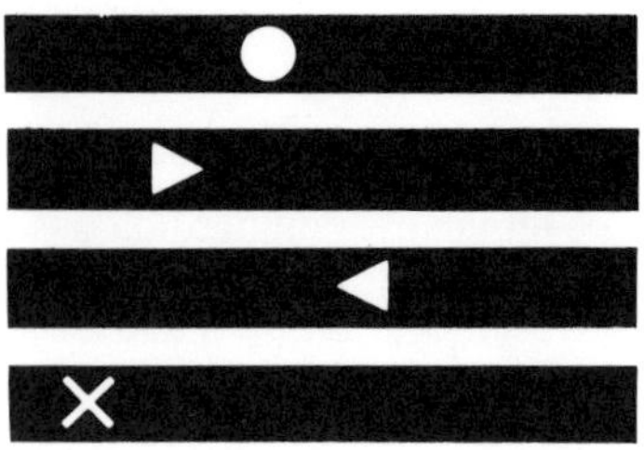

: In focus

: Front focus

: Rear Focus

: Focus not possible

Autofocus Motor: the autofocus gear train is driven by a coreless motor, which, despite being very compact, features very high torque, leading to super-fast acceleration and immediate response. Compared to the coreless motor used in the F-801 this one has been improved in torque and rotation speed by 15%.

Wide angle zoom lenses such as the AF Nikkor 28-85mm, *f*3.5-4.5 are ideal for travel photography because of their versatility. Anything from portraits to landscapes can be covered.

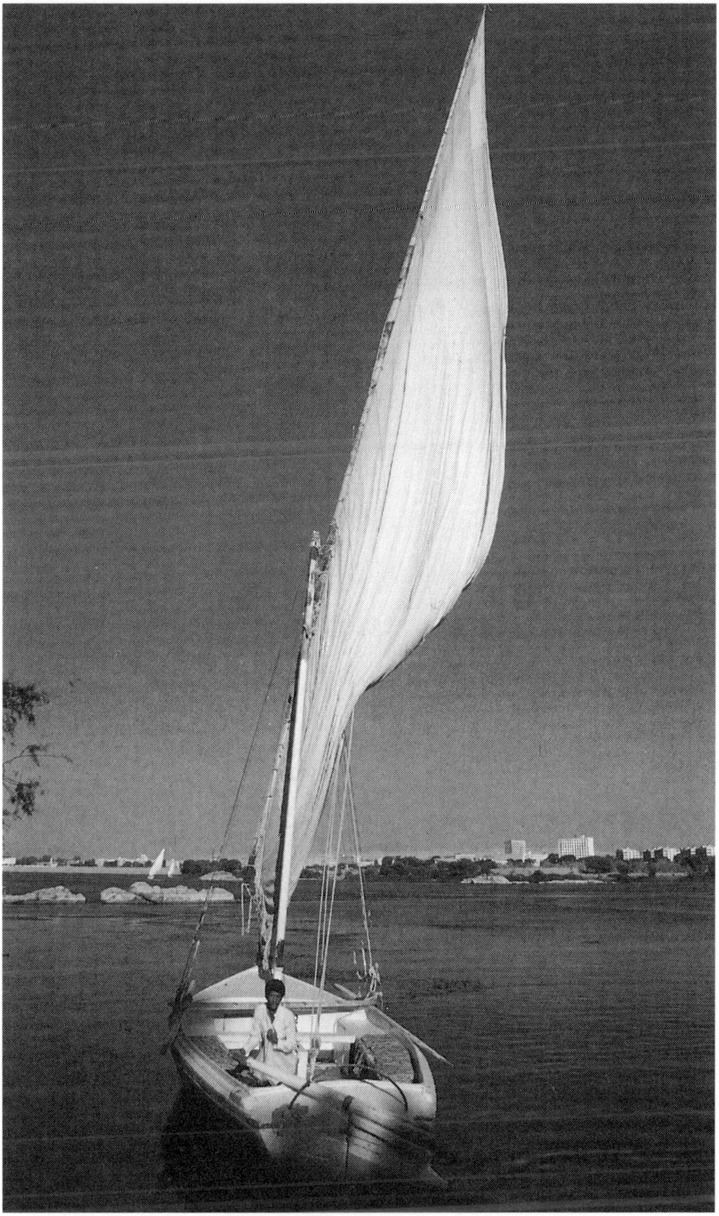

Exposure Metering

The Nikon F4 is equipped with three different exposure metering systems to cope with any kind of lighting. They are: Matrix Metering, Centre-Weighted Metering, and Spot Metering. Except for the spot sensor, the metering systems are incorporated in the viewfinder. They are switched with the meter selector dial located on the right side of the Multi-Meter Finder. Inside, the metering mode being used is also indicated in the bottom LCD row. The interchangeable viewfinders do not all offer all three metering modes but since the spot sensor is located in the camera body, this metering mode is available with all four viewfinders. The type of lens being used also determines which metering modes are accessible. Every metering and exposure mode the Nikon F4 has is available with Nikon AF and AI-P lenses. Depending on the type of mount the use of other lenses leads to certain limitations. Almost all Nikon lenses allow Centre-Weighted metering. Matrix Metering demands lenses with AI-standard mounts at least and is also available with AF-Nikkors for the F3AF. These types of mounts plus AI-modified lenses will also allow the centre-weighted mode, as do any of the teleconverters from AI-standard upwards. Matrix Metering is possible with teleconverters of AI-S standard. The lens chart in Appendix I will inform you as to the functional restrictions concerning focusing, exposure, and metering modes in combination with the different types of lenses.

Matrix Metering Mode

Matrix metering is ideal for automatic exposure modes and is also available for manual setting and for automatic flash output control with Nikon Speedlites. It is especially useful in difficult lighting, in high-contrast scenes, and in rapidly changing lighting conditions, and leads to correct exposures even when the main subject is off-centre. The Matrix Metering mode in the Nikon F4 represents the consequent development of the Multi Pattern Metering introduced with the Nikon FA in 1983. With this kind of metering a manual exposure compensation becomes unnecessary, even in the case of strongly differing levels of brightness in different areas of the frame, because it is done automatically. Two photo diodes, to the left and right of the viewfinder eyepiece, each consisting of three sensors, are employed for Matrix Metering and meter the frame in five segments. This is shown in the diagram top right. The right photo diode covers the upper and lower right segments as well as the one in the middle. The left photo diode takes over the upper and

The matrix metering sensor determines scene brightness by dividing the scene into five areas, analysing each area for both brightness and scene contrast. According to these key data, the scene is classified into one of 25 matrix "boxes", each containing one or more algorithm patterns.

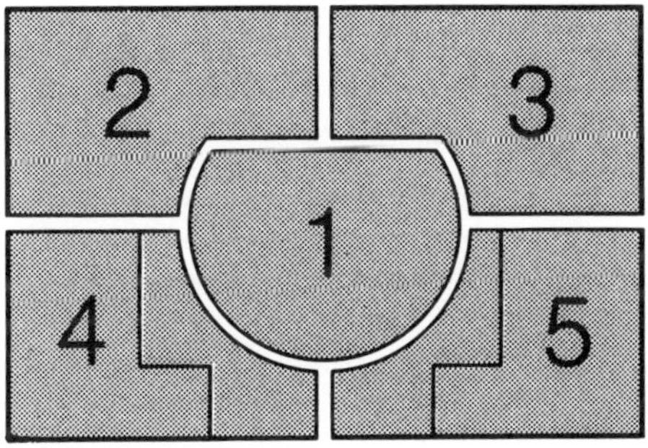

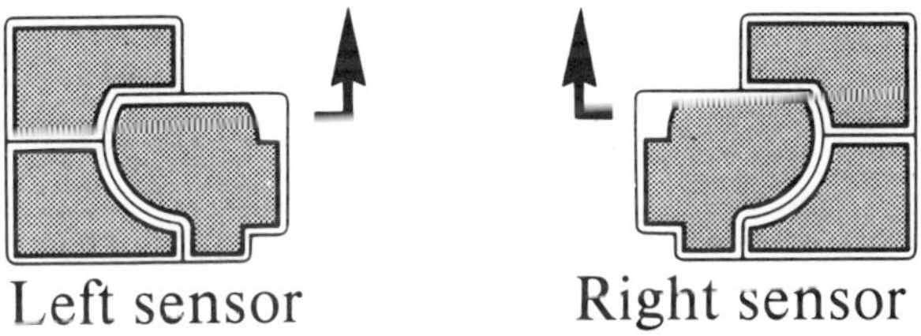

Matrix metering algorithm pattern

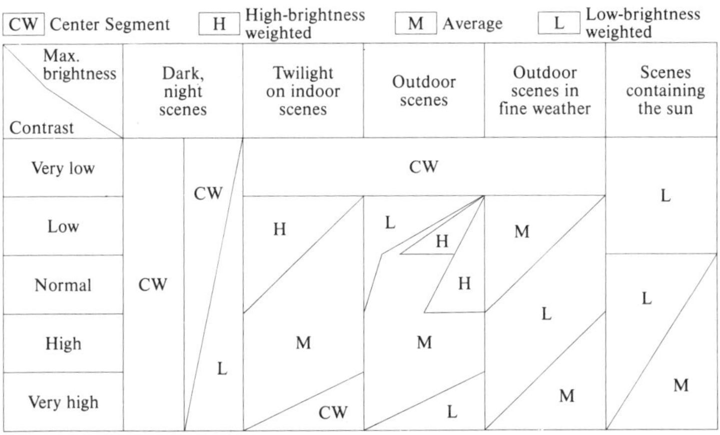

lower left segments and again the centre segment. The high-capacity computer uses software designed by Nikon to calculate the exposure data which employs an extensive range of algorithms to evaluate brightness and contrast, and arranges the information according to 25 Matrix boxes, each of which has one or more algorithms. Upon analyzing the scene's light patterns, it then determines the appropriate computation method. In the end the camera itself decides if the brighter or the darker areas should be emphasized, or if an average or a centre-weighted exposure is best for the lighting situation. Just like a professional photographer, Matrix Metering averages out extremes of brightness and darkness. Matrix Metering works efficiently in a vertical as well as a horizontal composition. When the camera is turned from the one to the other position the mercury switch enclosed in each of the two sensors is automatically activated, thus detecting the prevailing position and the metering output assignment of the five segments is changed accordingly. The diagram shows exactly how the segments are addressed in two positions.

Centre-Weighted Metering Mode

The centre-weighted mode of the F4 operates with 60% of the meter's sensitivity within the 12mm circle in the centre of the viewfinder, unlike the F3 which had a higher concentration of 80%. You can combine this metering mode with any automatic or manual exposure mode and it is available in the standard DP-20 Multi-Meter Finder as well as the AE Action Finder DA-20.

This is an appropriate metering mode whenever your main subject is not too small but not frame-filling either, although you do have to keep in mind that the important part of the picture should be arranged in the middle.

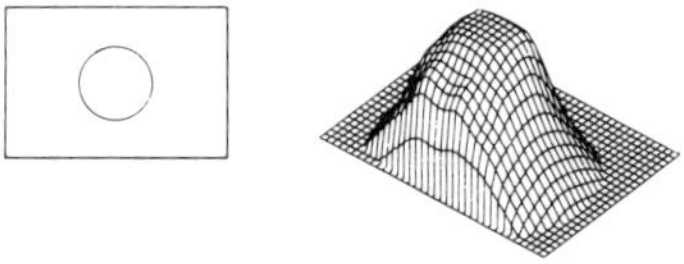

Sensitivity of Centre-Weighted Metering.

Spot Metering Mode

Spot Metering is best for the precise and selective metering of tiny subjects in manual exposure mode. The inner circle of 5mm diameter in the viewfinder defines the area covered by the spot. The spot sensor is an integrated part of the F4's autofocus module in the camera body. Therefore, this metering mode, which is so vital for individual compositions, is available with every interchangeable viewfinder. If you employ Spot Metering along with an automatic exposure mode, you will either have to aim the area of metering within the small circle at a part of your subject that you intend to have averagely bright or you will have to use the exposure lock function.

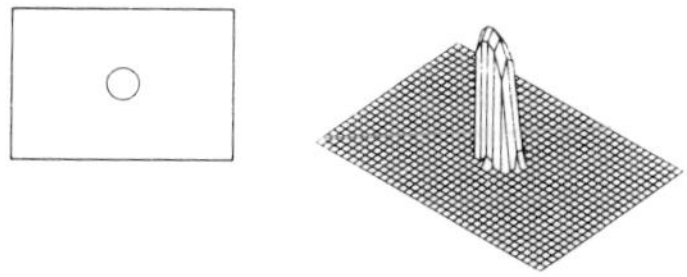

Sensitivity of Stop Metering.

The Exposure Controls

Five different exposure control modes are available in the Nikon F4. Depending on the situation you can choose between Manual mode, High-Speed and Normal Program modes and Aperture or Shutter Priority modes. Some of the lens types mentioned earlier do not allow all the above modes. The lens compatibility chart (Appendix I) shows exactly which modes will work with what lens. You will see that lenses with built-in microcomputers allow the use of any exposure mode.

In Aperture Priority and the Program modes the shutter speeds are controlled automatically and stepless from 30 to 1/8000th sec. The lower LCD in the viewfinder indicates the speeds in 1/2 steps, as well as any exposure compensation employed with automatic control. You can lock the exposure reading with the AE-L button. When you want to lock both the latter and the autofocus setting you can do so by switching the lever concentric to the AF-L button to its lower position and pressing the button.

The Multi-Control Data Backs MF-23 and MF-24 for 250 exposures also enable you to perform Auto Exposure Bracketing with a preset number of frames and differing exposure levels.

Manual Mode

The shutter speed and aperture are not only means of controlling the correct exposure but are also important for the picture composition. A camera claiming to be professional must offer the photographer the possibility of setting both elements individually according to his creative intentions. Fast shutter speeds will freeze movement or prevent blurred pictures due to camera shake whereas slower speeds give an image of blurred streaks or can be employed in panning your subject; creating the typically blurred background. For manual setting the mode selector must be set to **M**.

The aperture determines the depth of field, i.e. the area that also appears sharp in front of and behind the focal plane. Large apertures produce a shallow depth of field and smaller *f*-stops lead to larger areas of sharpness, so you can either let your main subject stand out or create in-focus pictures of overall uniformity.

The reliable automatic exposure controls and the fast AF system of the Nikon F4 guarantee excellent results without extensive preliminary technical adjustments and deliberation.

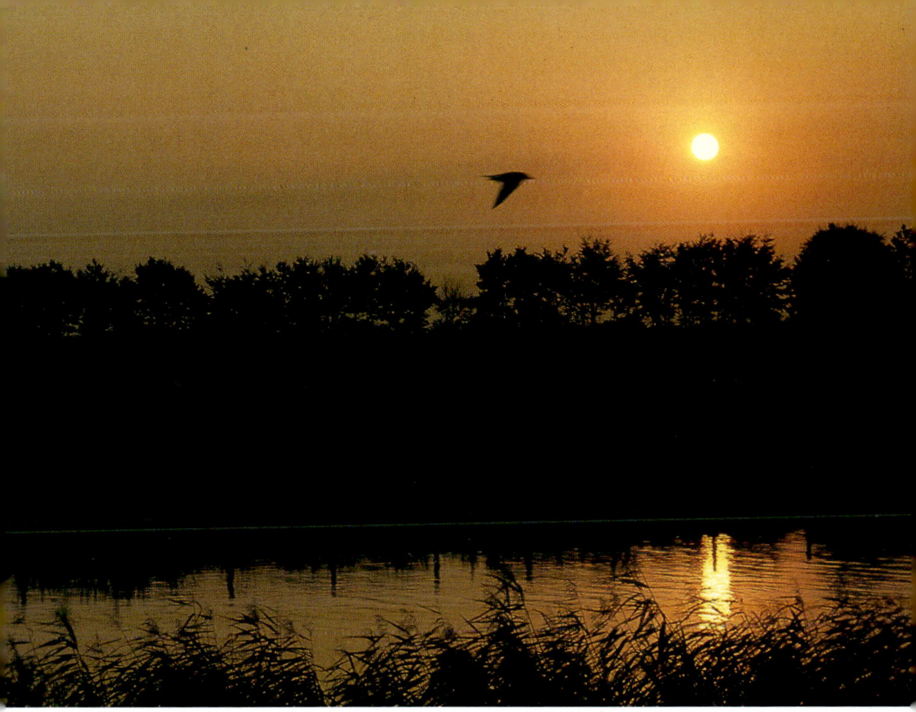

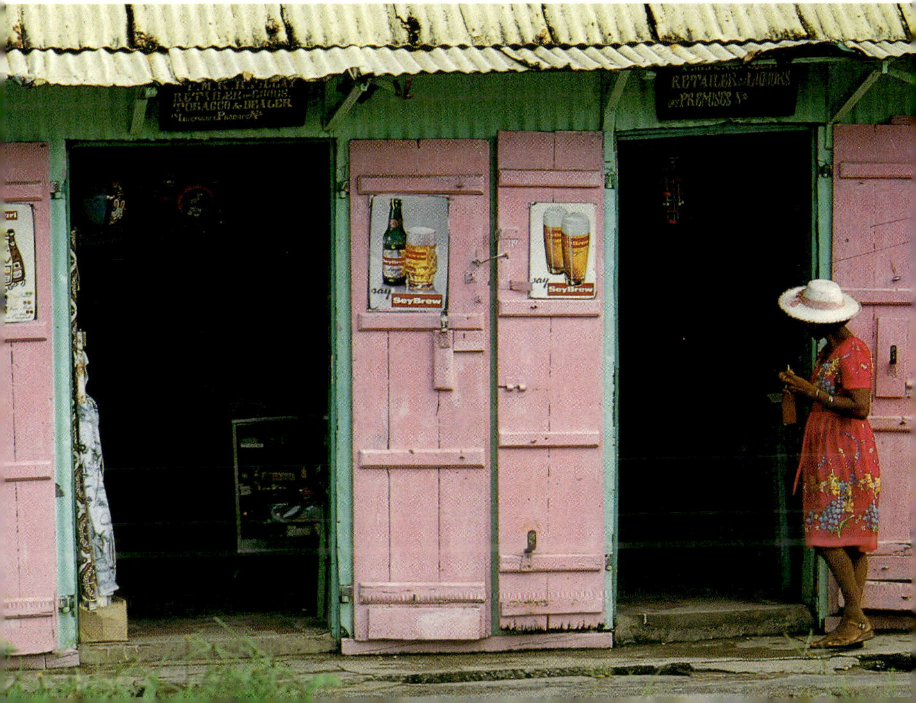
TOBACCO & DEALER
RETAILER LIQUORS
PREMISES
say SeyBrew
SeyBrew

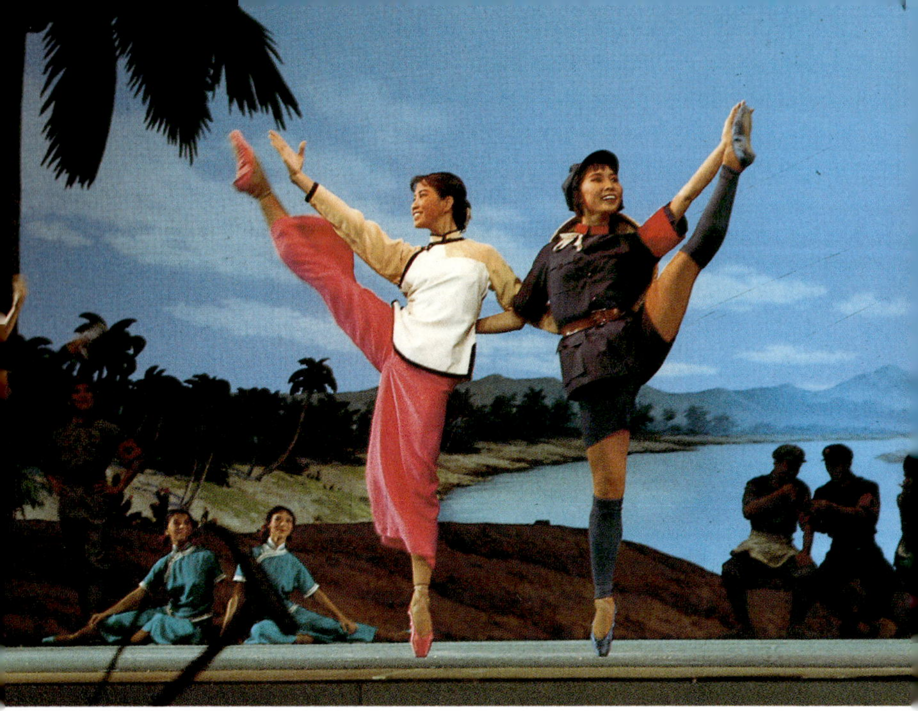

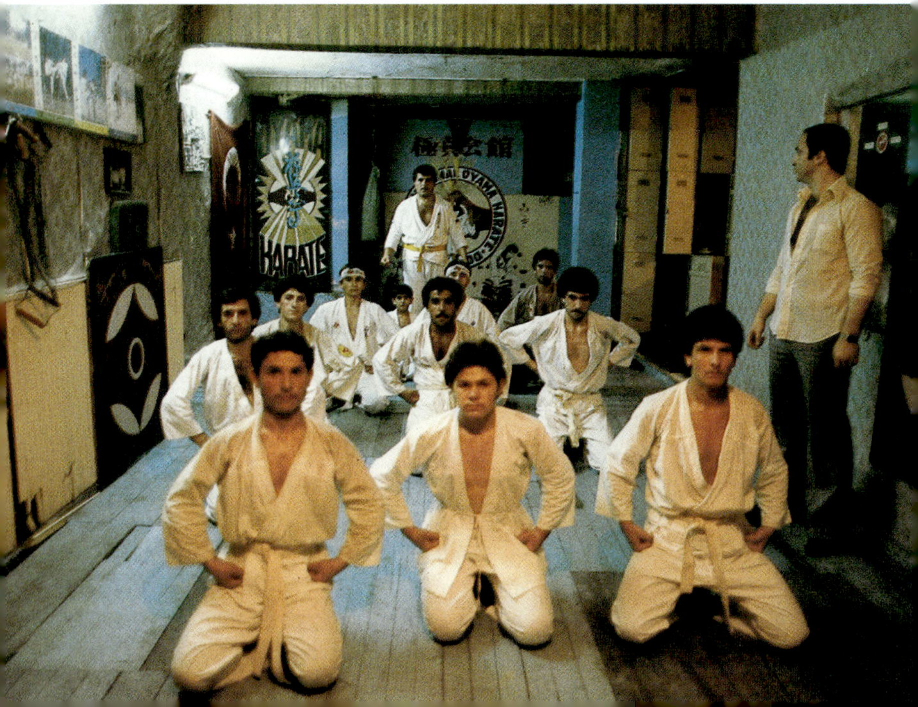
極真会館
KARATE

Shutter Speed: manual control of the shutter speeds is via the shutter speed dial which allows settings from 4 to 1/8000th sec. in whole steps. Whenever the shutter release button is lightly pressed the speed set is indicated in the viewfinder LCD.

Aperture: although Nikon lenses only offer click-stop diaphragm settings in whole steps intermediate settings are also possible and the Nikon F4 will react accordingly. The position of the aperture ring can be controlled through a window in the viewfinder.

Setting the Exposure: the proper aperture and shutter speed settings in manual mode are indicated by the electronic analog display in the Nikon F4's Multi-Meter Finder DP-20, which appears in the lower LCD of the viewfinder, whenever the exposure mode selector is set to **M**. The correct exposure is indicated by an exclamation mark symbol. The plus and minus signs indicate over or underexposure of +/–2 EV or more. The marks in between indicate deviating exposures of +/–1 EV.

A chain of marks starting from the centre indicate the manual setting's degree of deviation from the meter reading in 1/3rd increments. Every single mark stands for 1/3rd EV all through to +/– 2 EV. This type of display along with the possibility of setting the aperture steplessly allows for very precise exposure settings.

The deviation value is indicated by a digital display in the other viewfinders. Plus and minus marks and arrows inform you if the chosen setting would lead to over or underexposure. A correct setting is indicated by a **0.0**. The two arrows and the +/– marks are also shown.

Program Modes

Both aperture and shutter speed are set automatically in the program modes by the camera's controls to ensure a correct exposure. In order to cope with different picture-taking situations the Nikon F4 has two different program modes, indicated on the exposure mode selector by **PH** for High-Speed Program mode and **P** for Normal Program mode. The high-speed program is ideal for moving objects, snapshots, and when using a telephoto lens, since this mode employs faster shutter speeds which can prevent blurred images due to moving subjects or camera shake. The normal program mode employs smaller apertures for greater depth of field by beginning to stop down the lens at brightness values in which the High-Speed Program would still be operating at full

The Nikon F4's system is fast and reliable for all poorly lit scenes down to EV1 at ISO 100.

aperture, in order to achieve faster shutter speeds. The chart shows how the program modes differ according to the brightness values. Follow either line to where it intersects a diagonal line. These points show the combination of aperture – next to a horizontal line – and shutter speed – below a vertical line.

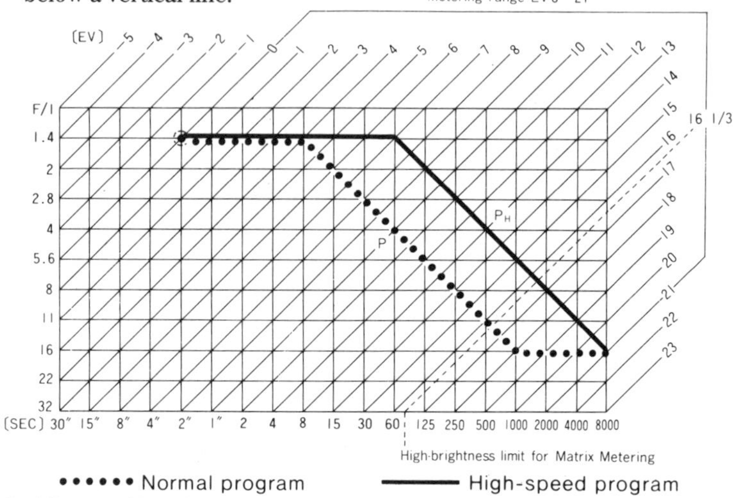

Dual Program Chart. This demonstrates the difference between the F4's normal and high-speed programs.

The automatic program modes are only available when lenses with integrated microcomputers are used. The Nikon F4 will switch to Aperture Priority if other lenses are mounted.

The ideal metering mode for the automatic program modes is Matrix Metering. This combination enables the type of quick and safe shooting needed for candid results.

Preliminary Settings: the exposure mode selector must be set to either **P** or **PH** and the aperture ring of the lens set to the smallest

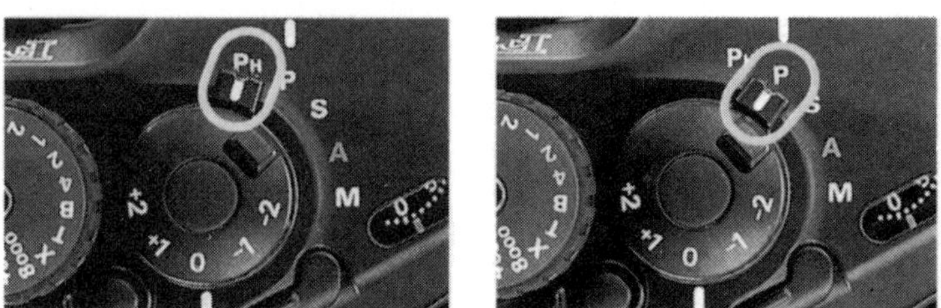

The Nikon F4 offers two program modes; **P** for normal or **PH** for high speed.

aperture if a program mode is to be used. AF-Nikkor lenses offer the possibility of locking the aperture ring in this position to prevent an accidental setting.

Viewfinder Display: the camera controls both aperture and shutter speeds from 30 to 1/8000th sec. steplessly in the program modes. Both values calculated by the camera are indicated in 1/2 EV steps in the lower LCD in the viewfinder. The exposure setting will be appropriate and the shutter can be released whenever numerals only appear. If even the fastest speed and the smallest aperture would not suffice to ensure a correct exposure, due to extreme subject brightness, the signal **HI** appears as a warning against overexposure instead of a number. The aperture indication will be that of the lens's smallest *f*-stop. In the reverse case when underexposure is threatening, the display will show **LO** and the lens's largest *f*-stop. If the lens aperture ring is not set to the smallest *f*-stop the display will show **FEE**. Perfect program mode operation is only possible when the lens is set to its smallest aperture. If a lens without a built-in microcomputer is mounted on the F4 and not set accordingly the camera will switch to Aperture Priority and the indications in the viewfinder will switch accordingly. When you use viewfinders other than the Multi-Meter Finder DP-20, only the **P** will appear, standing for program mode, next to the automatically-controlled shutter speed except if underexposure or overexposure is threatening, or the aperture ring is not set to the smallest aperture, when **LO**, **HI** or **FEE** will appear.

With Multi-Meter Finder — **With other finders**

Correct exposure.

Overexposure; use film with a lower ISO speed or use Nikon ND filter.

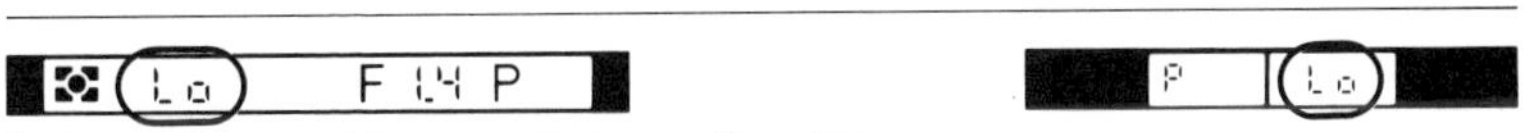

Underexposure; use a Nikon speedlight or use film with a higher ISO speed.

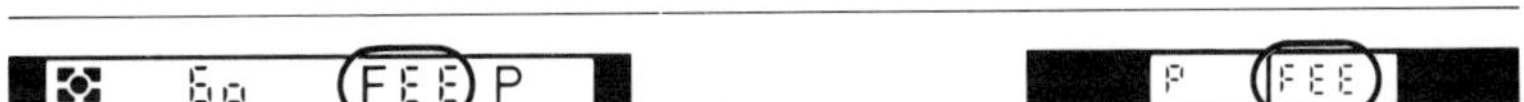

Lens is not set to the smallest aperture setting. Set lens to smallest aperture.

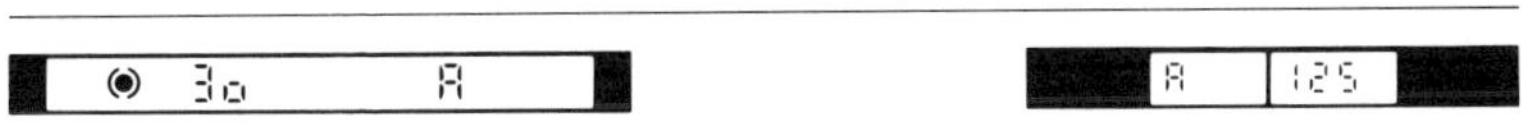

Non-CPU lens is used; automatically shifts to A mode.

Shutter Priority Mode

Whenever certain shutter speeds are necessary to achieve the intended effect the Shutter Priority mode, with its possibility of presetting the speed, is the ideal exposure mode. While the photographer can fix the speed the camera will automatically control the aperture setting to ensure a correct exposure. Depending on the situation, faster shutter speeds can be chosen to stop action or slower speeds for intentionally-blurred subjects.

Shutter speeds from 4 to 1/8000th sec. are available and can be set in whole steps with the shutter speed dial. Matrix is the most advisable metering mode here too, because of its simplicity and reliability. But, of course, you can also employ the other modes as well and, if necessary, the exposure lock function.

Shutter priority is only possible in connection when lenses with built-in microcomputers are attached. If others are used on the F4 the camera will automatically switch to aperture priority and the viewfinder LCD will inform you accordingly.

Preliminary Settings: the exposure mode selector must be set to S and the lens's aperture ring set to the smallest aperture, which can be locked on AF-Nikkors, when you want to use the Speed Priority mode.

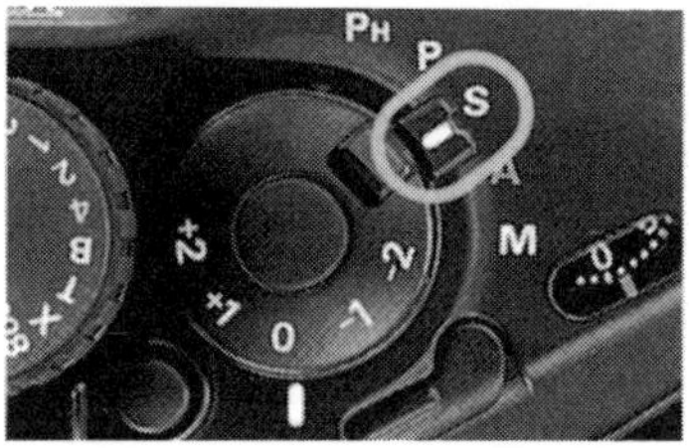

For shutter speed priority, set the dial to **S**.

Viewfinder Display: the exposure mode is indicated by an **S** in the lower LCD of the Multi-Meter Finder DP-20. As always the metering mode is displayed to the left, next to that is the manually-set shutter speed and to the right, the aperture, automatically controlled by the camera. If the manually-set speed happens to be too slow for a correct exposure, even with the smallest aperture, the aperture display will be replaced by **HI** warning against overexposure. In order to ensure a correct exposure you will either have to resort to a faster speed, use an additional neutral density filter, or a film with a lower ISO rating. If, in the opposite case, a preset shutter speed would lead to an underexposure, in spite of the largest aperture, the aperture display in the viewfinder would be replaced by **LO**. Then a slower speed, a film with a higher ISO rating or a flash unit would have to be used. In case the lens's smallest aperture has not been preset the warning signal **FEE** will be displayed instead of the automatically controlled aperture value. The ADR window of the viewfinder shows the current aperture of the attached lens. Whenever lenses without microcomputers are attached, the F4 will switch to aperture priority automatically which is indicated by the appropriate displays.

If other viewfinders than the Multi-Meter Finder DP-20 are used only the automatically controlled aperture values will be displayed, or the warning signals for over or underexposure, or a faulty aperture setting. Lenses without built-in microcomputers will lead to the display being switched accordingly, showing **A** and the manually-set shutter speed.

With Multi-Meter Finder | **With other finders**

Correct exposure

Overexposure; select higher shutter speed or use Nikon ND filter.

Underexposure; select slower shutter speed, or use a Nikon speedlight.

Lens is not set to the smallest aperture setting. Set lens to smallest aperture.

Non-CPU lens is used; automatically shifts to A mode.

Aperture Priority Mode

If you intend to control the depth of field precisely by presetting the aperture, aperture priority is the ideal exposure mode. You can choose a large aperture and blur out any background interfering with your subject or make sure everything is in sharp focus from front to rear. A typical example for controlled depth of field is portraiture when larger apertures are preferred to let the person's head stand out from the rest. Landscapes, on the other hand, call for smaller apertures with their larger in-focus areas. Aperture priority is possible with almost all Nikon lenses. After manually presetting any aperture the camera's computers will control the shutter speed automatically from 30 to 1/8000th sec. for a correct exposure. Matrix metering is easiest here, too, but you can also use any other mode. If your main subject is not framed in the circles on the viewfinder screen when you use Spot- or Centre-Weighted metering you will have to also employ exposure lock.

Preliminary Settings: the exposure mode selector must be set to **A** and the aperture manually set to the intended aperture. The position of the shutter speed dial is irrelevant in this case.

For aperture priority set the dial to **A**.

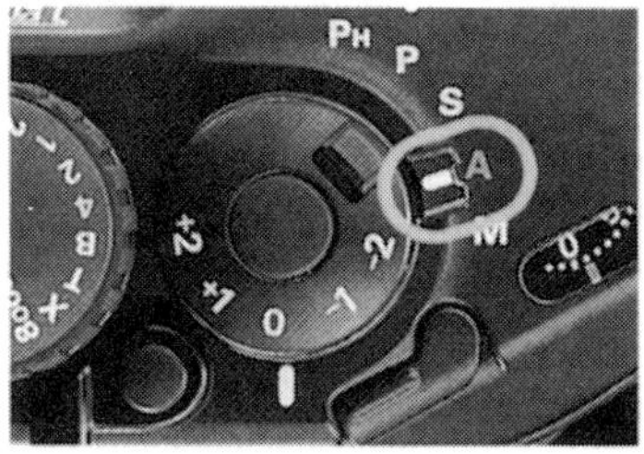

Viewfinder Display: the preset aperture can be seen in the ADR window. The automatically controlled speeds from 30 to 1/8000th sec. are indicated in 1/2 EV steps and **A** shows that Aperture Priority mode has been selected. If even 1/8000th sec. cannot prevent overexposure the display would show **HI** instead of a shutter speed, so you should set a smaller aperture or use a neutral density filter or a film with a lower ISO rating. In the opposite case **LO** would appear if even the slowest speed of 30 sec. would still not prevent underexposure. A larger aperture or a faster film may be solutions to the problem.

With Multi-Meter Finder

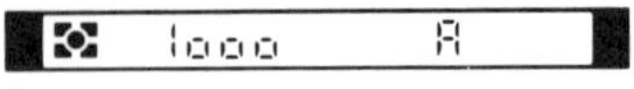

With other finders

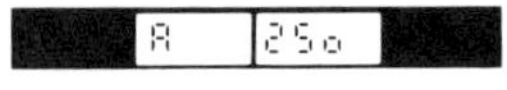

Correct exposure

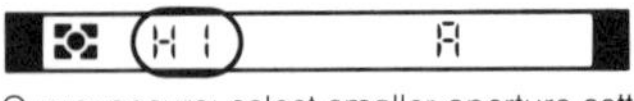

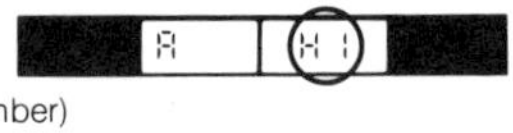

Overexposure; select smaller aperture setting (larger f-number) or use Nikon ND filter.

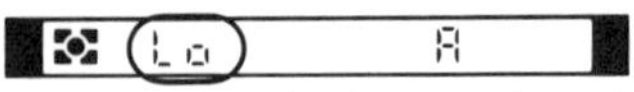

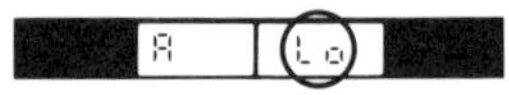

Underexposure; select larger aperture setting or use a Nikon speedlight.

Other viewfinders will display only the **A** symbolising aperture priority as well as the automatically-controlled shutter speed. Threatened over or underexposure will be signalled with the display **HI** or **LO** respectively.

Stop-Down Metering: if you employ lenses without automatic diaphragms, or where the diaphragm mechanisms do not couple with the F4, you will have to perform stop-down metering. It is advisable to focus at full aperture so you can check the setting on the screen at its brightest. After that you can stop the lens down for exposure metering and shooting. In aperture priority mode the F4 will automatically control the shutter speed necessary for a correct exposure according to the preset aperture. This is also true for lenses with fixed apertures such as Reflex Nikkors. When working with PC-Nikkors for perspective control, metering has to be done before shifting. The meter value can then be locked with the AE-L button, the lens shifted to its final position and the shutter released.

Exposure Compensation

Perfectly exposing a subject is not just a question of precise metering and automatic controls. A number of interdependent factors play important roles. This includes the real film speed, which can differ from the face-value, as well as the subsequent processing. Last but not least, personal taste can also be decisive. Intentional over and underexposing can also be effective. That is the reason why many photographers expose their films differently from the instructions. The Nikon F4 offers a number of methods for compensating the exposure. You can employ the compensation dial, the AE-lock, or manage with the help of the electronic analog display in manual mode. An alternative to this is to influence the exposure by changing the film speed setting. The latter is not to be recommended, because there is no indication in the viewfinder and it can only be checked by comparing the film speed printed on the cassette through the window in the camera with the film speed dial. Nothing tells the photographer to set the dial back to its original position, and, besides, in this case you would have to do without the automatic film speed setting.

Exposure Compensation in Automatic Modes

Automatic Exposure Lock Function: a very simple way to compensate the exposure is to meter an alternative but similarly bright subject in connection with the exposure lock. The best mode for this is Spot Metering because it enables you to evaluate the important subject details. Centre-Weighted Metering will also allow exposure lock and in

The AE-L button is used to lock the exposure meter reading. When operated, the function is indicated in the viewfinder.

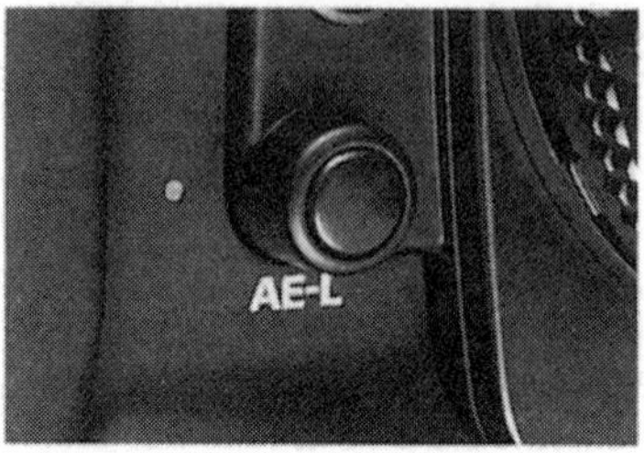

Matrix Metering compensation is automatic so any exposure mode can be used. After you have aimed the camera at the specific details, lightly press the shutter release and the AE-L buttons. While you keep them depressed you can recompose. As long as the exposure is locked **EL** will indicate this in the Multi-Meter Finder's lower LCD. If the focus mode selector is set to **S** you will have to refocus after you have composed the final picture. In order to do so and reactivate autofocus operation, let the release button go and then press it again. If the camera is set to Continuous Servo mode, focus will be continuously reset as long as you press the shutter release button. But this time your subject must be framed in the viewfinder brackets if it is to come out in focus. On many occasions it can be helpful to lock the focus and exposure settings simultaneously. This can be done by turning the lever located around the AF-L button into the lower position and then pressing just that button.

Exposure Compensation Dial: this dial allows a compensation of the automatic exposure control in the F4 in steps of 1/3rd EV within a range of +/–2 EV. The dial is secured against accidental setting by a lock lever which must be released before any compensation is possible. The scale on the dial indicates the amount of compensation, i.e. setting to a + value will lead to exactly that amount of overexposure, and vice versa a – value will lead to the according underexposure. Since both a compensation signal and the amount of deviation is displayed in the viewfinder you can do the setting without taking the camera from your eye. The amount of compensation you set will appear with the according + or – sign in the upper LCD of the viewfinder to the left of the frame counter.

The exposure compensation dial allows manual override of up to +/– 2 *f*-stops.

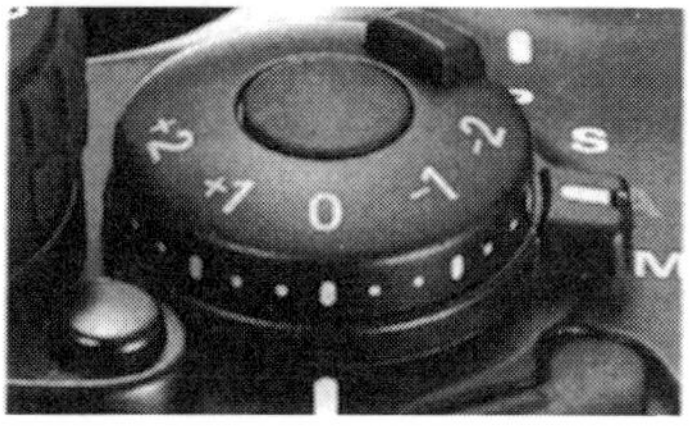

Exposure Compensation in Manual Mode

In order to prevent a faulty exposure in manual mode you can move in close to the subject detail you intend to emphasize until it fills the frame, using Centre-Weighted metering, and set the exposure according to the electronic analog display in the viewfinder. After that you can recompose and shoot. If you happen to be using a zoom lens, instead of closing in on your subject, you could just utilize its longest focal length until nothing else can influence the meter reading. This method is only possible, though, with zoom lenses that do not have changing maximum apertures with different focal lengths because a varying effective maximum aperture would lead to false meter readings. Experienced photographers can make use of the analog display when they intend to compensate with the help of the precise indication of deviations in 1/3rd EV steps from –2 to +2 EV.

Auto Exposure Bracketing

With the optional Multi-Control Data Backs MF-23 and MF-24, for 250 exposures, the Nikon F4 also offers the possibility of producing consecutive automatic exposures of the same subject. You can preset up to 19 exposures and predetermine the amount of deviation between them. Afterwards you can pick the one picture out of the series that suits your taste or your intentions best.

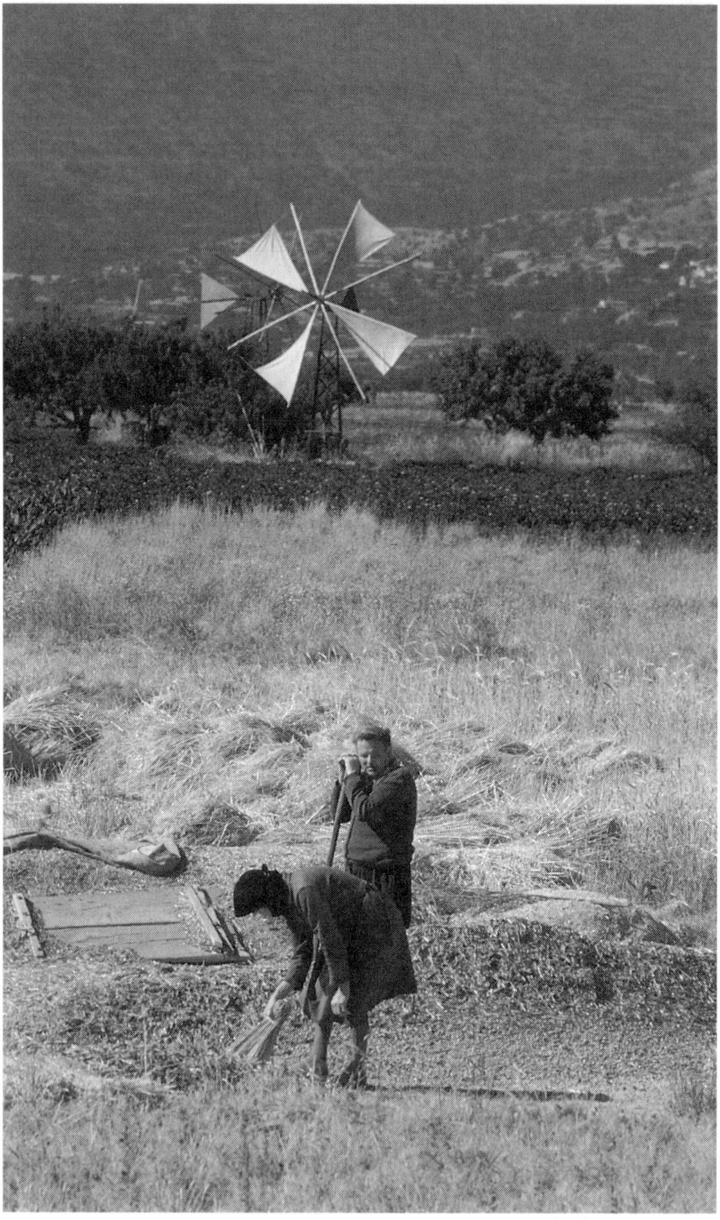

Flash with the Nikon F4

The Nikon F4 has two different connections for flash guns. The ISO type hot shoe takes most Nikon Speedlites and other units with the appropriate mounting foot. Some Nikon Speedlites can only be mounted with a compatible Nikon flash unit coupler. Four electrical contacts in the ISO type hot shoe, on the top of the Multi-Meter Finder, provide the following functions beside the ignition signal: proper synchronisation of the flash unit, automatic flash output stop, identification of a TTL flash unit, and both the viewfinder flash-ready indication and the automatic switching to the proper sync speed. The flash unit used must be dedicated in order to ensure these functions.

Nikon flash units SB-24, SB-23, SB-22, and SB-20 have a built-in AF illuminator allowing automatic flash photography with autofocus function in complete darkness. The LED in these units projects a pattern of stripes onto the subject whenever outside lighting conditions are poorer than -1 EV (at ISO 100) to enable the autofocus system to continue working.

The Nikon F4 also has a threaded sync terminal that accepts all standard PC-type plug-in sync cables for the use of studio flash equipment or torch-type flash guns. Threaded Nikon flash cables are recommended because they are safe against accidental loosening. Most of all reporters will be thankful for this because it puts an end to the constant checking of the camera-to-flash connection.

Cybernetic Fill-in Flash Operation

Nikon dedicated electronic Speedlites, including SB-24, SB-23, SB-22, SB-20, SB-18, SB-16B, and SB-15, take full advantage of the F4's fine-tuned cybernetic controls, which automatically synchronize the camera's shutter speed and the lens aperture to provide precisely controlled exposures with balanced and natural-looking fore- and backgrounds. The extremely short burst of the flash lightens up the foreground and will lead to a sharp image even when lighting conditions are generally quite good because the sync speed is controlled according to the prevailing light. Using cybernetic control the F4, together with a Nikon Speedlite, allows the photographer a choice of several different flash techniques, one of which will always be ideal for the specific situation. With the SB-24 you can synchronise the flash to the rear or second

Using telephoto lenses greatly flattens the perspective in landscape photography. Distances seem to be much shorter than in reality.

shutter blind. In normal TTL mode the slowest flash sync speed is 1/60th sec., but if you switch to rear blind sync photography in program or aperture priority modes, shutter speeds of up to 30 sec. are possible, depending on the prevailing conditions. The creative possibilities of rear blind sync photography are described further in the chapter about the Nikon AF-Speedlite SB-24.

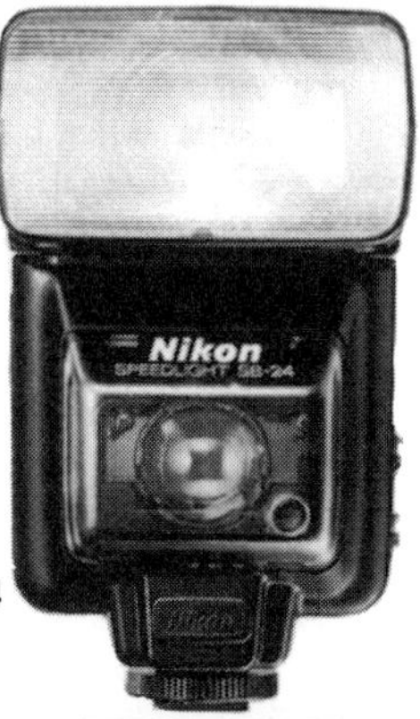

SB-24

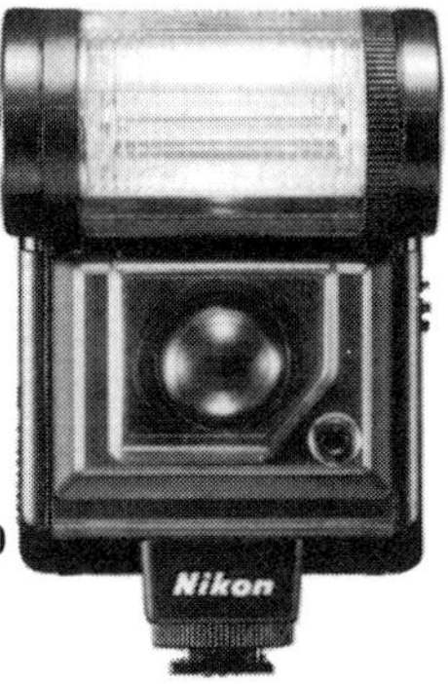

SB-20

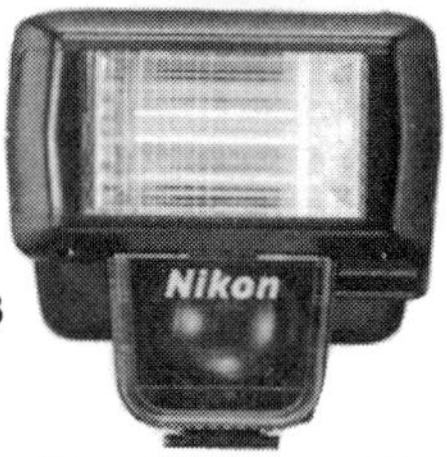

SB-23

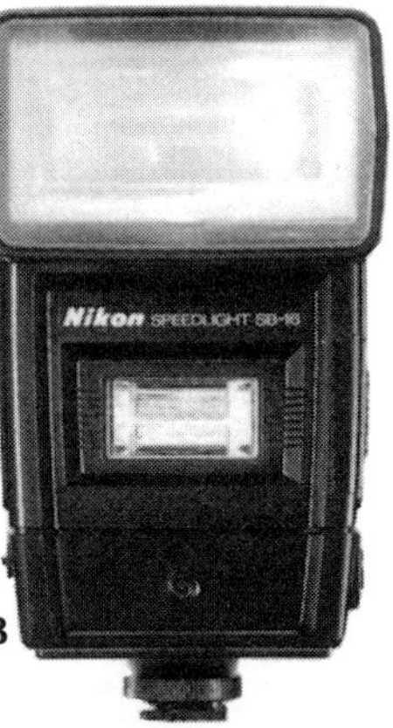

SB-16B

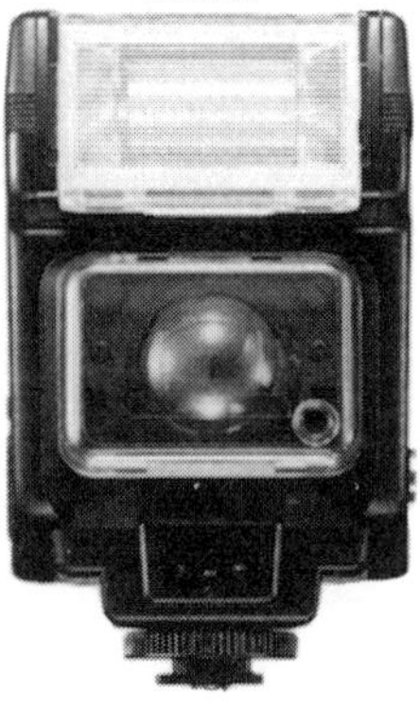
SB-22

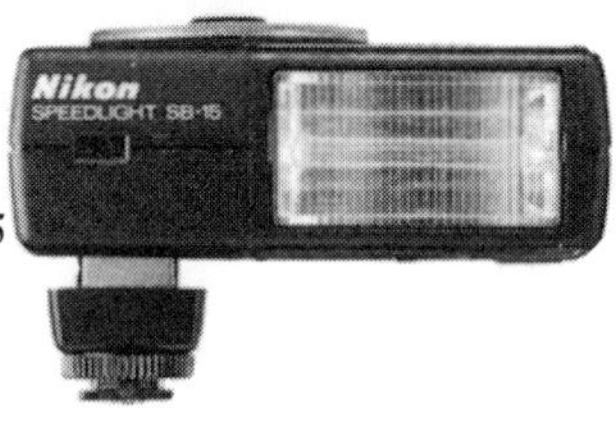

SB-15

Matrix Balanced Fill-in Flash

This combination of fill-flash and matrix metering controls the balanced exposure of both a subject's fore- and background by means of five comprehensive computation methods, based on general scene brightness and contrast. The camera then decides if the exposure should be low-brightness weighted, average, centre-weighted, or high-brightness weighted.

Background Exposure Metering
(In Matrix metering)

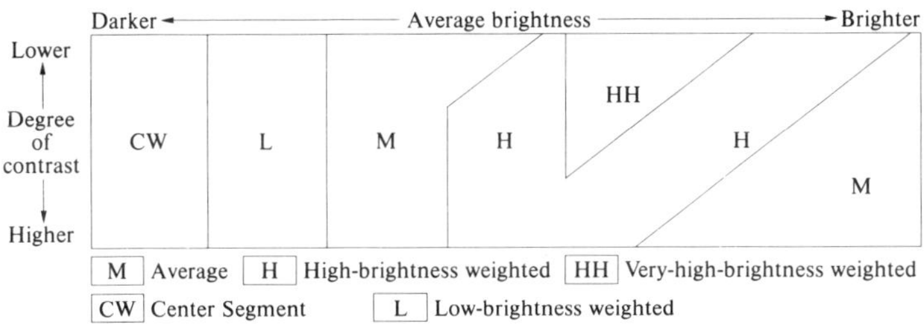

Flash Output Level
(In Matrix metering, with a lens f5.6 or faster)

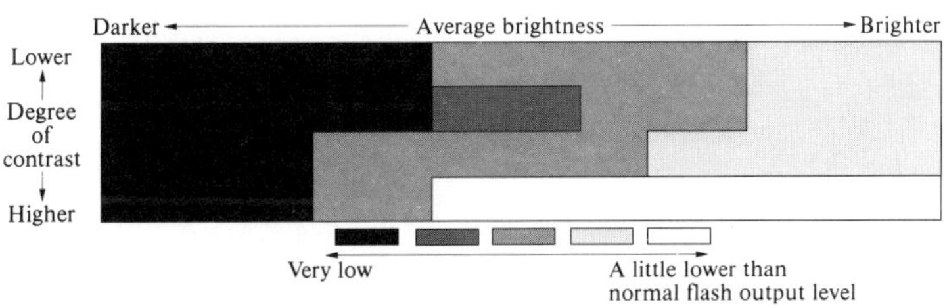

Balanced Fill-in Flash in Program Mode: when the exposure mode selector is set to **PH** or **P** the cybernetic flash controls always try to employ the fastest sync speed of 1/250th sec. When a correct flash exposure is only possible with slower speeds because the limit of the automatic aperture control – *f*4 or higher in the case of lenses with smaller maximum apertures – has been reached, the camera will utilize speeds down to 1/60th sec. When using an ISO 100 film the aperture is controlled between *f*4 and the smallest available aperture. The limit, as to the largest aperture, depends on the film speed. The chart shows the exact program lines.

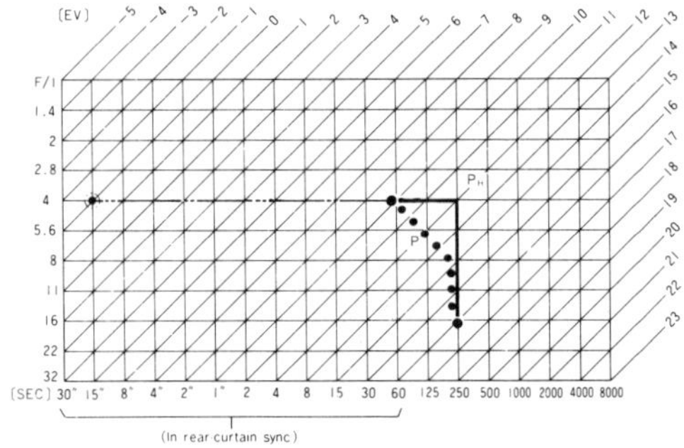

Matrix balanced Fill-in in **P** Mode

Balanced Fill-in Flash in Shutter Priority Mode: in this mode you are free to choose sync speeds from 4 to 1/250th sec. so it is ideal for night photography, for example a cityscape of night lights with the automatic flash exposure of the foreground subjects balanced to the background scenery. The aperture is controlled automatically with every *f*-stop available from the lens's smallest to its largest. In case a faster speed than 1/250th sec. has been set accidentally the Nikon F4 will automatically be switched to the fastest possible sync speed.

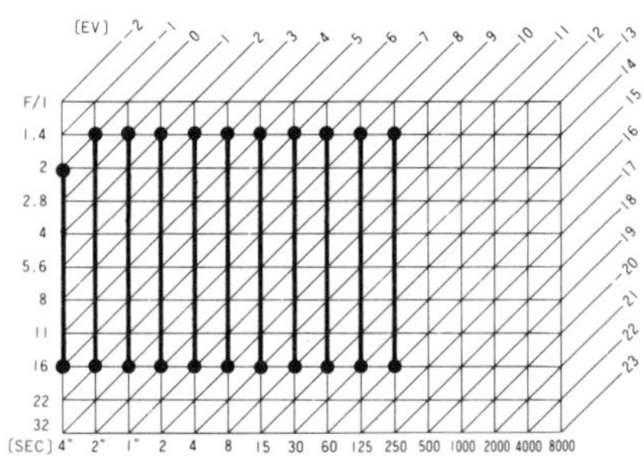

Matrix balanced Fill-in in **S** Mode

Balanced Fill-in Flash in Aperture Priority: you can preset any aperture when the exposure mode selector is set to **A**. The camera will choose a sync. speed between 1/60th and 1/250th sec. in order to achieve a natural-looking flash photo. The automatically controlled sync speed does not depend on the speed of the film in use.

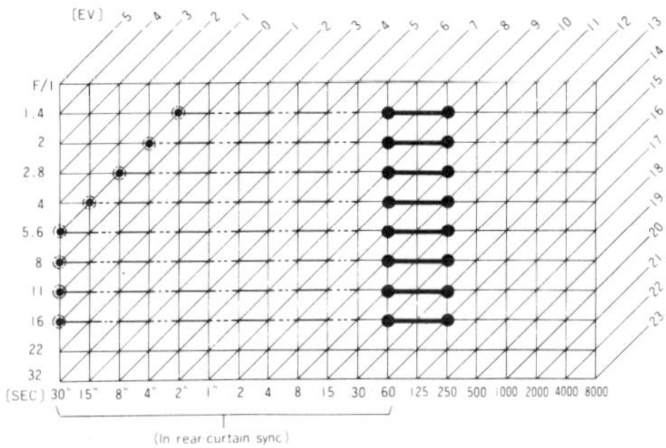

Matrix balanced Fill-in in **A** Mode

Balanced Fill-in Flash in Manual Mode: both aperture and shutter speed are set by the photographer in this mode while flash exposure is determined by the scene brightness and contrast registered by the camera's matrix metering system.

Centre-Weighted Fill-in Flash

The Nikon F4 can also offer centre-weighted metering in combination with regular TTL-flash photography. This mode is ideal to emphasize background details. If the exposure value measured in the centre segment is within the controlled shutter speed/aperture range, flash output will automatically be reduced by 2/3rd EV to achieve a natural effect. When the centre-weighted metering reading leads to an exposure value which is beyond the controlled range, the camera will automatically switch to normal TTL flash operation without compensation.

Nevertheless if you wish to compensate the flash output in centre-weighted TTL flash mode, you can do so manually within a range of +1 to –3 EV with the SB-24.

In Matrix TTL Flash, Centre-Weighted TTL Flash, or Spot TTL Flash modes, standard TTL flash is selected. In this flash mode, although exposure for the background is metered by each of the three systems, the flash output level is not determined automatically. However, the photographer can select the flash output compensation manually on the Nikon Speedlite SB-24 from +1 to –3 EV in steps of 1/3rd EV in these modes. Film speeds from ISO 25 to ISO 1000 can be used for TTL flash photography. For the non TTL flash modes the whole range from ISO 6 to ISO 6400 is available.

The Nikon Multiflash System

In order to achieve lighting conditions similar to those in a studio, you can utilize up to five different Nikon Speedlites such as the SB-24, SB-23, SB-22, SB-20, SB-18, SB-16B, or SB-15 linked to each other via Nikon TTL multi-flash sync cords. The F4's automatic flash controls will take care of each flash unit's output in such cases as well.

Further special flash techniques with the Nikon F4 in combination with the dedicated Nikon Autofocus Speedlite SB-24 will be described in the chapter about dedicated Nikon flash units.

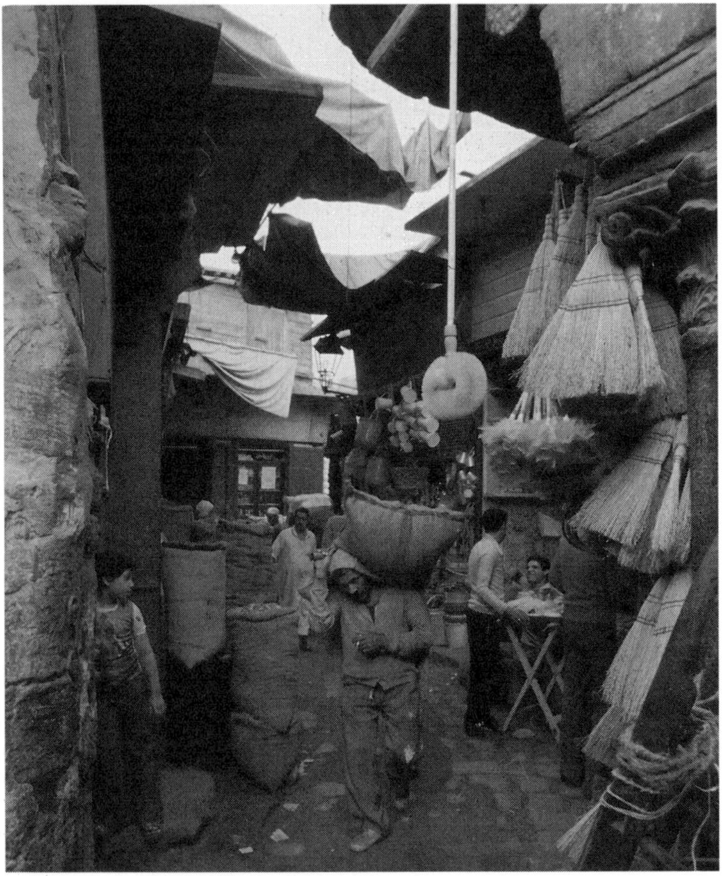

The Nikon F4's matrix metering system guarantees automatic correctly exposed quick snapshots even in complex lighting situations.

The Predecessor – F3

Even though the Nikon F4 is without doubt the top – and the most advanced – model in the Nikon SLR camera program, it will not replace the F3 immediately; a camera proven in the hands of professionals day after day for many years. The F3 will remain a desired piece of equipment for professionals for some years to come.

The moment the Nikon F3 was presented in Tokyo, on 6th February 1980, everybody knew that it was going to be the camera design concept of the '80s. The Nikon F3 was the first professional camera to offer an automatic exposure system which is always available, regardless of the viewfinder being used, because it is incorporated into the camera body. The Nikon engineers equipped the F3 with an LCD in the viewfinder which can be illuminated for better visibility in dim light – another Nikon

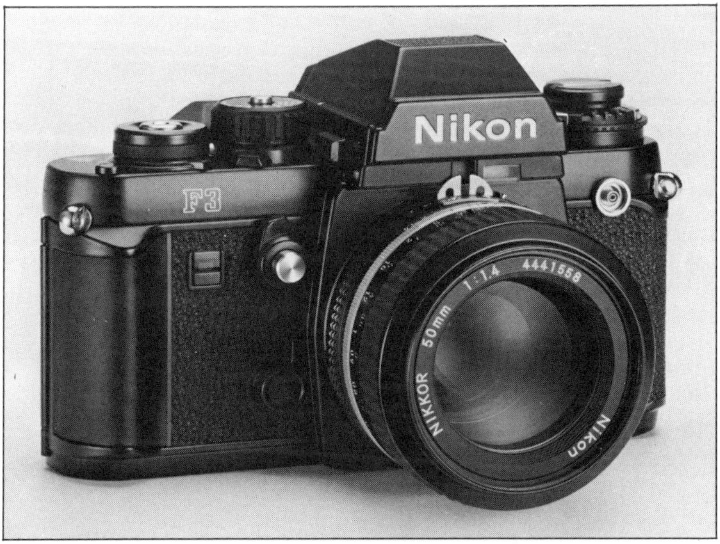

The Nikon F3 with standard DE-2 pentaprism finder. A High-Eyepoint viewfinder is also available, converting the camera to model F3 HP.

first! The manual shutter speeds and the self-timer operation are quartz-controlled. In addition to the electromagnetic shutter release, the F3 is also equipped with a mechanical one that works without battery power in case of emergencies.

The optional Motor-Drive MD-4 is considered to be the fastest serially-produced unit for 35mm SLR cameras. It is capable of running at up to 6 fps. Automatic TTL flash output control is also possible with the Nikon F3.

Exposure Metering System of the F3

The Nikon F3 utilizes a silicon sensor placed at the bottom of the mirror-box for its metering system. This location has a number of advantages. First of all the sensor is exceptionally secure against stray light in this position and secondly it makes compensation unneccessary when you change focusing screens. The light coming through the lens is reflected to the screen by the reflex mirror and onto the eyepiece by the prism. Part of the light passes through the central, semi-silvered area of this reflex mirror onto a secondary mirror which finally reflects it onto the sensor. The same sensor meters the light reflected off the surface of the film during the time the shutter is open in the TTL flash metering operation.

The metering system is strongly centre-weighted. The F3 concentrates about 80% of its sensitivity on the 12mm dia. circle in the centre of the focusing screen. The areas at the edges hardly register.

The metering system is activated by lightly pressing the two-step shutter release button and it remains active for 16 seconds after you let the button go. After that it is switched off for the sake of energy conservation. The release button can be locked to prevent battery drain, for example, when it is accidentally pressed in the camera case.

Film Speed Range: this can only be set manually, from ISO 12 to ISO 6400. The numbers on the film speed dial represent the full ISO steps and the dots in between them are the intermediate settings.

Automatic Exposure Control of the F3

The F3 offers an aperture priority automatic exposure mode when, depending on the film speed and aperture setting, the controls will choose an appropriate shutter speed steplessly and automatically. The shutter speed dial must be set to the A position and automatically-controlled shutter speeds from 1/2000th to 8 sec. are available. In order to ensure a correct exposure, even in the case when important subject details are off-centre, the F3 offers an exposure-lock function. It is also possible to compensate the automatic exposure by up to +/– 2 stops.

Manual Exposure Control

The F3 is quartz-controlled to secure absolutely precise manual shutter speeds. In order to prevent accidental settings the shutter speed dial is locked in the A position. A little button on top of the dial has to be pressed to unlock it. After that you can choose one of the fifteen click-stop positions for manually-set shutter speeds from 1/2000th to 8 sec. There are also the settings **B**, **T**, and **X**. When you choose the **X** position the shutter will run at its fastest flash synchronised speed of 1/80th sec. The shutter will remain open as long as you keep the release button pressed when the dial is set to **B**. The **T** position will also result in the shutter remaining open, but you can let the release button go immediately. Moving the dial to another position will close the shutter again.

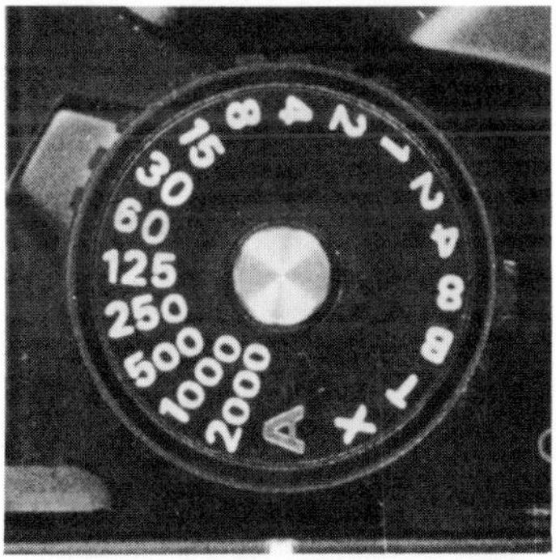

The Nikon F3 shutter speed dial with speeds from 1/2000th to 8 seconds and **B**, **T**, and **X**. There is also an **A** position for automatically-controlled shutter speeds.

Whenever the batteries are exhausted you can trip the shutter of the F3 with the mechanical backup release lever next to the bayonet. The resulting speed will be 1/60th sec. Long time exposures should also be released using this lever, with the dial in the **T** position.

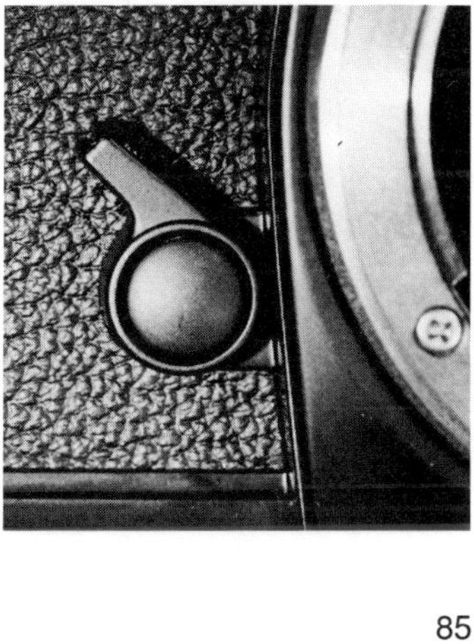

The mechanical backup release lever.

Viewfinder Display

Even though shutter speeds are controlled steplessly in the aperture priority mode, the LCD in the viewfinder will indicate the next value. A +/– sign to the left of the number 2000 serves as a warning of overexposure and, correspondingly, a – sign in front of the number 8 warns of underexposure. Manual operation is indicated by an **M** in front of the selected shutter speed. Over- or underexposure of at least 1/4 *f*-stop is indicated again with the + and – signs, respectively. In the **T** and **B** positions **M–** will appear and when the dial is set to **X** the display will show **+M 80**. The manually preset aperture is reflected directly into the viewfinder. A flash-ready signal is the third display in the viewfinder. It lights up as soon as the capacitors of dedicated Nikon flash units are fully loaded. The displays can be illuminated for better visibility in poor lighting conditions by pressing the small red button on the right side of the viewfinder.

The Electronics

Nikon has incorporated very sophisticated electronic controls in the F3. Instead of the soldered electronic components common in earlier cameras, they employed a method utilized by NASA to connect electronical parts in their space flight program. Three of the F3's ICs are produced in this process, which is called "Chip on Board" and they are in charge of the exposure metering and controls, the quartz oscillator, and the liquid crystal display. These IC's and further electronical components are placed on a flexible printed circuit. These circuits contribute to the camera's reliability as they render soldered wire connections, which are prone to defects, unnecessary. Embedded in synthetic resin they are also protected against moisture and dust. Besides, they can be wrapped around the other components which also leads to the modest dimensions of the camera.

Focal lengths between 85 and 135mm are ideal for portraits. Zoom lenses prove to be very convenient for pictures similar to the ones on pages 86/89 because they allow precise framing without having to change position.

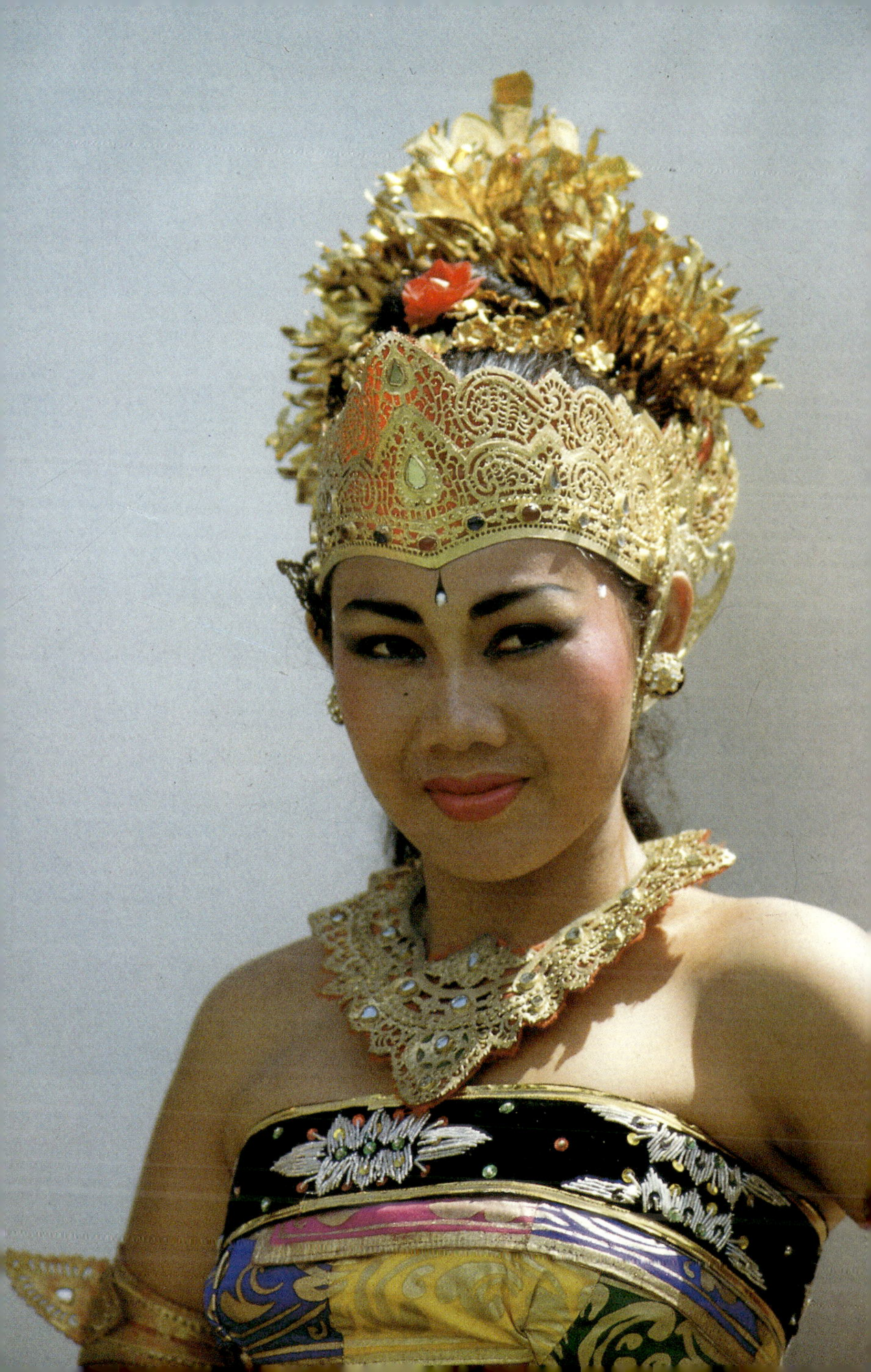

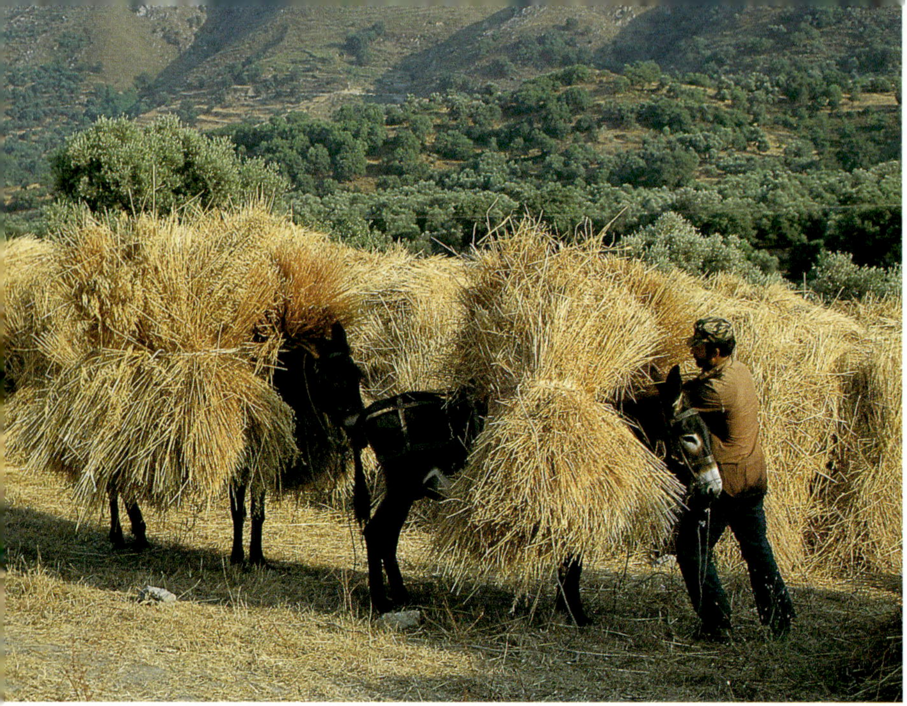

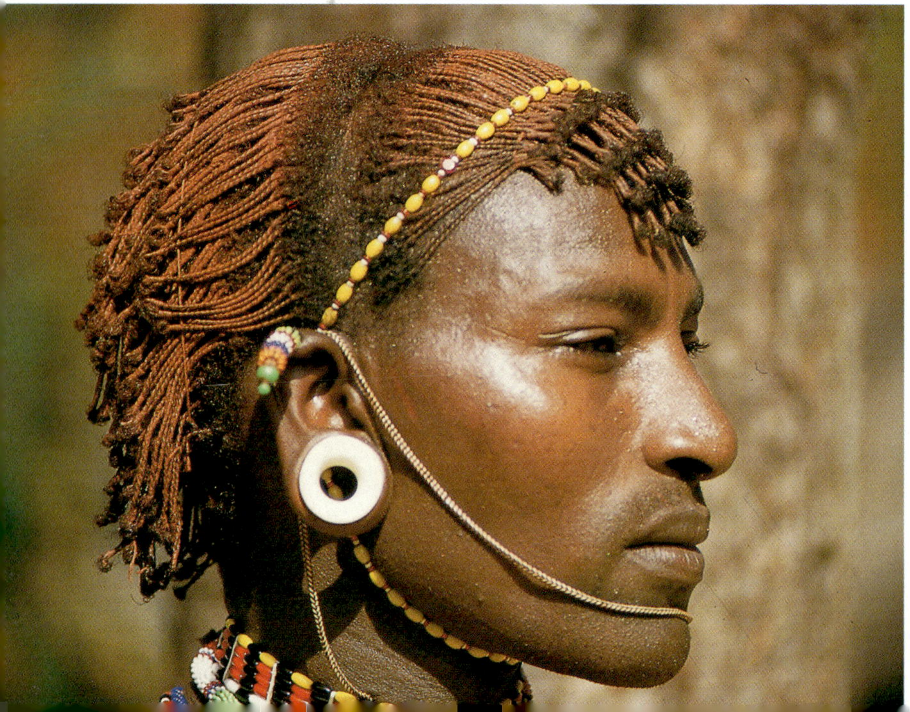

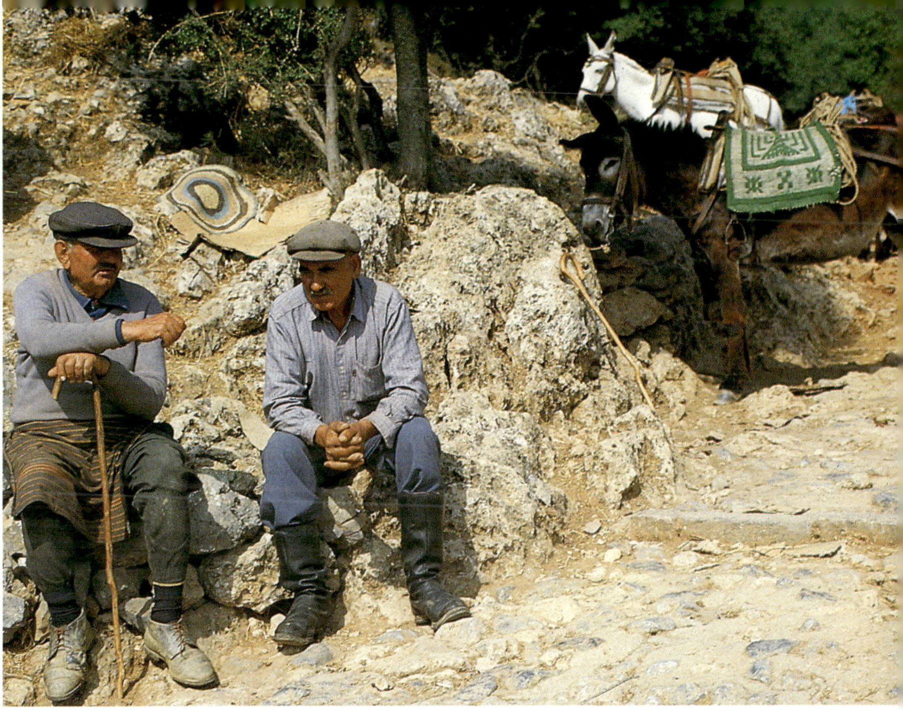

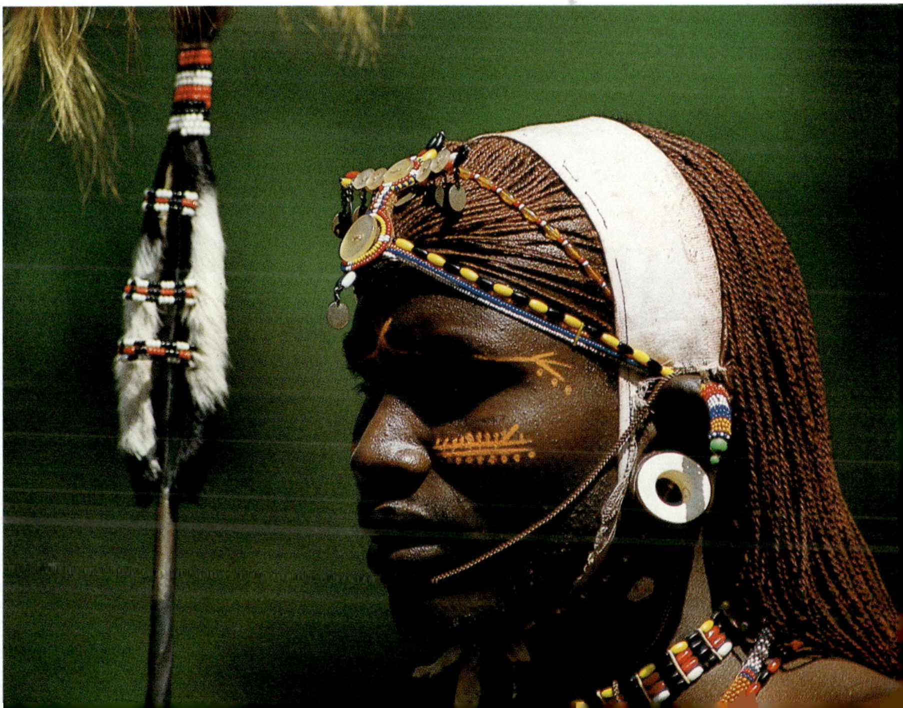

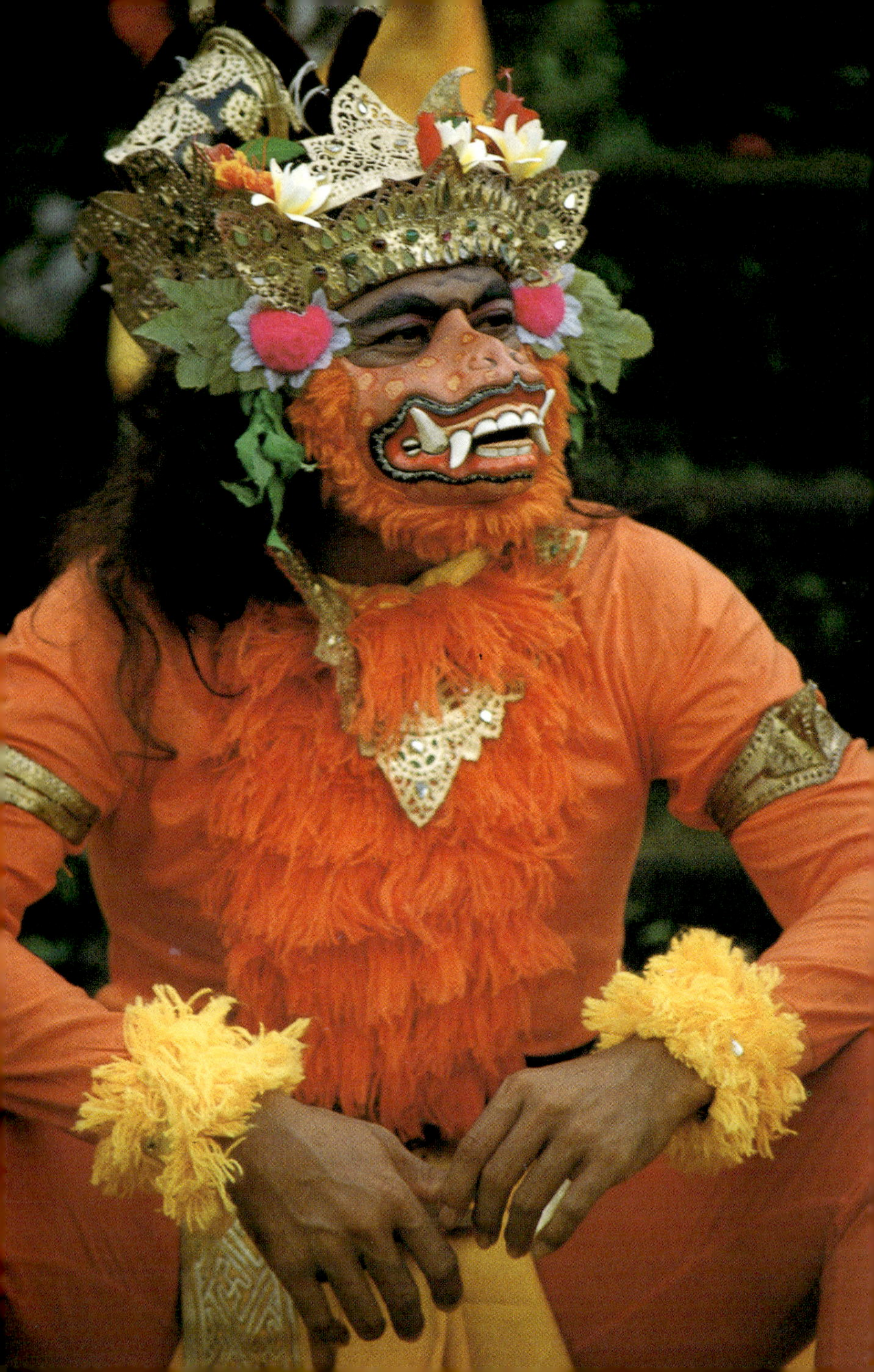

The Mechanics

The F3 is a good example of advanced precision mechanics which were developed for a completely new film transportation system. Additionally, ball bearings ensure extra smooth operation. Besides, the main transporting shaft is not located directly between the film advance lever and the take-up spool any more. It is placed eccentrically by employing a special connecting shaft which allows the shafts of the shutter drum, the sprocket, and the take-up spool, to be located immediately next to each other. This greatly simplifies the construction of the gear train. A smooth operating system with hardly any play could be realised by utilizing a very long connecting shaft with widely spaced ball-bearings. All of these factors improve power transmission and reduce torque, which is nearly the same with or without a film loaded in the camera. This is important for the use of the Motor-Drive MD-4 since it saves energy and enhances the possible exposure frequency.

The mirror-box is mounted into the F3's body as a partly prefabricated unit. Nikon engineers employed a combination-magnet in the design of the electrical mirror operation for the first time, which greatly improves its function. It is also equipped with a pneumatic damper to reduce vibrations caused by the mirror reaching its final position. A mirror brake stops the movement when it returns to its original position. This is especially neccessary for high-frequency motor-operation with the MD-4.

The Shutter

Unlike the F4, the F3 has a shutter that travels horizontally, which is also a Nikon development. Its special characteristic is the existence of only one drum; that is, the drums of both the first and second shutter blinds have a mutual axis. The simple design contributes to its reliability. The blinds are made of strong and especially light-weight titanium. In order to improve their dimensional stability a relief pattern is pressed into the thin foil blinds. A matt-black coating prevents reflections. The shutter is mounted into the body as a prefabricated unit just like the mirror-box. Precision, especially that of the faster shutter speeds, is guaranteed by an extra-strong magnet controlling the second shutter blind. The first blind is released mechanically. Drag and inertia during shutter operation is reduced by ball-bearings in the main shutter drum. The shutter's vibrations are absorbed by a highly effective braking system for both blinds, consisting of silicon rubber dampers and a big brake-drum. The

Zoom lenses are ideal for quick snapshots with autofocus and matrix metering. The AF 80-200mm, *f*2.8 zoom was used for this picture of a Balinese dancer.

use of especially wide blinds ensures the shutter is absolutely light tight. The complete unit is designed to operate without a single adjustment becoming necessary for at least 150,000 cycles.

The Five Nikon F3 Models

The F3 used to be available in five different versions. Apart from the standard model you could choose between the Nikon F3T with extra strong titanium body-caps, the F3HP with the High-Eyepoint viewfinder for short- or long-sighted users, the F3P which is only available to press-photographers, and the F3AF with its additional autofocus function. The AF-Nikkors can be used on any F3 model. Numerous accessories such as flash units, remote control, and close-up equipment is also available.

Nikon F3HP: this version is equipped with the High-Eyepoint viewfinder, especially for short or long-sighted photographers, so that the complete frame can be viewed even at a distance from the eyepiece. The F4 is also equipped with this viewfinder which makes working with goggles or helmet a lot more convenient. The complete frame can be viewed from a distance of 25mm from the eyepiece. Except for the High-Eyepoint viewfinder the F3HP is indentical to the F3.

Nikon F3/T: titanium is considered to be the strongest and, at the same time, lightest metal in the world. In order to endure in especially difficult circumstances, the F3/T's body castings were all made out of this material. Nikon has now ceased using titanium for environmental reasons, after over thirty years of experience in working with this high-tensile metal which is about twice as scratch-resistant as brass. It is about as corrosion-proof as platinum. No further 'F3 Titan' cameras will be made, Nikon announced in September 1989.

Nikon F3P: Nikon developed a special model of the F3 together with the biggest Japanese news agency Kyodo which is meant to meet the needs of press photographers. For one thing, all of the features unneccessary in a press photographer's everyday work were excluded, for example the multiple-exposure lever, the self-timer, the camera back lock-lever, the eyepiece shutter, the cable release terminal and the fixed 1/80th sec. shutter speed. The F3P is equipped with a High-Eyepoint viewfinder with a titanium cap and a ISO-type hot shoe, including an additional contact for the flash-ready light in the viewfinder. This hot-shoe does not allow TTL flash output control.

The shutter speed dial extends a bit higher and the main switch was designed so that it can be operated with gloves. The shutter release button is covered by a silicon-rubber coating, giving it a more definite touch. The frame counter window is round and the numbers are white on a black background. The camera back is equipped with an additional film-guide shaft to ensure that the film is absolutely level in front of the film gate. The film speed dial window is covered with a piece of plastic to further improve the camera's resistance to moisture.

Nikon F3AF: this was the first professional autofocus camera. Its "brains" were built into the interchangeable AF viewfinder, DX-1. Unlike the F3, the autofocus drive motors were not built into the camera body but into each of the two AF lenses. The DX-1 AF viewfinder can also be employed on other F3 models. These combinations do not allow autofocus operation but the electronic rangefinder function is available. This camera has been discontinued.

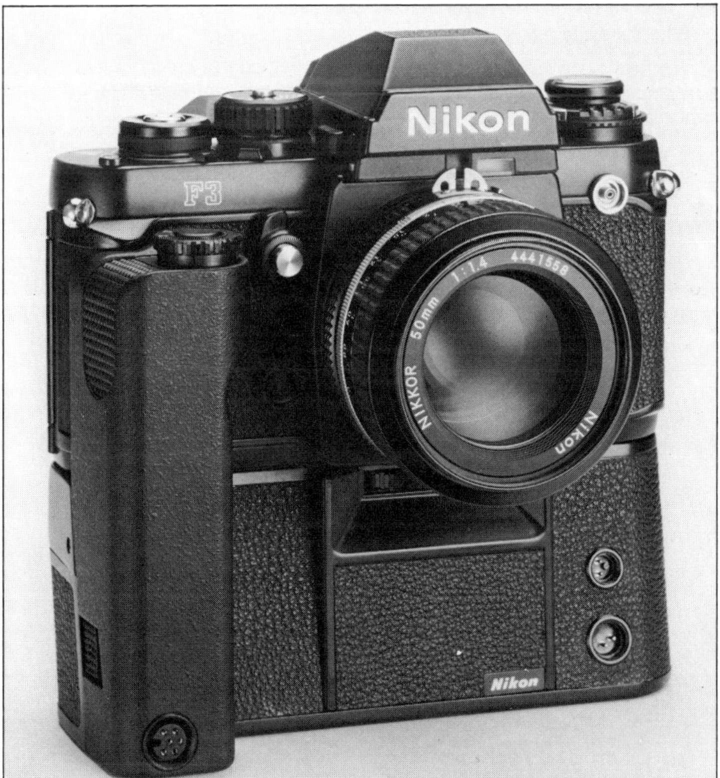

With the Motor Drive MD-4 it is possible to expose up to 5.5 frames per second with the Nikon F3.

Interchangeable Lenses

F4 owners have a choice of 19 different AF-Nikkor lenses with focal lengths from 20mm to 300mm with which almost any photographic task can be mastered. They all have built-in microcomputers for relaying data to the camera body, without which not all of the F4's functions would be available. Further AF-Nikkors are being introduced regularly.

Apart from the new AF lenses, driven by a motor in the camera body, you can also use the two older AF-lenses with the Nikon F4 in autofocus mode. These have their own motors and were introduced with the F3AF.

The P-type Nikkor with an integrated microcomputer also allows the use of all the Nikon F4's automatic controls except autofocus. So, you will have to focus this lens manually with the help of the electronic rangefinder or the clear matte screen.

In addition, about 50 Nikkor lenses between 6mm and 2000mm are available for manual focusing. Even 30-year-old Nikkors with the F-bayonet can still be used on the Nikon F4. Many of them can even be used as autofocus lenses together with the AF-Teleconverter TC-16A.

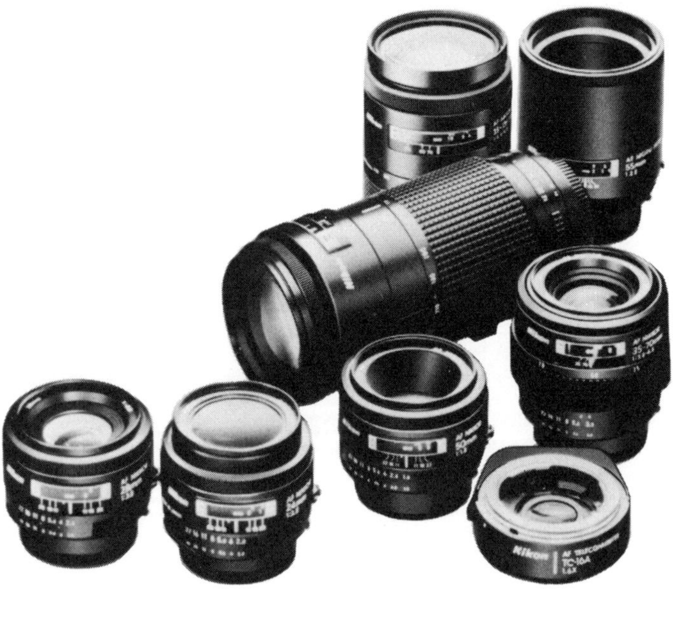

Aperture priority and manual modes as well as centre-weighted and spot metering modes can be utilized with nearly all of these lenses. The features of the different types of lenses in connection with the F4 will be discussed on the following pages.

Nikon Integrated Coating

Nikon began apply microscopically thin layers of anti-reflective materials, each of them matched to the type of glass being used, to almost all of the glass/air lens surfaces in Nikkor and Nikon Series E lenses. As a result of the NIC-multicoating, image contrast is dramatically increased by a decisive reduction of stray light.

Close Range Correction

Close Range Correction, CRC for short, greatly improves the flatness of field for wide-angle lenses at short distances and also nearly eliminates resolution flaws at the maximum aperture of the medium telephoto Nikkor 85mm, *f*1.4 lens. Technically this improvement uses "floating" elements; in the Nikkor 24mm, *f*2.8 the last three elements move further to the front than the others at short distances.

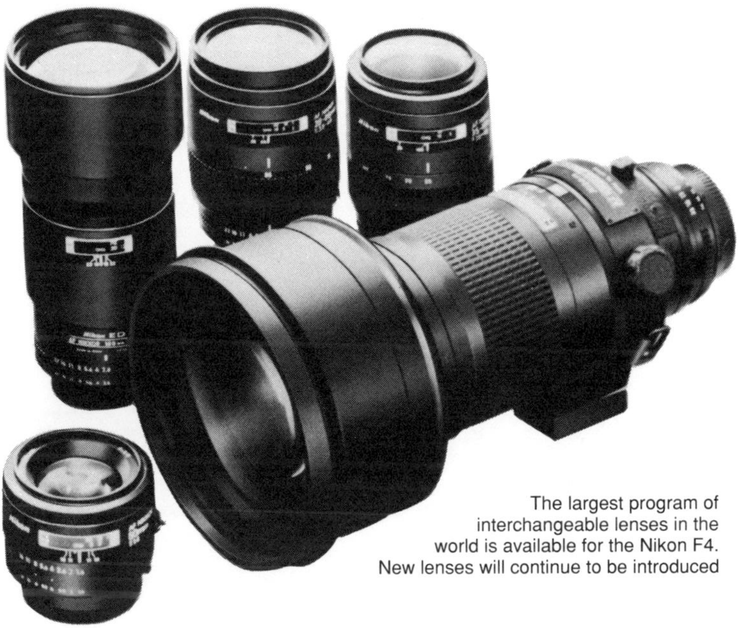

The largest program of interchangeable lenses in the world is available for the Nikon F4. New lenses will continue to be introduced

Schematic drawing of the Nikkor 24mm, $f2.8$. The three rear elements move further forward than the rest when the lens is focused to 0.3m

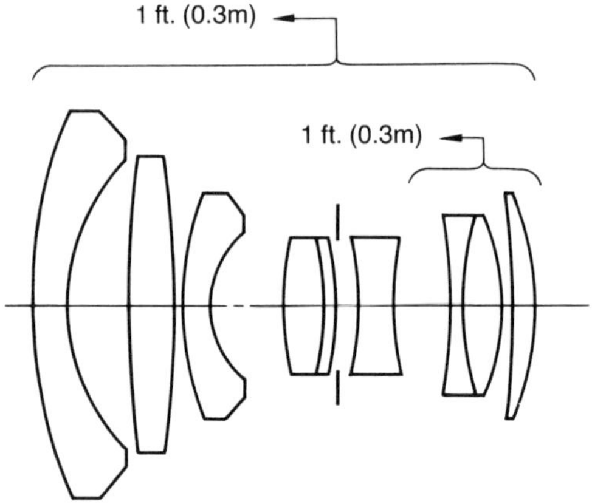

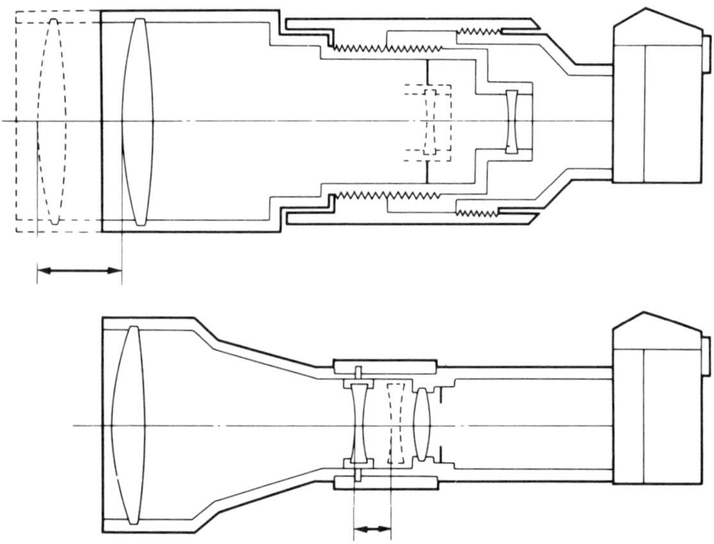

Above: a conventional telephoto lens with heavy helical focusing mount, the entire optical system has to be moved for focusing.
Below: modern Nikon lens with internal focusing. Only a relatively small optical element within the system has to be moved for focusing. Consequently the lens is much slimmer and lighter in construction.

Internal Focusing

Nikon introduced lenses with so-called internal focusing as early as 1977. This makes long telephoto lenses much lighter and easier to handle. With IF, only some internal elements shift during focusing and not the complete optical system. The physical length of IF lenses remains unchanged and is much smaller compared to conventional designs, as too is their weight, so hand-held telephoto shooting first became possible. In addition focusing became faster and easier due to the shorter shifting distance of the internal elements.

Another advantage of IF lenses is also the result of this type of focusing mechanism. The typically poorer image quality at shorter distances could be overcome and their closest focusing range improved impressively. This makes IF telephoto lenses interesting for close ups, for example, when shooting small animals when you have to keep your distance.

ED Glass with Extra-Low Dispersion

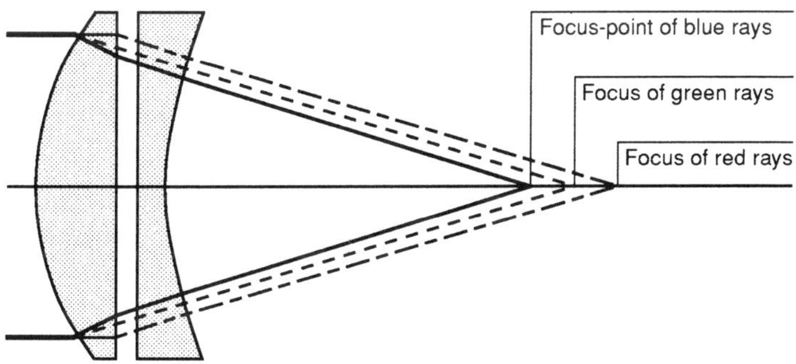

The colours which make up visible light do not come to focus at the same plane. The longer the focal length of the lens being used, the larger the focusing error. The above diagram shows the three colours – red green and blue. Nikon ED glass elements almost completely correct this error, which is known as chromatic aberration.

ED glass has an extremely low dispersion index which allows extraordinary colour rendering. Unlike glass types employed earlier to avoid chromatic aberration, ED glass is not sensitive to varying temperatures and humidity. It is relatively hard and scratch-resistant permitting its use in exposed front and rear lens elements. Stunning sharpness and high contrast even at maximum aperture is typical for lenses with ED glass.

Conventional lenses cannot offer this high degree of colour saturation and sharpness. Telephoto lenses are employed when shooting distant objects. A natural deterioration of image quality in such cases is due to the air masses between the lens and the subject with their contents of haze, smoke, and tiny dust particles. Colour aberrations in conventional lenses will be added to the above-mentioned deterioration of image quality. As a result, even photos made with the help of a tripod look unsharp and flat. Lenses with ED glass, on the other hand, deliver natural-looking, crisp colours, high contrast, and outstanding sharpness over the complete distance range. They even do away with the usual refocusing necessary when using conventional lenses for infrared photography.

AF-Nikkor Lenses

The Nikon F4 focuses automatically on the object framed in the AF-brackets when you use the new AF-Nikkor lenses. The built-in

The Nikon Bayonet

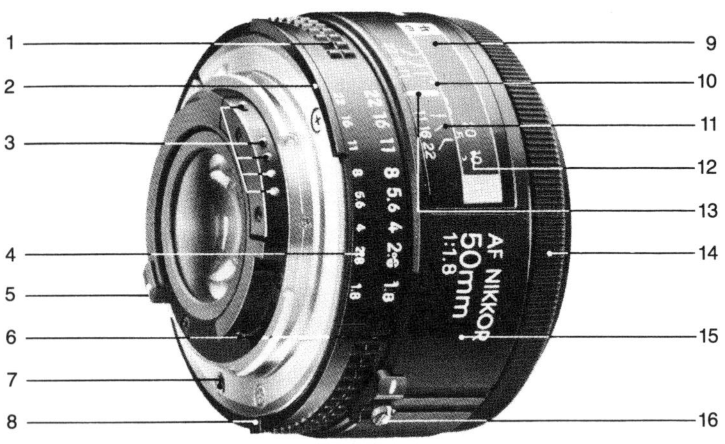

1. Aperture ring
2. Aperture cam for transfer of aperture value or aperture value coupling
3. AF contacts
4. Aperture scale
5. Focal length contact or focal length control cam
6. Auto diaphragm lever
7. AF motor coupling
8. Lens speed contact or control cam
9. Distance scale window
10. Infrared compensation index for focusing with infrared films
11. Depth of field scale
12. Distance scale
13. Aperture/distance index, lens alignment marker
14. Focusing ring
15. Lens housing
16. Aperture lock

microcomputer in these lenses relays all the data necessary for fast and precise autofocus operation as well as exposure control to the central processing unit in the camera. In order to ensure correct and reliable data transfer, make sure the contacts are never damaged or dirty.

The time-tested F-bayonet allows the AF-Nikkors also to be mounted on conventional Nikon SLR cameras. The wide and ribbed focusing ring of the newer-generation AF-Nikkors enables fast and handy manual focusing. The AF-Nikkors introduced earlier still have a much slimmer focusing ring. Perhaps in the course of evolution they may also be modified? Nikon is concerned that lenses meant for professional use especially offer easy manual focusing. One example for this company philosophy is the replacement of the earlier AF-Nikkor 70-210mm, *f*4 zoom by the AF-Nikkor 70-210, *f*4-5.6 zoom which not only has a focusing ring with a much better grip but also further improvements. We can expect all future AF-Nikkors to have such a ring.

Five contacts in the lens bayonet are responsible for transmitting data between the camera and the lens. A small protruding ridge on the aperture ring couples with the light metering system and the smaller pin controls the aperture setting. Other elements in the bayonet are the AF-coupling and the aperture indexing post. The switch that enables the minimum aperture to be locked, for program and aperture priority modes, is located on the right side of the lens just behind the aperture ring. The older AF-lenses have a somewhat clumsy turning pin which has been replaced in the newer models by a handy sliding bar. The aperture ring itself has two aperture scales. One is for setting the aperture, with the help of the index on the lens barrel, the other one is intended for direct aperture readout through the window in the viewfinder. Manual or automatic focus settings can be controlled through the distance scale window. Next to the index line for distance there is another index mark for the focus setting in infrared photography. On zoom lenses there are often a number of such marks for different focal lengths. Lenses with fixed focal lengths also have depth of field indicators. Differing details for specific lenses will be dealt with when they are presented on the following pages.

AF Standard Lenses

Lenses with focal lengths of around 50mm are called normal or standard in 35mm photography. These focal lengths are close to the length of the diagonal of the 35mm frame. The picture angle of 43° results in a perspective very similar to that of the human eye. Pictures made with normal lenses have a natural perspective due to this and can be universally employed. In addition they are also the fastest lenses of the whole system, built compactly and of light weight, so therefore they are, good to include in your equipment. Normal lenses are also quite reasonably priced. Nikon offers two AF Nikkors with fast maximum apertures of $f1.8$ and $f1.4$. This fast maximum aperture results in a clear and bright viewfinder image which is a decisive factor in controlling focus and composition.

AF-Nikkor 50mm, f1.8: this is one of the longest-running designs of all the interchangeable AF Nikkors. The optical design is the same as that of the non-AF version. It weighs a mere 210g and measures nearly 5cm. It is ideal for general photography.

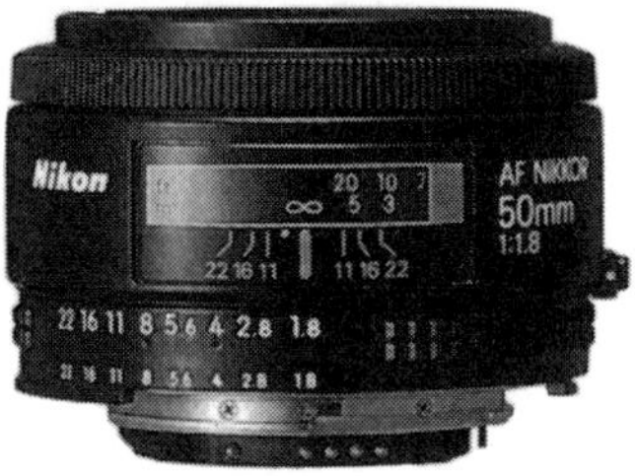

AF-Nikkor 50mm, f1.4: this very fast lens is the suitable choice for pictures to be made without flash and in low-light conditions. The very bright viewfinder image, due to the large maximum aperture, proves to be especially helpful in these dim conditions. This lens also corresponds to the earlier manual focusing model in its optical design.

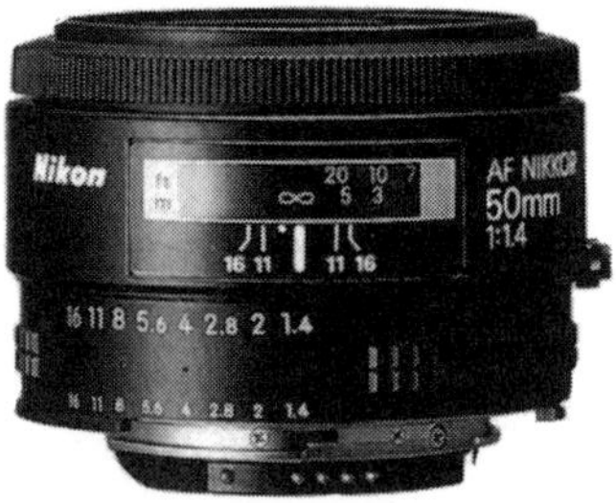

AF Wide-angle Lenses

You can cover large objects from relatively short distances with wide-angle lenses. Because of their extensive angle of view you can take your pictures in small rooms. The large depth of field obtainable with lenses of shorter focal lengths, make them very well-suited for snapshots, architecture, landscapes, and indoor photography. In the case of the latter their relatively large maximum aperture comes in handy and makes them ideal for available-light photography. The range of AF-Nikkor wide-angle lenses available embraces four models with focal lengths of 20mm, 24mm, 28mm, and 35mm. Even though manual focusing is less critical in wide-angle lenses, due to their greater depth of field, autofocus can be a welcome help and make things easier with these focal lengths as well.

AF-Nikkor 20mm, *f*2.8: this fast lens is already one of the super wide-angles. Its optical design is identical to the non-AF lens with the same specification. It is especially compactly built and its 12 elements in nine groups weigh only 260g. The shortest focusing distance is 25cm. The wide focusing ring is convenient for manual focusing. In spite of the large angle of view, distortion and vignetting have been reduced to a minimum, even at full aperture.

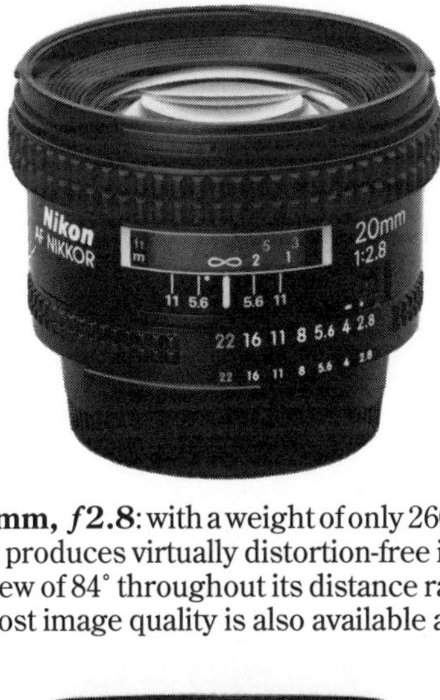

AF-Nikkor 24mm, *f*2.8: with a weight of only 260g and a length of just 56mm, this lens produces virtually distortion-free images in spite of the large angle of view of 84° throughout its distance range from 0.3 metres to infinity. Utmost image quality is also available at close range thanks

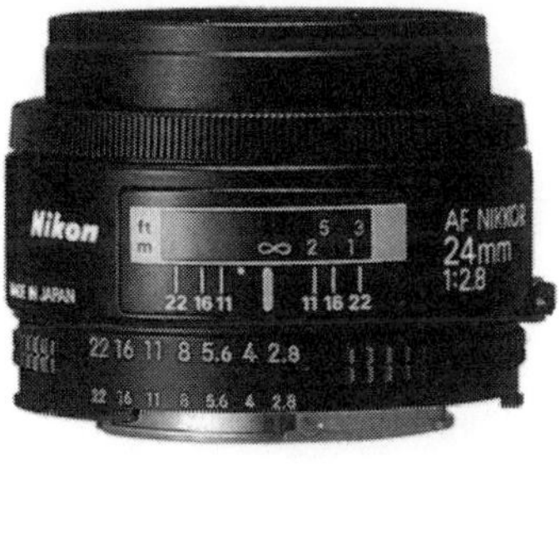

to Nikon's CRC system. The retrofocus design prevents vignetting in the corners of the picture that normally occur at full aperture. The optical design is identical to that of the non-AF type. The maximum aperture is relatively fast for this focal length but if you need an even faster model you can find one in the non-AF Nikkor range.

AF-Nikkor 28mm, *f*2.8: this is a completely new lens. Its optical design consists of only 5 elements in 5 groups. The non-AF Nikkor with the same specification has 8 elements in 8 groups. As a result the AF-Nikkor weighs 50g less and is more than 4mm shorter. A concession was made in the case of the shortest focusing distance which is 0.3m in the newer model as opposed to 0.2m in the earlier one. The retrofocus design prevents vignetting in the corners of the picture even at full aperture. Distortion can be reduced to a minimum even at the shortest focusing distance of 0.3m. The manual focusing range of lenses offers a faster model of this focal length, too.

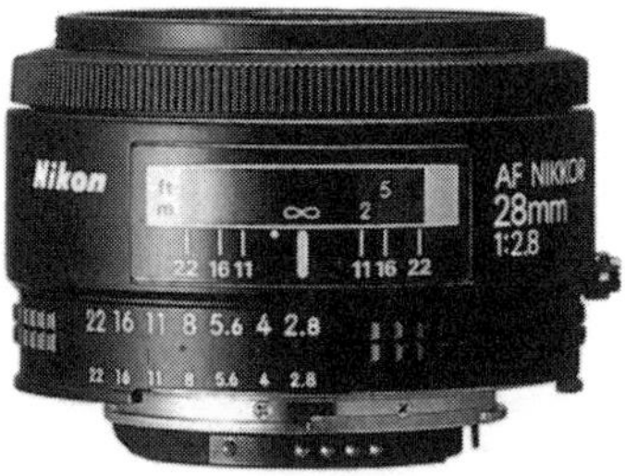

AF-Nikkor 35mm, *f*2:

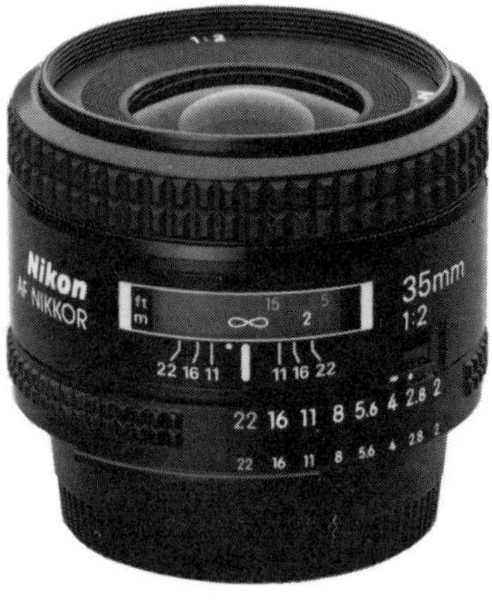

this model is also a new design. It is a moderate wide-angle with a large maximum aperture and consists of 6 elements in five groups. It weighs only 215g and is not quite 44mm long. The shortest focusing distance is 25cm. Again, the non-AF lens program offers an even faster model for available-light photography with a fastest aperture of *f*1.4. On the other hand, this lens weighs and costs about twice as much. This focal length with its moderate wide-angle impression and without very obvious perspective distortion allows the lens to be employed universally. Many professionals use this lens instead of the normal 50mm because it is ideal for news photography and snapshots.

Autofocus Telephoto Lenses

All in all Nikon has introduced five autofocus telephoto lenses with focal lengths from 85mm to 300mm. With the exception of the 85mm AF-Nikkor, all of their optical designs include extra-low-dispersion glass and the internal focusing which Nikon has offered for several years to ensure quick and easy manual focusing. An outstandingly large maximum aperture is typical for all five lenses.

Telephoto lenses are used to pull in distant scenes and to get frame-filling shots without being close to the subject. While wide-angles seem to stretch the perspective, telephoto lenses tend to compress it, an effect that gets stronger with the longer focal lengths. The depth of field also gets shallower with the longer lenses. Portrait photographers use this to make their subjects stand out better from the background. If you wish, the very large maximum apertures of the AF-Nikkor telephoto lenses will allow you to limit the depth of field to a very small area. These fast telephoto lenses are also employed for sports and candid shots as well as portraiture.

AF-Nikkor 85mm, *f*1.8:

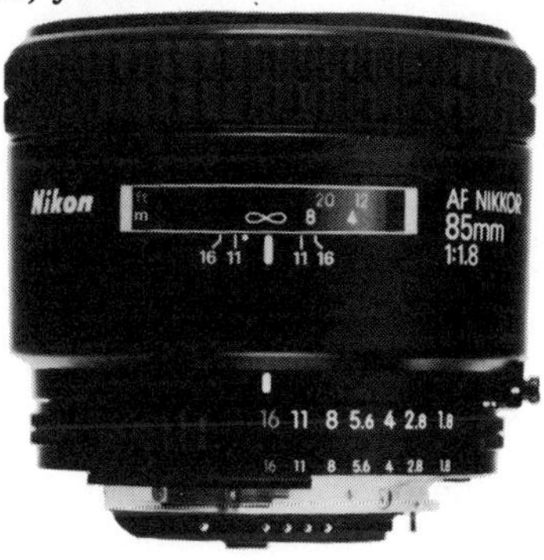

the 85mm has been one of the photographer's favourite focal lengths in the Nikkor lens program from the very start. This lens seems to continue the triumphant advance of this focal length which is so ideal for portraiture and news reporting. The fast aperture of *f*1.8 has a lot of advantages. One of them is the suitability for photography in poor lighting conditions without a flash, another the possibility of reducing the depth of field with the maximum aperture, and also the super-bright viewfinder image which allows a perfect control of focus and composition even in twilight. One of its special features is its rear element focusing mechanism. In this design, only the optical element in the rear is shifted, which allows even faster focusing in autofocus operation. The lens has a ribbed rubber-coated ring for easy manual focusing. Due to the weight of only 415g this compact and versatile lens is also recommended for travel photography.

AF-Nikkor 180mm, *f*2.8 IF-ED: this focal length also has a long tradition in the selection of Nikon's long and fast telephoto lenses. The large maximum aperture of *f*2.8, the easy internal focusing, and the light weight, compared to the complex design, make this lens an ideal companion in sports and news photography. Internal focusing also reduces the noise caused by autofocus operation. By utilizing ED glass with an extremely low dispersion index the lens is almost completely free of chromatic aberrations and provides high-quality images even at maximum aperture. It weighs 750g and is only 153mm long. The shortest focusing distance of 1.5m enables you to shoot frame-filling portraits at the closest range.

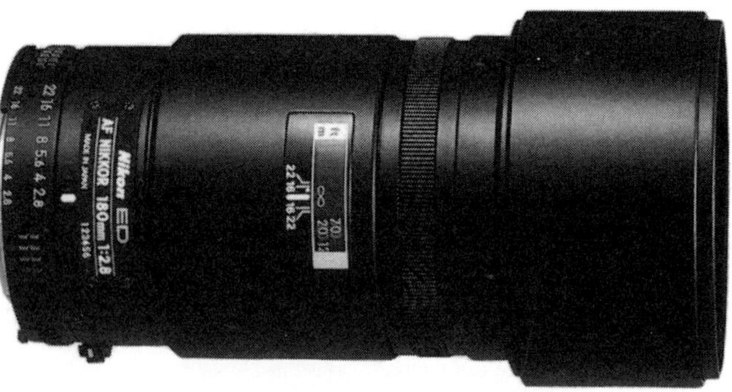

AF-Nikkor 300mm, *f*4 IF-ED: this is a newly-designed lens with a slightly larger maximum aperture than the earlier manual focusing type. As in all the newer long telephoto lenses, Nikon also employed ED glass with an extremely low dispersion index in this model. The lens delivers an extraordinary image quality right from the maximum aperture. Because of its compact size, compared to the focal length, and its relatively light weight it is an ideal lens for travel photography. The shortest focusing distance is 2.5m. It is only 227mm long and weighs about 1330g. Its optical design consists of 8 elements in 6 groups.

In order to mount it on a tripod it comes equipped with a tripod collar which can be rotated through 360°. The focusing ring has an **A/M** switch with which the lens can be set to manual focusing. This mode is especially recommended for tripod shooting, since operating the autofocus lock would be quite clumsy in such a case. If the main subject were off-centre you would first have to loosen the tripod head, lock the focus setting, recompose, and finally tighten the tripod head again before you could release the shutter. The focus limiting ring is a very practical feature with which you can confine the focusing range to the distance area the subject can be expected in. Autofocus operation will not cover the complete range of the lens from its shortest focusing distance to infinity but will only work within the preset range. So, if the photographer knew beforehand that his subject is not going to get closer than 10m he can set the limiting ring accordingly. The autofocus system will not have to operate in the shorter distance range between 2.5 and 10m, where more adjustment is necessary for the lens's focal setting, so it can focus much faster than before. This advantage is especially important for sports, action, and fashion photography.

The lens takes normal threaded filters in a special slip-in type holder which is installed into the lens barrel. A filter must always be used as it is an integral part of the lens design. For this reason the L37c filter is included with the lens.

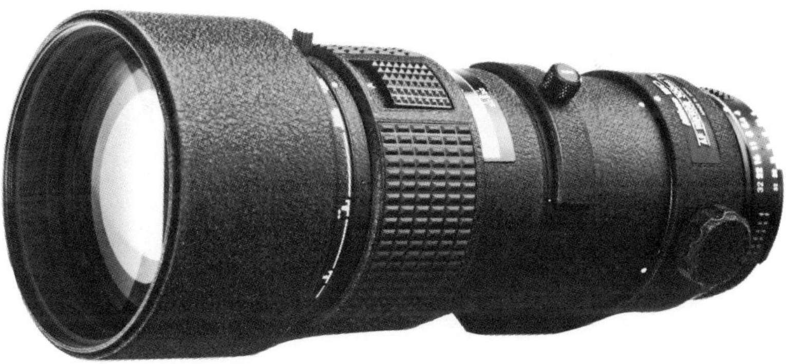

AF-Nikkor 300mm, *f*2.8 IF-ED: this super-telephoto lens is designed without compromise for available-light photography. It will prove its advantages, especially in those low-light conditions where the photographer's most important goal is to utilize fast shutter speeds. Since it produces a spectacular image quality even at its full aperture, thanks to the use of ED-glass, this lens will be used mainly by sports photographers working in poorly-lit gymnasiums or arenas. It will also help wildlife photographers who also constantly have to cope with dim light. But not only the technical advantages and the high image quality contribute to this lens's popularity. The creative possibilities, especially, of such a large maximum aperture, with its extremely shallow depth of field, allows a photographer to let annoying background details disappear and the main subject to stand out crisp and clear. Many fashion photographers take advantage of this in their outdoor shooting. In many cases the resulting faster shutter speeds will even allow hand-held shooting.

This lens can also be used for manual focusing and on non-AF Nikon cameras. The lens can be set from autofocus to manual mode with the **A/M** switch on the focusing ring. In manual mode you can mark any focus setting. If, for example, a photographer wanted to shoot a runner at the starting line and at the third hurdle, he would first focus on that third hurdle, mark the position with the little knurled screw on the

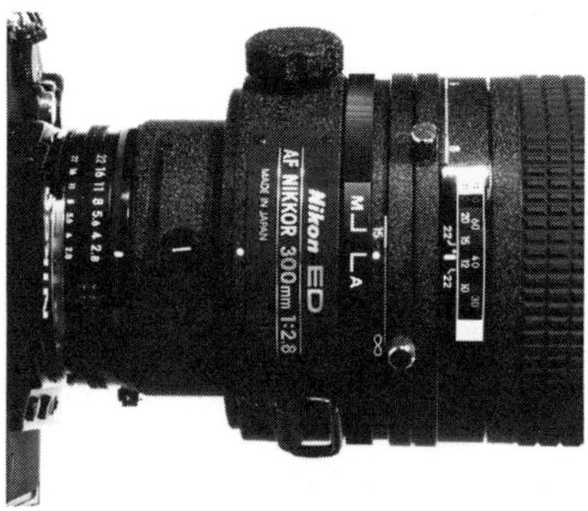

marking ring, and then set the focus back to the starting line for his first shot. After that he would rotate the focusing ring quickly into the preset position. If he wanted to follow the runner he could focus beyond the index mark.

Two more small knurled screws are for limiting the focusing range which can speed up the autofocus operation. If he knew beforehand in which distance range his subject would be moving he could mark both ends of the range with the little screws. Autofocus operation will be limited to the preset range and will, therefore, be much faster. Normal threaded filters in slip-in type holders are also an integral part of this lens's optical design. So a filter must always be screwed into the holder. In spite of the complex design and the large maximum aperture the lens weighs only 2700g and is only 225mm long. Of course, it has a tripod collar, allowing the lens to rotate a full 360°. Since the lens is heavier than the camera you should not hold the combination by the camera alone as this could damage the bayonet. This is why the tripod collar has eyelets for attaching a shoulder strap.

AF-Nikkor 600mm, *f*4 IF-ED: so far this extremely fast super-telephoto lens has only been presented as a dummy prototype. Like the 300mm it has focusing limiter rings to enhance autofocus speed. The **A/M** switch allows the lens to be set from autofocus to manual mode. A filter holder is also installed in the lens barrel to keep the filter size small. Wildlife photographers especially, who prefer to work at dusk, would be very fond of this lens. Since rather large masses must be shifted for focusing, in lenses with longer focal lengths than 500mm, Nikon engineers are thinking about integrating special focusing motors into future super-telephoto lenses. These motors could be matched to the specific needs of the lens design.

Speculation about this has been aroused by the electrical contact pins in the bayonet which are not being used by any present equipment. This lens also has a sturdy tripod mount exactly in the center of gravity. Eyelets for a shoulder strap are located on the barrel near the bayonet

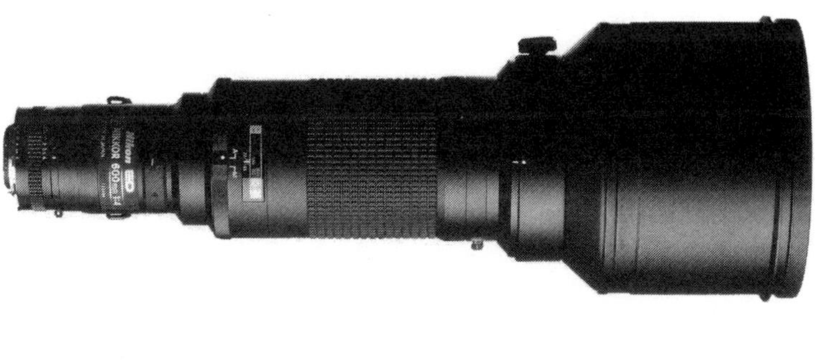

AF Zoom Lenses

With a zoom lens you can change frame coverage without having to alter your position. As a result the perspective of your picture will not change since it is not dependent on the focal length but on the shooting position.

Very roughly, you can divide the 9 AF zooms in the selection of interchangeable Nikon lenses into two groups. To distinguish wide-angle and telephoto zooms; all zooms that have a shorter focal length than 50mm are wide-angle zooms, as opposed to the normal or medium telephoto range. Most of the Nikon wide-angle zooms begin at 35mm. There are five different models in all. They differ in their longest focal length and in their maximum aperture. Many zooms have varying speeds, i.e. the actual maximum aperture becomes smaller when you zoom to longer focal lengths. The automatic exposure controls, including automatic flash metering, recognize these changes and compensate the exposure accordingly. The light meter also reacts to the changing situation since it monitors the light through the lens. Problems can only arise when metering is done externally without taking into consideration the changing aperture.

Autofocus really proves to be a big advantage with zoom lenses. Whereas a photographer would have to set the focus and the focal length with one or two separate rings in manual mode, today he can concentrate on his composition. The Nikon F4 will focus perfectly, automatically. Slight defocusing when changing the focal length, common earlier especially with one-ring zooms, are most certainly a thing of the past today. AF zooms make news-reporting, action, sports, and travel photography even faster. They render the constant changing of lenses unnecessary and are replacing many fixed focal length lenses with their own ever-expanding focal ranges. Today the image quality of zooms equals that of fixed focal length lenses. Concessions are only necessary with respect to their not so fast and varying speed. The AF-Nikkor lens program already offers two zooms in the popular ranges of 35 to 70mm and 80 to 200mm, both of which have a fast and consistent maximum aperture of *f*2.8 in the whole focal length range.

AF Wide-Angle Zooms

Most of the zoom lenses Nikon offer are wide-angle. They add up to about two-thirds of all the zooms. Most of these have a shortest focal length of 35mm. Only two of them start at 24mm and 28mm. Wide-angle zooms are especially appropriate for news reporting, fast snapshots, and indoor photography.

AF Zoom Nikkor 24-50mm, *f*3.3-4.5: this is the zoom with the shortest focal length of the whole Nikon lens program. It can replace the traditional fixed focal length wide-angles of 24mm, 28mm, and 35mm and also includes the standard 50mm. It is quite compact and, therefore, favoured by news and travel photographers. The separate rings for focusing and the focal length allow easy handling even when focusing manually. The focusing ring's ribbed rubber coating also makes manual focusing a pleasure. The relatively large fastest aperture of *f*3.3 at 24mm is also remarkable. The shortest focusing distance is 0.6m and can be reduced by another 10cm to 50cm in the macro-position. The lens weighs only about 375g and is just 74mm long.

AF Zoom Nikkor 28-85mm, *f*3.5-4.5: this is a very versatile autofocus zoom lens that covers all the focal lengths from wide-angle and normal to the medium telephoto range without exception. Focusing is done by rotating a ring. It is ideal for snapshots and news photography

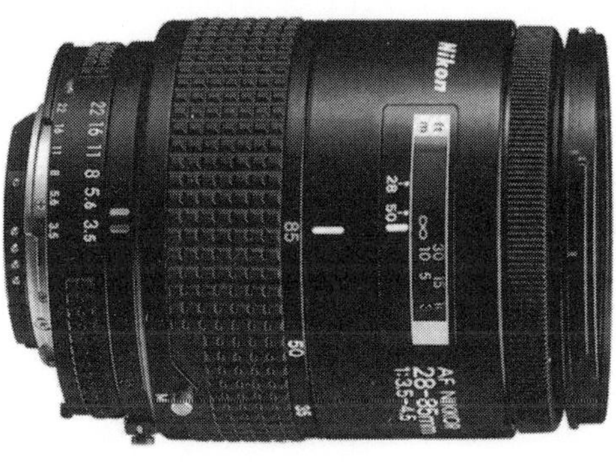

indoors and out. The large focal length span allows landscape as well as portrait photography. The focal length setting ring is engraved with the positions for 28, 35, 50, and 85mm. In order to do close-ups to the ratio of 1:3.4 the macro position must first be unlocked with the small silver button on the focal length setting ring. You will have to focus manually with the ring mentioned above in this case, though. The electronic rangefinder or the clear matte screen will show you when your subject is in focus. The lens is just 98mm long and weighs a mere 540g. The optional lens hood HB-1 has a diameter of 63mm and is mounted on the lens with a bayonet. Lens hoods are important accessories because they fend off stray light and, therefore, help improve contrast.

Even at night matrix metering proves its effectiveness. It allows automatic photography without any need for compensation.

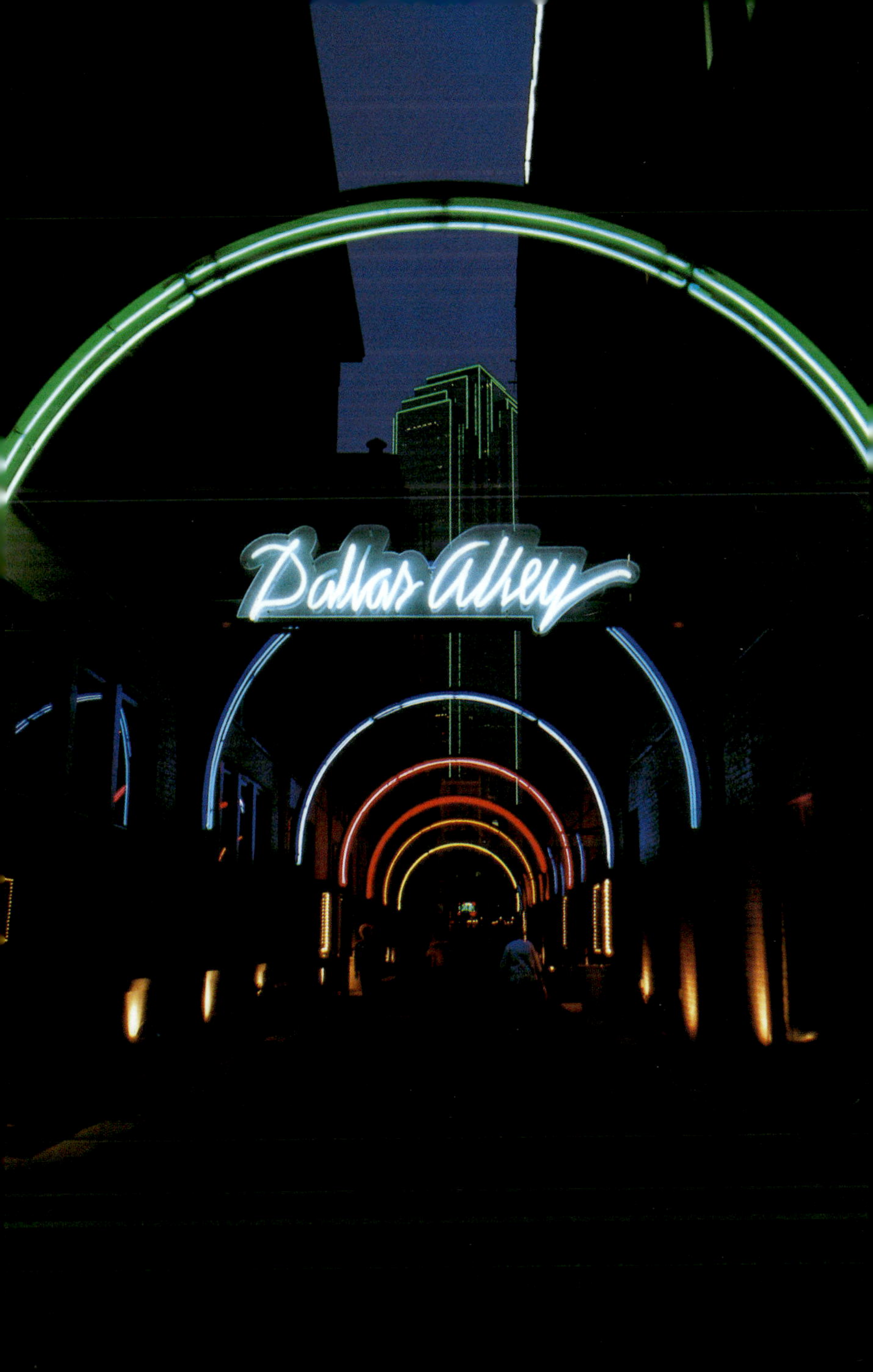
Dallas Alley

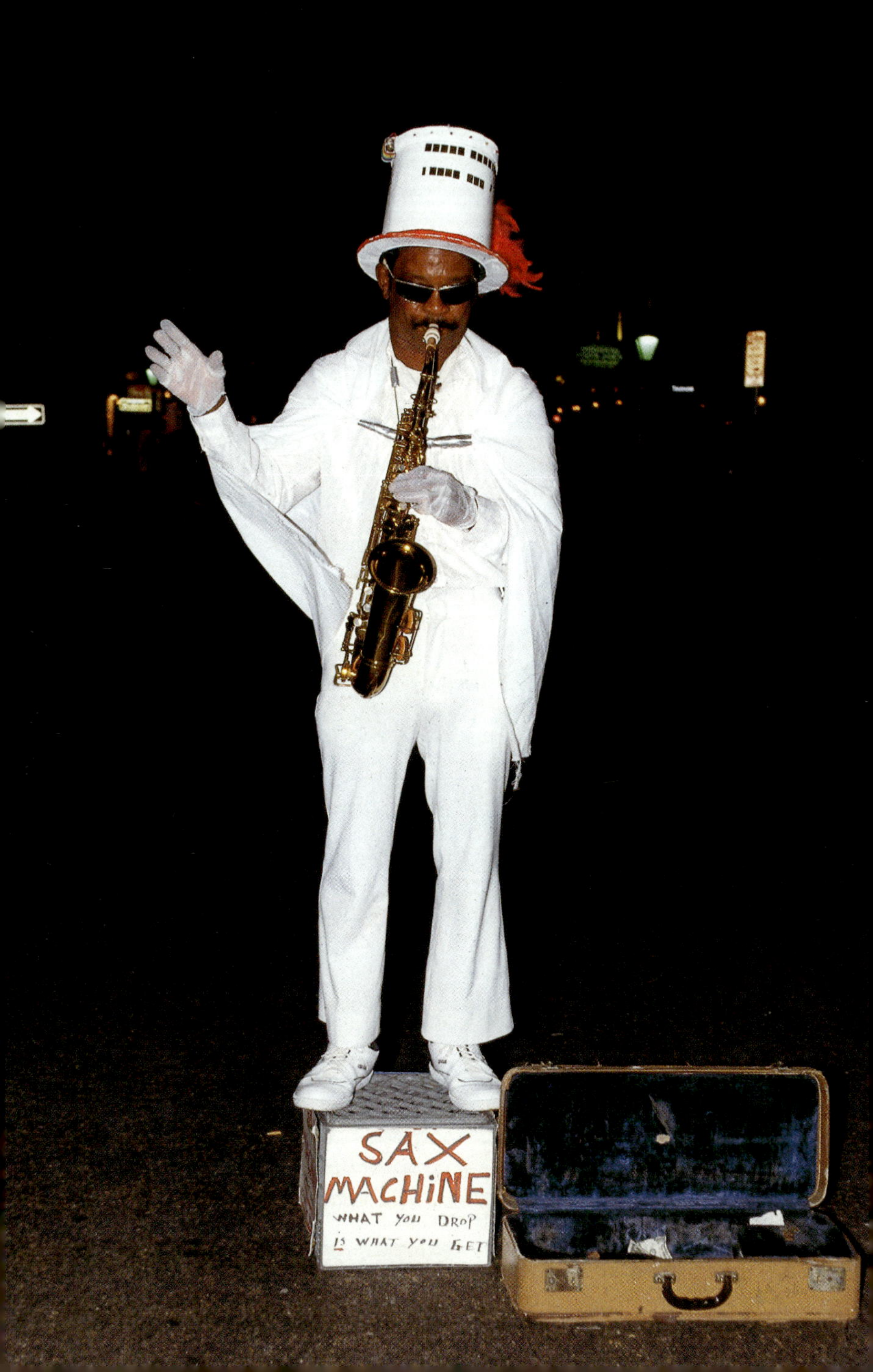
SAX
MACHINE
WHAT YOU DROP
IS WHAT YOU GET

AF Zoom Nikkor 35-70mm, *f*2.8: this is the fastest of all the wide-angle zooms in the selection of interchangeable Nikon lenses. It is a high-performance zoom with a consistent maximum aperture of *f*2.8. Unlike the zooms described above, this lens has a combined two-part focusing/zooming ring, so you change the focal length by sliding the ring back and forth and not by rotating it. Focusing in manual mode is done by a separate, wide ring with a handy ribbed rubber coating. The lens allows close-ups to a ratio of 1:4 at a focal length setting of 35mm and a focusing distance of 28cm. Thanks to the complex design which called for 15 elements in 12 groups, image quality defects such as distortion and vignetting is reduced to a minimum. This fast wide-angle zoom weighs 665 grams and is 95mm long. The lens hood HB-1 can also be employed for this lens.

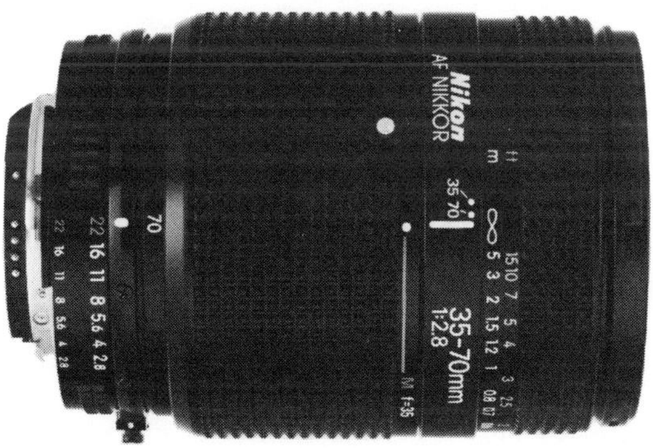

Difficult contrast situations as in the picture on the left are mastered automatically by the combination of an F4 and a matrix controlled electronic Speedlite.

AF Zoom Nikkor 35-70mm, *f*3.3-4.5: this zoom lens is not only smaller and lighter than the AF zoom Nikkor 35-70mm, *f*2.8, but is also cheaper. On the other hand it is not so fast and does not have a consistent maximum aperture. Its really light weight of only about 255g and its length of just 61mm makes it the ideal lens when you are on the go. It has two separate rings for focusing manually and changing the focal length. Macro-photography with manual focusing is available at all focal lengths. The shortest focusing distance in autofocus mode is 50cm and can be reduced to 35cm in the macro mode. The HN-2 hood is used with this lens.

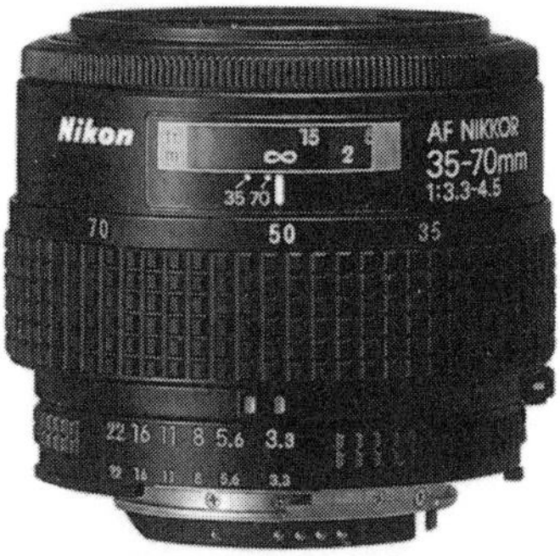

AF Zoom Nikkor 35-105mm, *f*3.5-4.5: this autofocus zoom covers a triple range from medium wide-angle to moderate telephoto. 16 elements in 11 groups were necessary for its design. The shortest focusing distance is 1.4m but you can utilize the macro position for closer shots up to a ratio of 1:3.5. In spite of the large focal length span this triple zoom weighs only 460g and is 96mm long. It is especially suitable for snapshots, news photography and portraits. Because of its light weight it is also ideal for travelling. The appropriate lens hood is the model HB-2.

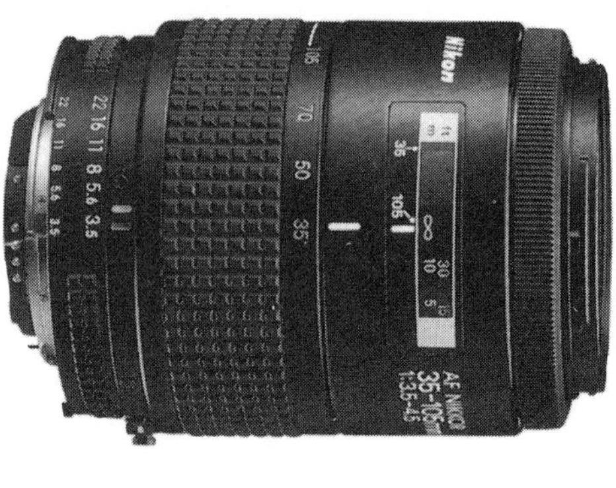

AF Zoom Nikkor 35-135mm, *f*3.5-4.5: with an almost quadruple coverage ranging from medium wide-angle to moderate telephoto this autofocus zoom is universally suitable for snapshots, news, and travel photography and ideal for landscape and portraits as well. Its design consists of 15 elements in 12 groups. The shortest focusing distance in autofocus mode is 1.5m. An additional macro position is available at thelongest focal length from a closest distance of 40cm, which results in a maximum reproduction ratio of 1:3.5. Unlike the earlier model, perhaps still in stock at some dealers, the newer type has been redesigned mechanically and is now also one of the zooms with a combined, two-part focusing/zooming ring. The new lens takes the same HB-1 lens hood the previous model did but the more complex mechanics of this kind of ring design led to slightly more weight – 685g – and length – 117mm, as opposed to that of its predecessor; 630g and 109mm.

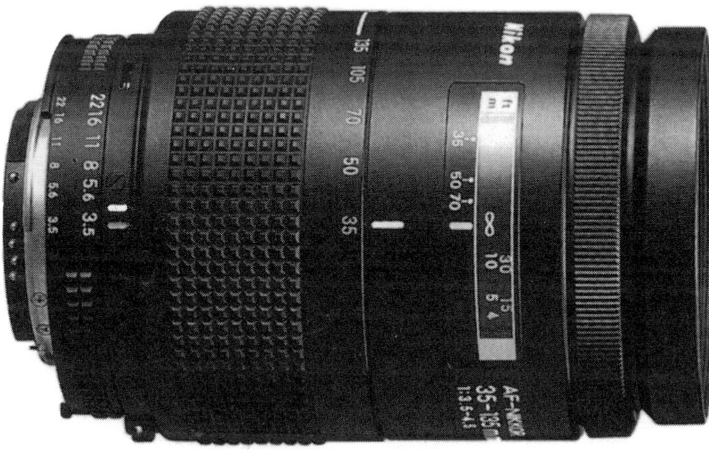

Angles of View

Fisheye 8mm

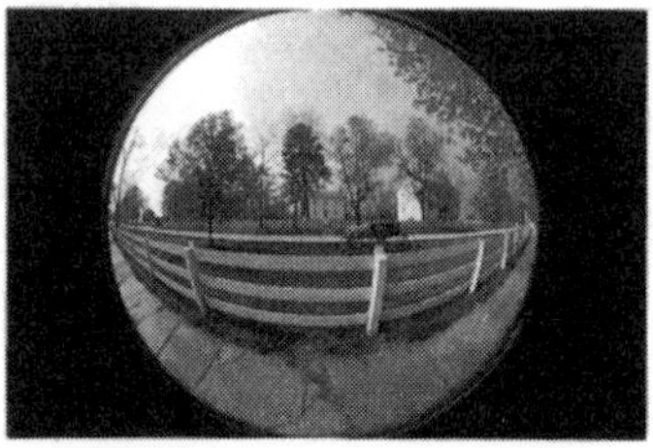

Ultra-wide 15mm

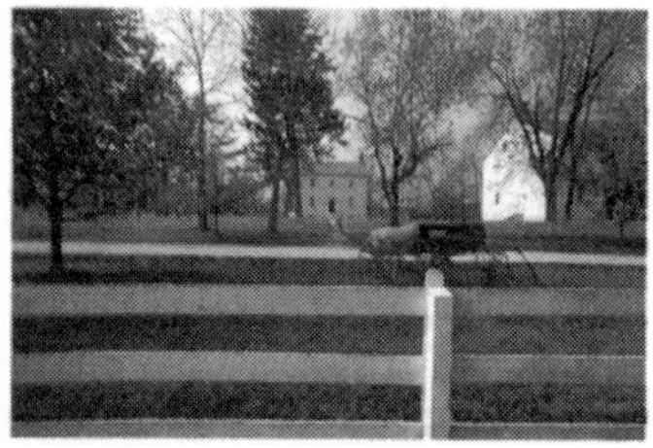

Normal 50mm

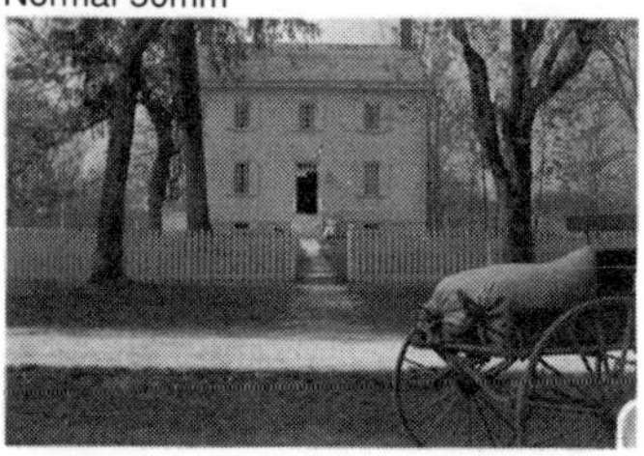

Tele 85mm

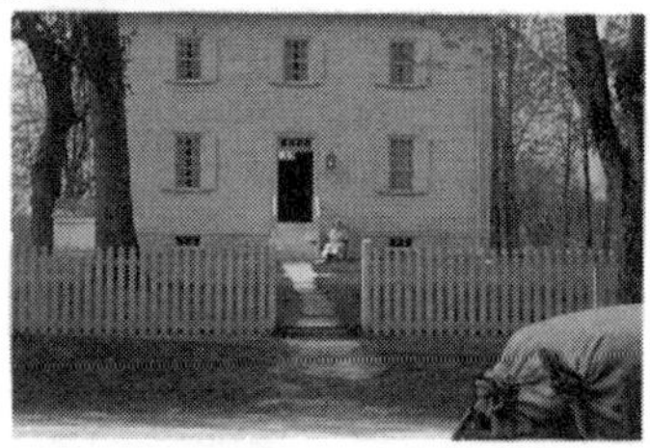

180mm

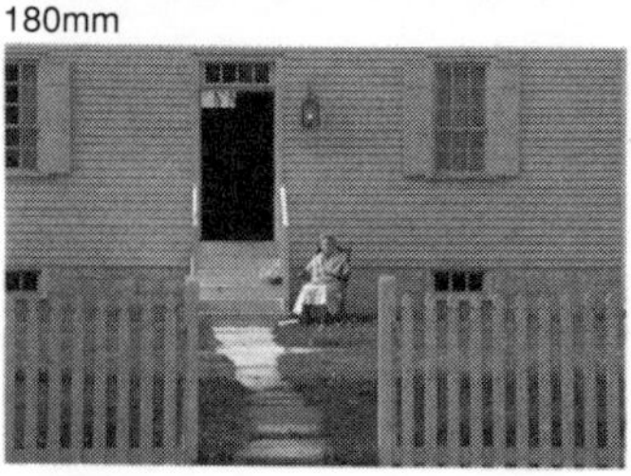

200mm

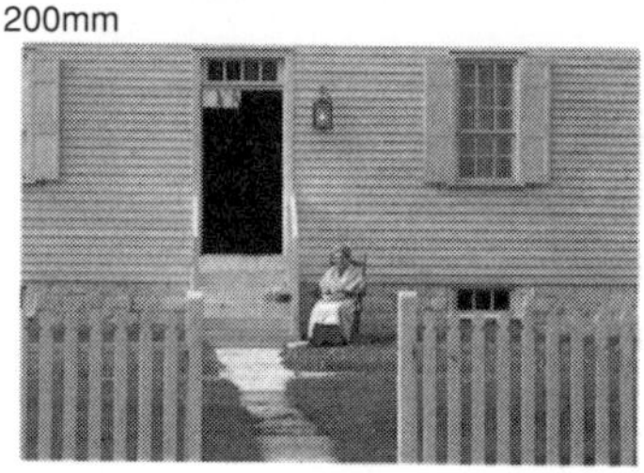

800mm

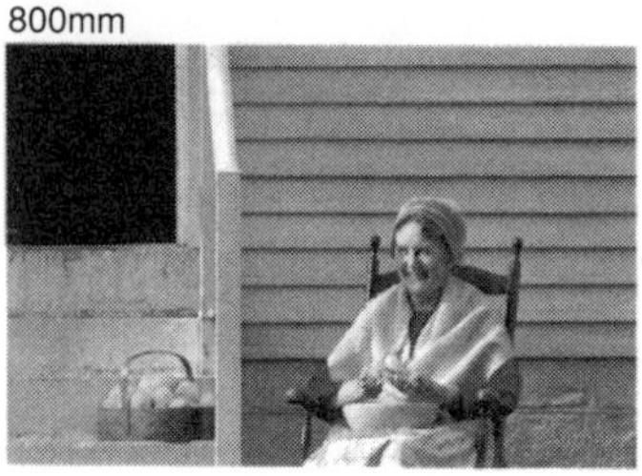

1200mm

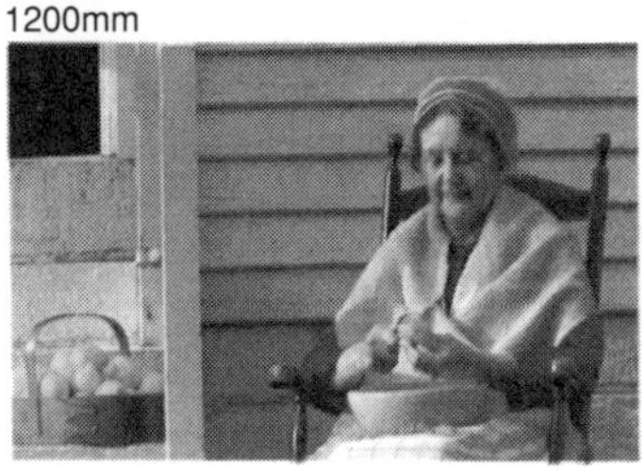

Wide-angle 24mm

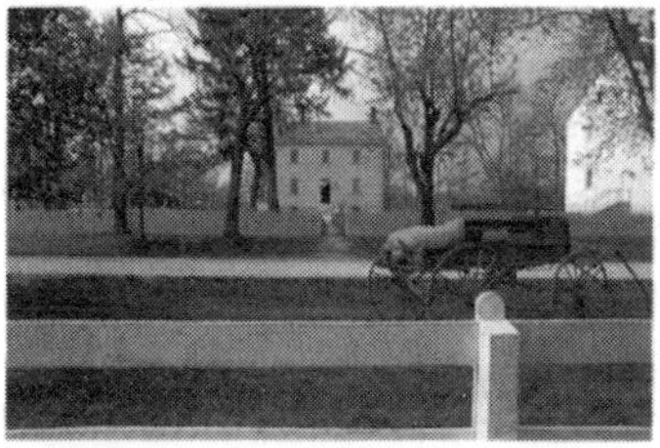

35mm

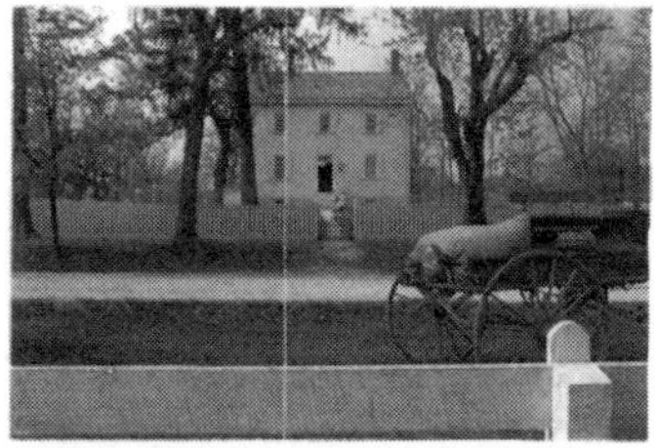

105mm

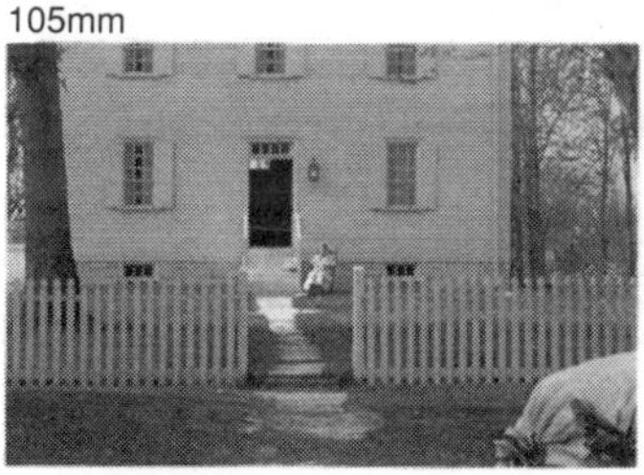

135mm

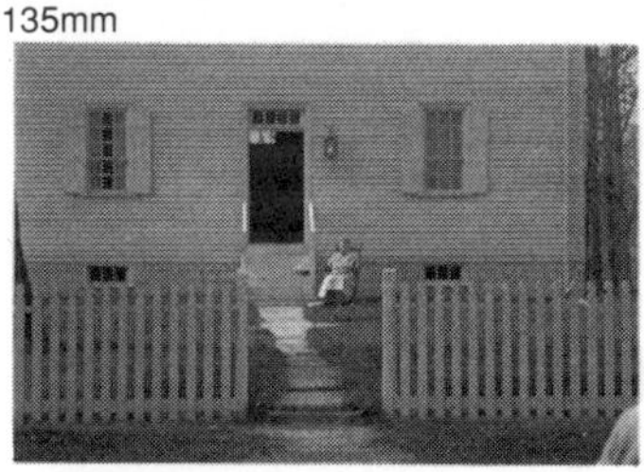

400mm

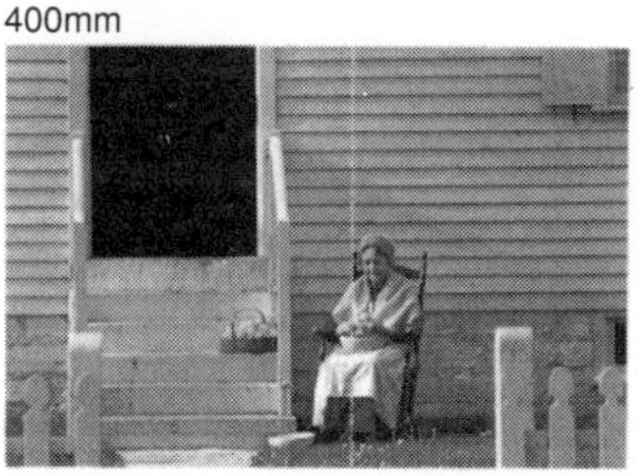

600mm

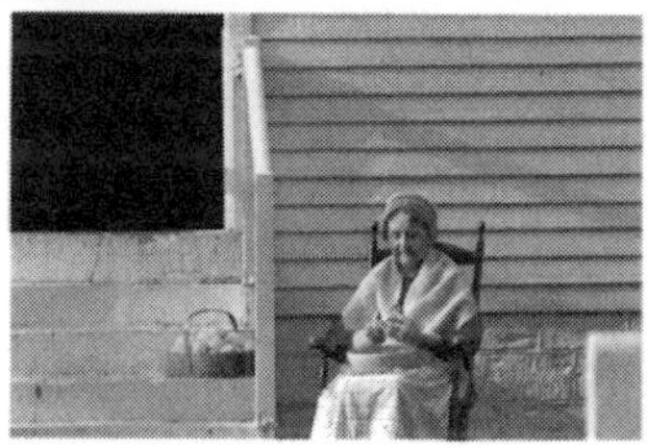

Comparison of focal lengths: pictures taken with different focal lengths from the same position do not show any change in perspective. Because of the different angle of view, wide-angle lenses show more, but represent the view on a smaller scale; telephoto lenses select a smaller frame, but represent it on a larger scale.

AF Telephoto Zoom Lenses

At present Nikon offers only three telephoto zooms in the AF program. The selection is restricted to the most popular focal length ranges of 70-210mm, 80-200mm, and 75-300mm, which have proved their usefulness in the hands of professionals hundreds of thousands of times for many years. These zooms can be employed universally and represent an ideal supplement to a wide-angle zoom or several single wide-angle lenses. They can be seen as a sort of link between the normal and wide-angle ranges and the super-telephoto lenses. They differ mostly in terms of their maximum aperture and focal length span.

AF Zoom Nikkor 70-210mm, *f*4-5.6: this lens already represents the second generation of the AF Zoom Nikkor lens series which was introduced in 1986. The previous model was replaced by a much improved new design only a year after it was put on sale. The new lens is not only smaller and lighter but has also been improved in terms of optical construction and image quality. In order to achieve this it had to do without a consistant maximum aperture throughout its focal length range which allowed it to be 170g lighter and 32mm shorter.

Unlike the older two-ring type zoom, the new lens is a zoom with a combined, two-part focusing/zooming ring and has a handy ribbed rubber-coated ring for manual focusing. This also shows the superiority of the new lens. Its shortest focusing distance is 1.2m which results in a reproduction ratio of 1:4.5. The appropriate lens hood is model HN-24.

AF Zoom Nikkor 80-200mm, *f*2.8 ED: all the shortcomings normally associated with zoom lenses were avoided in the design of this exceptional lens. It is an AF zoom of a very high quality with a fast maximum aperture of *f*2.8. Taking into consideration that this fast maximum aperture is consistent throughout the focal length range, the lens is rather light and compact. Its dimensions are only slightly greater than those of the popular manual-focusing Zoom Nikkor 80-200mm model with *f*4 as the maximum aperture. The same ED glass used in the fast telephoto lenses, to correct defects in colour rendering, is also employed in this case to ensure high image quality even at full aperture. Chromatic aberrations are almost completely eliminated. The whole construction is designed to withstand the toughest working conditions. The lens is delivered with case CL-43 but the very advisable lens hood HN-28 is optional. Like the longer telephoto lenses, this zoom also has an additional ring to preset a limited focusing distance span, in order to enhance the focusing speed in autofocus mode. The photographer can preset the lens to work within a range of less than or more than three meters. Depending on this setting the autofocus system will then cover only the shorter or the longer distance. This reduces shifting inside the lens and therefore results in a much quicker autofocus operation which helps a lot in action photography. Especially high speeds are achieved in focusing at long distances since much less shifting is necessary than in short range focusing. In normal operation the shortest focusing distance is 1.8m. In the macro position you can get as close as 1.5m to your subject at all the focal length settings.

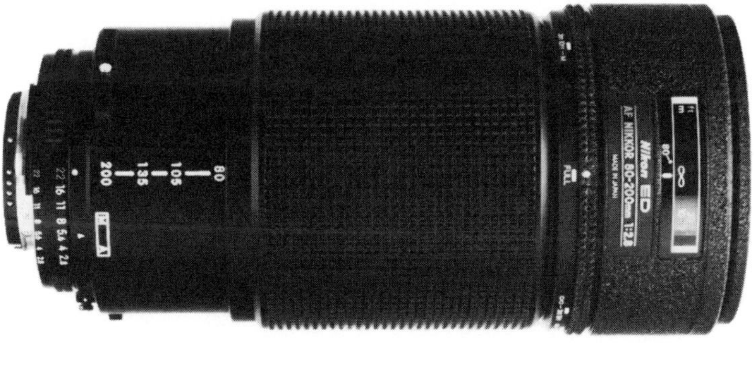

AF Zoom Nikkor 75-300mm, *f*4.5-5.6: travel photographers especially will have been waiting for a compact lens in this focal length range, which has not existed before in the Nikon program. This zoom of only 850g and 166mm covers the complete medium telephoto range with its quadruple focal length span. The optical design consists of 13 elements in 11 groups. The shortest focusing distance is 3m which allows frame-filling portraits from a relatively far-away position.

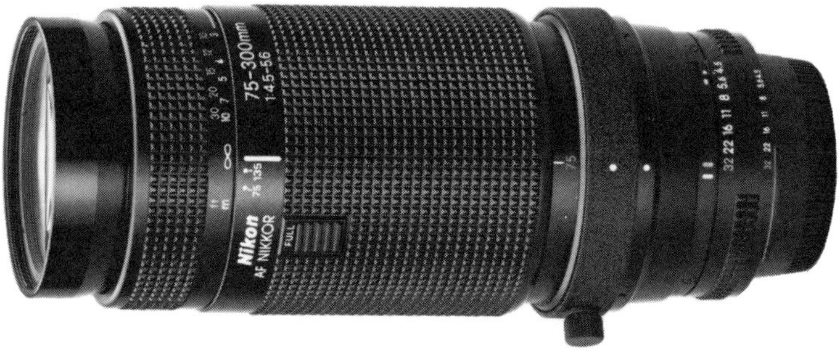

AF Macro Lenses

The object of macro photography is to reproduce small items on a large scale. This is still best done with manual focusing accessories. There are three ways leading into the miniature world. These are extensions such as bellows or automatic extension rings, close-up lenses, and macro lenses especially corrected for short focusing distances. Whereas normal lenses are corrected for medium to long range focusing, macro lenses show an excellent image quality at shorter focusing distances as well, which sometimes improves further still at long distances. This makes macro lenses universally ideal for close-ups and normal shots. The most popular focal length for a macro lens is 50 to 60mm and the only one available up to now in the Nikon AF program is situated half-way between. Unlike all the other companies who call their special lenses for close-up photography macro lenses Nikon has named theirs Micro Nikkors.

AF Micro Nikkor 55mm, *f*2.8: this lens, which is specially corrected for close-ups, allows up to life-size photography. The shortest focusing distance is 0.229m. Fast autofocus operation calls for extra-smooth focusing. On the other hand it might shift by itself due to its own weight when you focus manually and hold the lens in a vertical position. That is why the degree of friction in the focusing ring can be set from very smooth to more resistant. Thanks to the extraordinary degree of correction the Nikon Micro Nikkor will produce an extremely high image quality virtually free of distortion. Many photographers use the Micro Nikkor instead of a normal lens because of its extended range of use, even though its maximumn aperture is less.

It is also quite compact and measures only 74mm. When the barrel is extended completely for a reproduction ratio of about 1:1 the length will be 82mm. It weighs a lot more than the normal lenses at 420g.

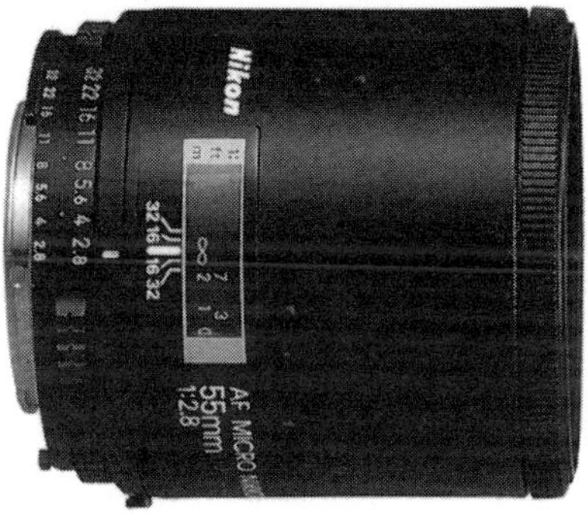

Nikon AF Teleconverter TC-16A

You can use non-AF Nikkors with autofocus operation in connection with this converter, provided the lens used has a maximum aperture of at least *f*3.5. More than half of the manual focusing lenses in the Nikon program fulfil this condition. Lenses modified to the AI standard cannot be used with the TC-16A. The converter, which is only 3cm long, is simply mounted between the camera and the lens. It produces a 1.6x increase in the focal length of the lens used and also causes a 1 1/3rd - *f*-stop decrease of the lens speed.

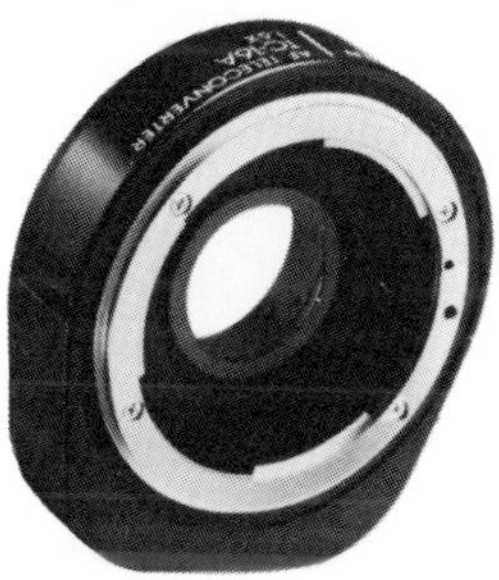

Metering is done the usual way at full aperture, but not all exposure modes are available. The lens compatibility chart shows you exactly which lens/converter combinations allow what operational modes. The optical design of the converter, weighing a mere 150g consists of 5 elements in 5 groups.

The following lenses can be used in autofocus mode in connection with the TC-16A:

Zoom Lenses
80-200mm, *f*2.8 ED

Wide-Angle Lenses
24mm, *f*2
24mm, *f*2.8
28mm, *f*2 (from serial no. 540021)
28mm, *f*2.8 (from serial no. 500001)
35mm, *f*1.4 (only AI-Standard models)*
35mm, *f*2 (from serial no. 931001)
35mm, *f*2.8 (from serial no. 880001)

Telephoto Lenses
AF 80mm, *f*2.8 (for the F3AF)
85mm, *f*1.4
85mm, *f*2
105mm, *f*1.8
105mm, *f*2.5
135mm, *f*2
135mm, *f*2.8 (only between infinity and 1.7 metres)**
180mm, *f*2.8 ED (only between infinity and 2.5 metres)**
200mm, *f*2 IF-ED
300mm, *f*2 IF-ED
300mm, *f*2.8 IF-ED

Standard Lenses
50mm, *f*1.2
50mm, *f*1.4 (from serial no. 3980001)
50mm, *f*1.8 (N)

Fisheye Lenses
6mm, *f*2.8
8mm, *f*2.8
16mm, *f*2.8

Special Lenses
Noct 58mm, *f*1.2
Micro 55mm, *f*2.8
Micro 105mm, *f*2.8 (only between infinity and 55cm)

*...AI-S standard lenses can be recognised by the orange-coloured smallest aperture marking

**...Correct focusing is only possible within a limited distance range.

AF-Nikkors with Built-In Motor

Nikon introduced the first professional camera with autofocus, the F3AF, as long ago as 1982. The autofocus system, which was sensational at the time, consisted of three parts. First, the camera body which was developed from the standard F3 body, proven in tough everyday work, the new AF Finder DX-1 designed as a control centre for automatic rangefinding and focusing, and finally two completely new lenses with motors incorporated for automatic focusing. The AF Finder DX-1 could be mounted on a conventional F3 and offered electronic rangefinding with certain lenses. Autofocus operation was not possible in connection with a normal F3 body.

Those first AF Nikkors were designed so that only a few of the lens elements had to be shifted in the AF Nikkor 80mm for focusing. Considering the time, this accounted for quite quick autofocus operation. The AF Nikkor 200mm was designed with internal focusing and the use of ED glass, so not only automatic focusing could be improved but also excellent sharpness and high contrast could be achieved, thanks to an almost complete correction of chromatic aberration.

Both lenses already had the AF-Lock buttons for locking the focus setting in the case of a composition with an off-centre main subject which would not be within the AF focus brackets. The Nikon F3AF already had an electronic rangefinder display for use with conventional non-AF lenses. You can employ the F3AF's AF Nikkors in unrestricted AF operation on the F4.

When you focus manually with the assistance of the electronic rangefinder, and the camera is set to Single Servo autofocus, you can only release the shutter when the green in-focus indicator LED lights up and the **A/M** switch on the lens is set to **M**. Neither the program nor the shutter priority automatic exposure modes will be available. All the other camera functions can be employed without limitation. The bayonets of these two lenses have six electrical contacts instead of the usual five of the new type AF Nikkors. This is because the camera must relay additional control information to the motors in the lenses.

AF-Nikkor 80mm, *f*2.8: in spite of the built-in autofocus motor this lens weighs only about 390g and is just 70mm long. Its optical design consists of 6 elements in 4 groups. The lens has a push-pull type switch to change from autofocus to manual operation. This switch can also be used for the autofocus-lock function. You can also employ the AF-Lock button on the F4. To facilitate easy manual focusing the lens has a handy, ribbed, rubber-coated focusing ring.

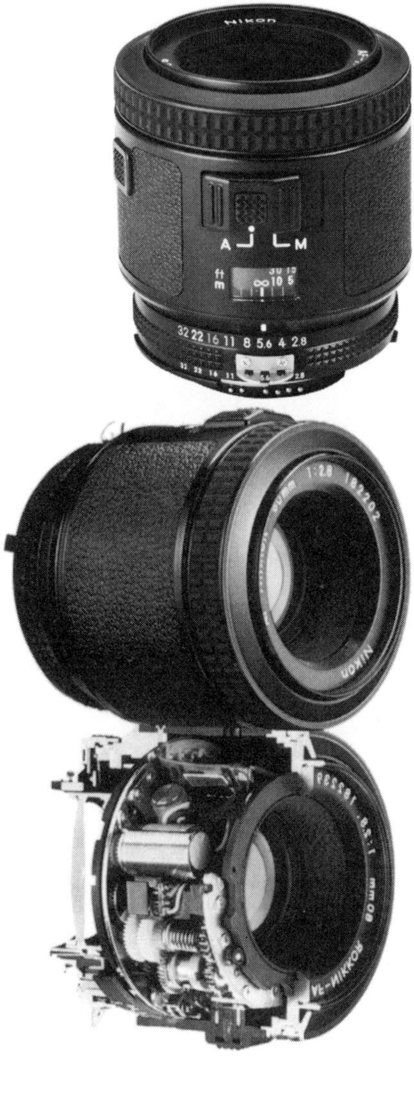

AF-Nikkor 200mm, *f*3.5 IF-ED: this lens is a really delightful in optical as well as mechanical terms and weighs only 870g. Its optical design consists of 8 elements in 6 groups. The rear filter is also an integral part of the optical design. In order to speed up autofocus operation you can limit the focusing distance to one of three ranges. Choose between 5m to infinity for long distance shots, 3 to 10m for medium range photography, and 2 to 5m for close range work. When set to these positions the AF systems will not be forced to run through the complete distance range but only the preset one. This reduces shifting within the lens and increases the focusing speed.

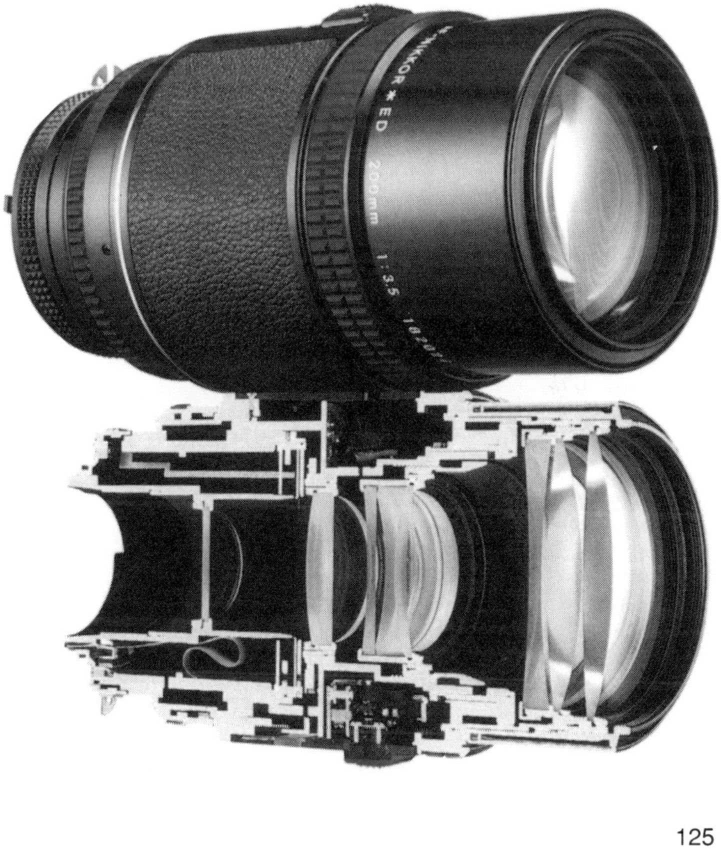

P-Nikkor with Built-In Microcomputer

P-Nikkor 500mm, *f*4 IF-ED: this is a new development for professional news photography at long distances. It is the first non-AF lens in the entire Nikon program with a built-in microcomputer containing all lens data which all Nikon AF cameras can read. Therefore all the exposure modes and the electronic rangefinder in the Nikon AF-cameras can be employed without exception.

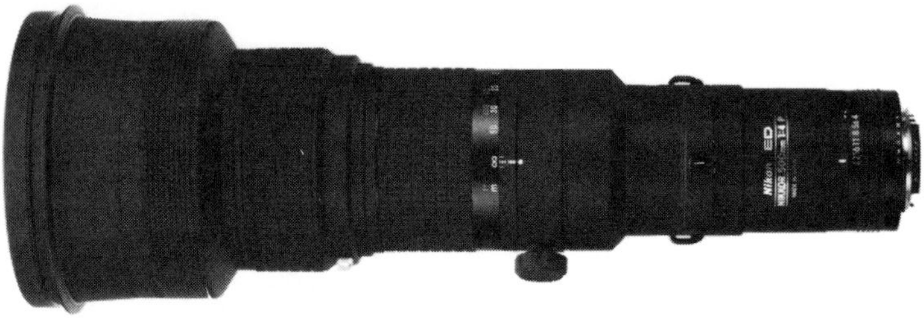

Its compact size and moderate weight, compared to other lenses of this focal length and maximum aperture, even allow hand-held photography. Due to these features this new 500mm super-telephoto lens will probably become the favoured of many reporters and sports photographers. It is also ideal for wildlife shots. The handy internal focusing technique makes focusing fast and easy without changing the length of the lens barrel. A sturdy tripod mount at the centre of gravity is also provided. The tripod mount collar allows the camera to be rotated a full 360° so that changes from horizontal to vertical format shooting from a tripod are quick and easy.

The optical design, consisting of 8 elements in 6 groups, includes the use of some elements made of ED glass with an extremely low refractive index, in order to avoid chromatic aberration common to other fast super-telephoto lenses. The shortest focusing distance is 5m. Screw-in filters with a standard thread mount of 39mm are used, mounted on a slip-in filter holder which, in turn, fits into the lens barrel. The hood HK-17 is provided with the lens. The weight of the lens amounts to only about 3kg. It also allows you to mark a preset focusing distance with a click-stop index so you can find a certain focal plane during action photography very quickly. Because of the click-stop index you do not run the risk of focusing beyond the preset distance. This feature is especially useful in sports and wildlife photography.

Since conventional lenses without built-in microcomputers do not allow you to employ all the F4's automatic operation modes, it might be expected that future manual focusing lenses from Nikon will also have such microcomputers incorporated.

Although we have stated that the AF-teleconverter TC-16A can only be used with lenses with a maximum aperture of at least *f*3.5 on the F4 for autofocus operation, experience has shown that it also works with this lens in all but the worst lighting conditions. This would turn the lens into a 800mm, *f*6.4 but, due to the converter being unable to convey the electrical data, shutter priority and program exposure modes will not be available with this combination.

Manual Focusing Lenses

Nikon have been producing lenses for 35mm SLR cameras for more than thirty years. Even today most of them can still be used on the most modern camera of the Nikon program, the F4. Nearly half of them, all the lenses with a maximum aperture of at least *f*3.5 to be specific, can be used with autofocus operation in connection with the converter TC-16A. The electronic rangefinder will also function with all lens/converter combinations with an effective combined maximum aperture of at least *f*5.6. A few restrictions concerning the exposure and metering modes will have to be accepted but this will not bother the photographer because the same restrictions are also valid for the use of lenses without built-in microcomputers, even without the TC-16A.

AI and AI-S standard Nikkors allow the use of all three of the F4's metering modes. The AI-system was introduced in 1977 and increased the amount of information exchange between the lens and the camera. AI stands for "Automatic Maximum Aperture Indexing". This system allows much easier and faster lens mounting, as a coupling ridge on AI standard lenses takes over what photographers used to have to do themselves, rotating the aperture ring back and forth once after mounting the lens, in order to inform the exposure meter about the maximum aperture of the lens being used. Older lenses can easily be modified to the AI standard at Nikon service facilities, but such lenses do not allow autofocus operation in connection with the AF-teleconverter TC-16A.

The introduction of the AI-S standard lenses in 1981 allowed even more information about the focal length and the type of lens to be transferred from the lens to the camera. This information is also transmitted mechanically via levers and tappets. AI-type lenses can be recognised by their typical coupling ridges whereas the special characteristic of the AI-S types is their orange-coloured smallest *f*-stop. The economy-priced E-series Nikon lenses introduced in 1979 have an AI-S standard mount but they have been discontinued.

Whenever you mount a non-AF lens on the Nikon F4 the autofocus-coupling is automatically interrupted. This mechanical coupling is also inactive when you mount AF lenses for the F3AF. The centre-weighted metering mode is available with nearly all Nikon lenses. With AI and AI-S standard lenses you can also utilize the matrix metering mode. This is also true when you use them together with the AF teleconverter TC-16A or any AI-S standard converter.

You can employ the manual and aperture priority exposure modes with every type of lens but not the shutter priority and program exposure modes. Everything you need to know about the usable features with the different lenses can be found in the lens table.

Thanks to the fact that you can mount nearly every Nikon lens on the F4, you have access to the largest program of interchangeable lenses in the world. When you consider autofocus operation to be suitable you can choose from about twenty AF-Nikkors. The non-AF Nikon lenses proven with time, are available for special purposes such as the ultra wide-angle range, the superfast telephoto range, close-up photography, or for perspective-control. We will describe the most important ones on the next pages. The table in Appendix II lists the lenses available.

Standard Lenses

Nikon offered four different lenses with the standard 50mm focal length in the conventional lens program, only three of which are still available. The E-series lens has been discontinued. The lenses have maximum apertures of *f*1.2, *f*1.4, and *f*1.8. The latter two are already available in the AF program. The extremely fast Nikkor 50mm, *f*1.2 is especially interesting as an alternative to the AF lenses for available light situations. The unusually bright viewfinder image further increases manual focusing accuracy.

Nikon offers a good choice of 50mm lenses. They are fast, compact and deliver a high quality image as well as having an angle of view similar to that of the human eye. All this combined with their moderate price make these lenses very appealing.

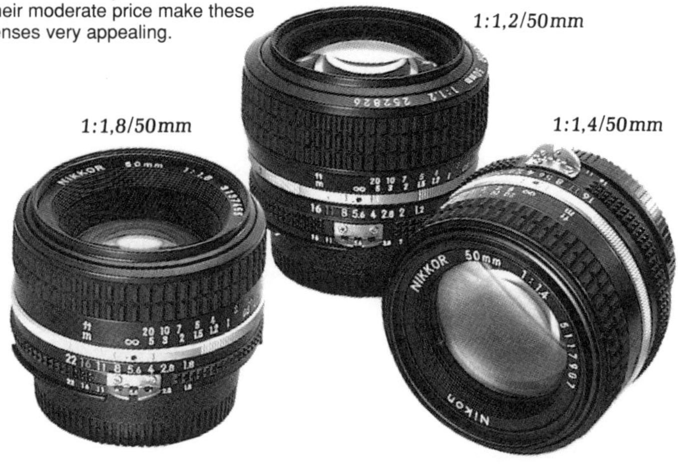

Fisheye Lenses

Fisheye Nikkors reveal highly unusual perspectives with their extreme angle of view of 180°, and more, and also because of their equally extreme barrel distortion. They are preferably employed to create extraordinary effects. The Nikon program offers three fisheye lenses with different angles of view and frame coverage. There are two types of fisheye. The Nikkors 6mm, *f*2.8 and 8mm, *f*2.8 produce circular pictures. The 6mm fisheye has the largest coverage of all Nikon lenses – 220°. With this lens you might even have problems keeping yourself out of the frame. The 8mm fisheye with a 180° coverage is of a much more compact construction than the extreme 6mm lens. The other type of fisheye represented by the Nikkor 16mm, *f*2.8 fills the full frame. Unlike the former two lenses this fisheye has the additional advantage of dimensions hardly exceeding those of a normal lens.

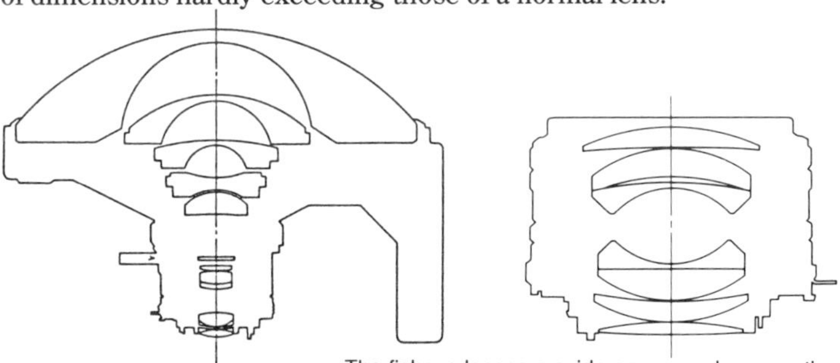

The fisheye lenses provide an unusual perspective. The cross-section shows the comparison with a normal lens.

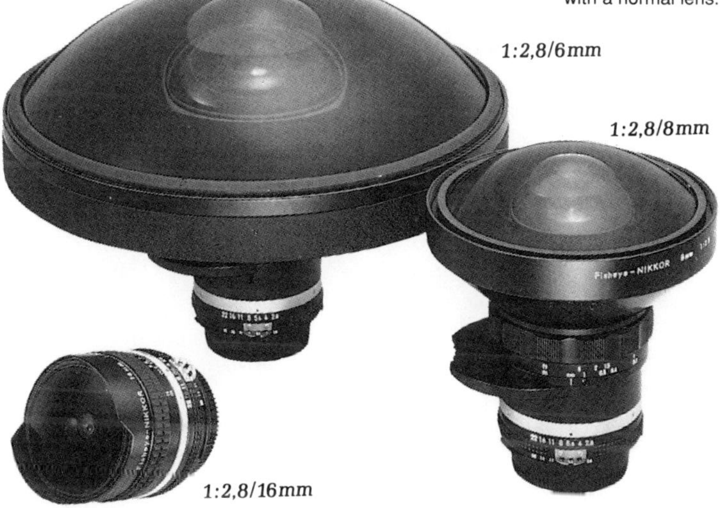

Ultra Wide-Angle Lenses

Nikon offers four different ultra wide-angle lenses in the non-AF program from 13 to 20mm, only one of which, namely the 20mm with the longest focal length, is also available as an AF model. Ultra wide-angle lenses show an extremely exaggerated perspective due to their very large angle of view. Objects at close range will appear much larger and distant subjects much smaller than normal. Pros know how to employ such effects for dynamic picture compositions. Ultra wide-angle lenses are also important for architecture, interiors, and landscapes. These subjects call for a large depth of field in addition to the immense angle of view. The Nikkor 13mm, *f*5.6 with its angle of view of 118° is unique. In spite of this it shows virtually no distortion, an even illumination of the whole frame, and high sharpness. The Nikkor *f*3.5/15mm also produces the highest image quality and already represents the second generation in this focal length. Its predecessor had a maximum aperture of *f*5.6. Both the 13mm and the 15mm lenses are equipped with the close range correction system, designed to keep up the high image quality even at the shortest focusing distance. This is also true of the Nikkor 18mm, *f*3.5.

The two 20mm Nikkors, one non-AF and one AF model, are of indentical optical design, both having a fast maximam aperture of *f*2.8 which is 1/2 *f*-stop faster than the non-AF predecessor with its *f*3.5.

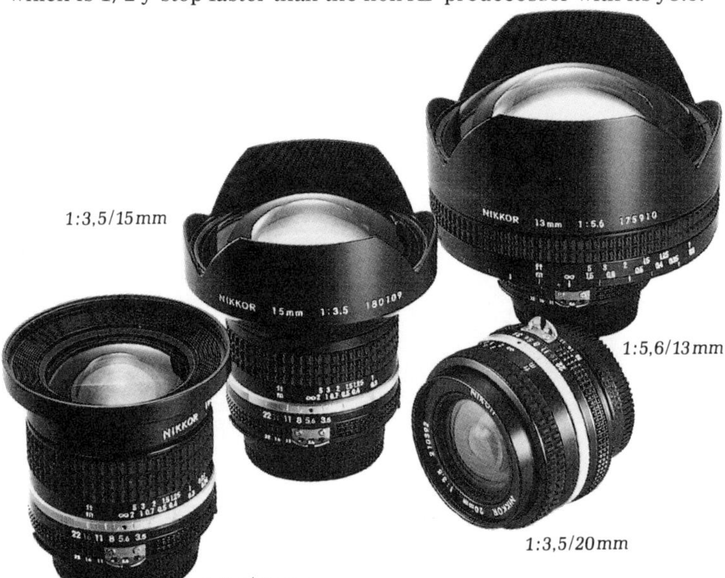

Wide-Angle Lenses

You can choose between fast maximum apertures or compact dimensions in the non-AF program of focal lengths of 24mm, 28mm, and 35mm. Depending on his personal interests and the assignment one photographer will go for light weight while another will insist on extremely large apertures. All three focal lengths are represented in the AF program as well. The 24mm Nikkors are available as *f*2 or *f*2.8 models. The increase of just one *f*-stop accounts for differences in weight and price. Whereas the weight differs only by about 50g to the advantage of the slower model, the faster lens will cost a good third more.

Only two of the previously-offered three lenses with a focal length of 28mm are still available. The slowest *f*3.5 model has been discontinued as well as the two E-series 28mm, *f*2.8 and 35mm, *f*2.5. So now the photographer also has a choice between a faster *f*2 and an *f*2.8 model. The relationship of the prices and dimensions is comparable to the situation of the 24mm lenses. There are still three 35mm Nikkors with differing maximum apertures available. You can choose between *f*1.4, *f*2, or *f*2.8. The very fast Nikkor 35mm, *f*1.4 is equipped with the CRC system for consistently high image quality even at its shortest focusing distance.

Moderate Telephoto Lenses

These lenses with their moderate focal lengths offer creative possibilities thanks to their slightly flattened perspective and their shallow depth of field at large apertures. The Nikon program offers two alternatives with both focal lengths. On the one hand there is a compact, light-weight, and slower version and on the other a one *f*-stop faster and distinctively more expensive model. The two 85mm lenses are the fastest with maximum apertures of *f*1.4 and *f*2. For the faster lens you would have to pay with twice the weight and price.

The maximum apertures of the two 105mm lenses are *f*1.8 and *f*2.5. They differ in weight by about 150g. Even though many photographers hardly ever need the maximum apertures they still prefer the faster lenses because the brighter viewfinder image provides easier control of focusing and the composition. The former E-series 100mm, *f*2.8 has been discontinued.

Only two of the previous 135mm lenses are still available – the fast *f*2, and the *f*2.8 model. The Nikkor 135mm, *f*3.5 and the E-series 135mm, *f*2.8 have both been discontinued.

Telephoto Lenses

With the exception of the 180mm lens, at least two versions of every focal length with differing speeds are available in the telephoto lens range. Surprisingly, the manual focusing Nikkor 180mm, *f*2.8 ED is more expensive than the newer version with autofocus option and internal focusing mechanism. Perhaps the latest model will soon replace it completely.

The super-fast Nikkor 200mm, *f*2 IF-ED is especially popular with sports photographers and is also often used for fashion photography. The extremely bright viewfinder image which enables fast and precise focusing, as well as high image quality at full aperture, are the main reasons for the popularity with professional photographers of this unique lens.

The price of the 200mm, *f*4, which is just one-tenth of that of the above lens, in spite of its high image quality and its compact size, has led to the enormous numbers in circulation.

The 300mm, *f*2.8 IF-ED Nikkor is also an optically brilliant lens which has become available in a slightly less expensive but slightly heavier AF-version. The Nikkor 300mm, *f*4.5 IF-ED is a similar case

Medium telephoto lenses such as the 180mm *f*2.8 ED are ideal for portraiture and landscapes. The use of ED glass guarantees immaculate image quality even at maximum aperture.

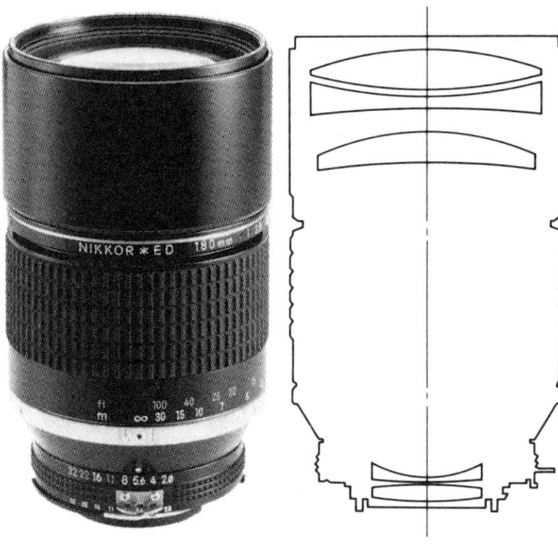

Both these pictures were taken with a 200mm lens, a focal length that is exceptionally well-suited to photography at medium and longer distances.

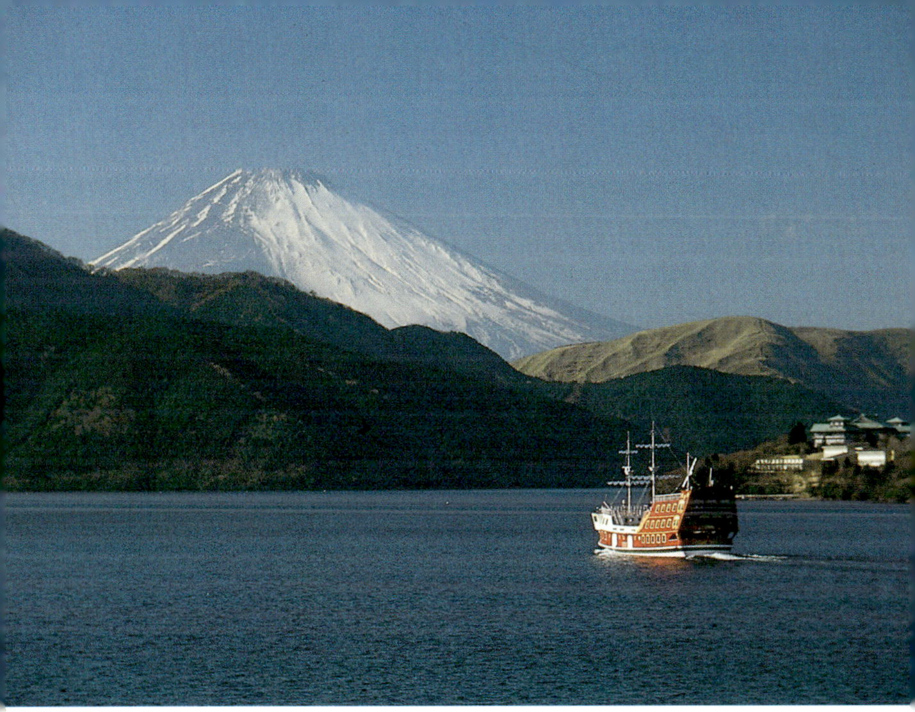

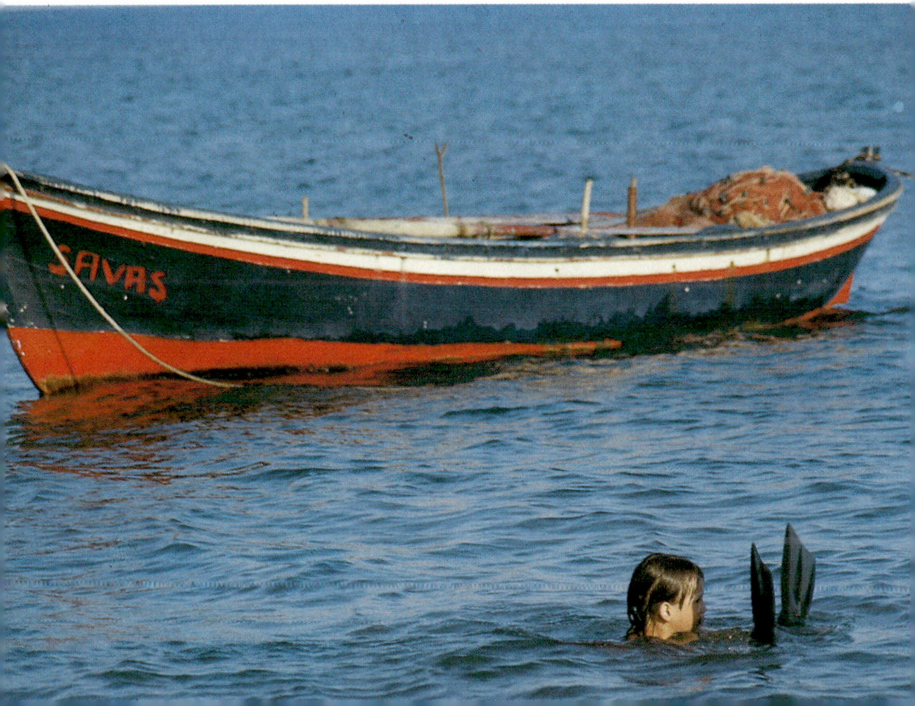
SAVAS

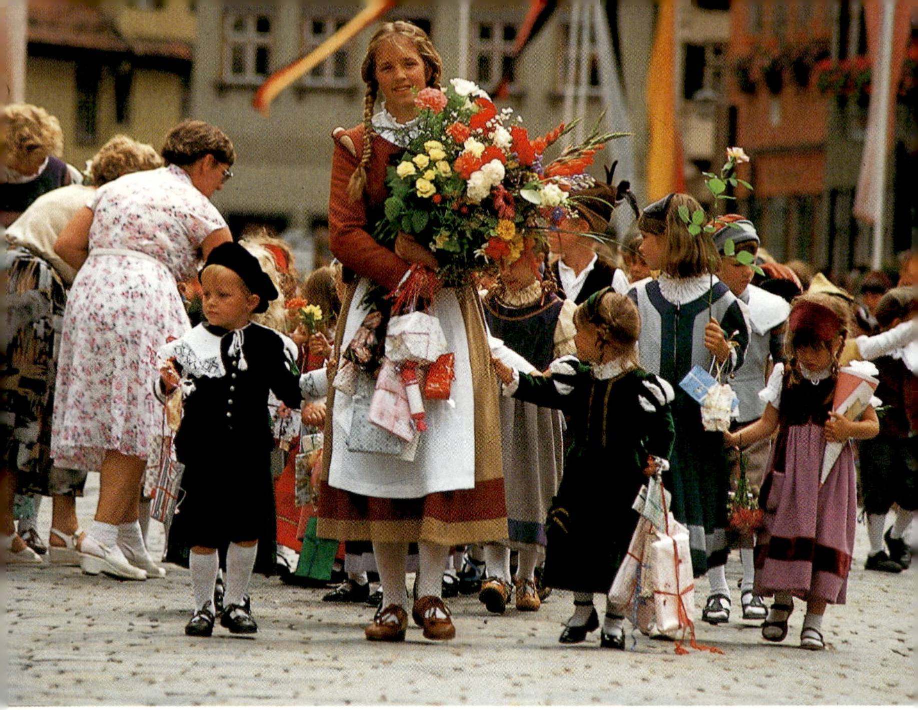

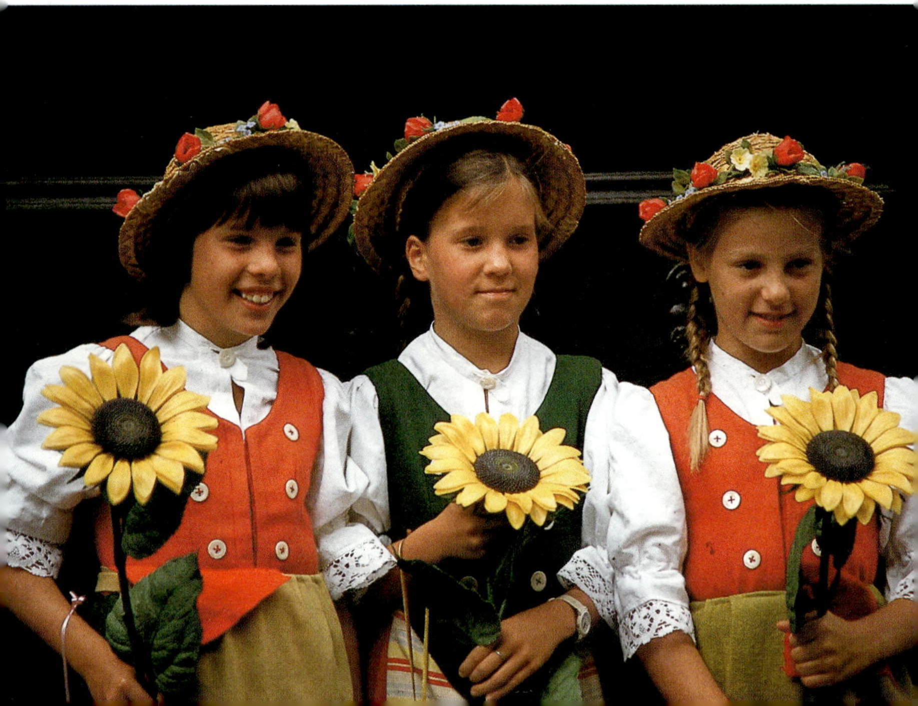

although the slightly less expensive, new AF 300mm, *f*4 IF-ED at 340g lighter, and about 19mm shorter, is a completely different design. The non-AF model's removeable tripod collar is a convenient feature making hand-held shooting easier.

The Nikkor 300mm, *f*4.5, without internal focusing and ED glass, is especially moderate in price and also has the removable tripod collar for hand-held photography.

Super-Telephoto Lenses

From focal lengths of 400mm onwards the Nikon program offers only manual focusing lenses, although an AF Nikkor 600mm, *f*4 IF-ED has been presented as a prototype but is not available yet. All of the Nikon super-telephoto lenses are designed with the internal focusing system and employ ED glass. They are all equipped with a tripod collar which can be rotated easily for horizontal as well as vertical format shooting. All of them take screw-in filters with 39mm or 52mm standard threads in slip-in holders. The lens hoods are either delivered with the lenses or built-in. In addition a preset focusing distance can be indexed.

Sticking to the principle of offering the ideal lens for every purpose, there are at least two versions of every focal length available in the super-telephoto range, too. In the case of the 400mm lenses, three models are available. Again, the main differences are in speed, size, and price. Whereas you would have to pay as much for the fastest *f*2.8 version as a small car might cost, you could acquire the Nikkor 400mm, *f*5.6 IF-ED for a third of that sum, with the still very fast Nikkor 400mm, *f*3.5 IF-ED costing about half.

There is only one 500mm lens – the already mentioned P Nikkor 500mm, *f*4 IF-ED, but two 600mm lenses are available. The faster one has a maximum aperture of *f*4, the more compact model begins at *f*5.6. The Nikkor 600mm, *f*4 IF-ED is the most expensive telephoto lens in the Nikon program, surpassed only by the ultra wide-angle lenses.

Zoom lenses allow variable, stepless framing without a change of shooting position. They prove extraordinarily helpful when a photographer is forced to cover an event from one position.

The two 800mm super-telephoto lenses cost much less. Photographers can choose either the rather large Nikkor 800mm, *f*5.6 IF-ED or the more compact Nikkor 800mm, *f*8 IF-ED. Both are equipped with a rotatable tripod collar for easy switching from horizontal to vertical format shooting. The faster lens takes 52mm screw-in filters whereas the more compact model has the smaller 39mm types, in both cases mounted in the slip-in holders. The Nikkor 800mm, *f*5.6 IF-ED is delivered with one additional lens hood which has to be mounted separately and both lenses are delivered with cases. The Nikkor 800mm, *f*5.6 IF-ED is a fairly new lens, introduced in 1986, which will replace the older model in the near future. As the Nikkor 1200mm, *f*11 IF-ED has been discontinued one might expect a new version in the course of time.

The Mirror Lenses

These telephoto lenses are very popular due to their compact design. They have fixed apertures and are only available as manual focusing models. The longest, the Reflex-Nikkor 2000, *f*11, is only made to order. The Reflex-Nikkors 1000mm, *f*11 and 500mm, *f*8 are available in the usual way. Neither lens can be stopped down, so they are delivered with a neutral density filter ND-4, to help control the shutter speed, plus 4 coloured filters.

The use of mirrors in the optical design allows the light path to be folded, permitting a significant reduction in length compared to conventional lenses. Mirror lenses are virtually free of chromatic aberration, eliminating the need to refocus in infrared photography. The doughnut-shaped blur of any point of light and reflections in out-of-focus areas of the image are a characteristic of mirror lenses.

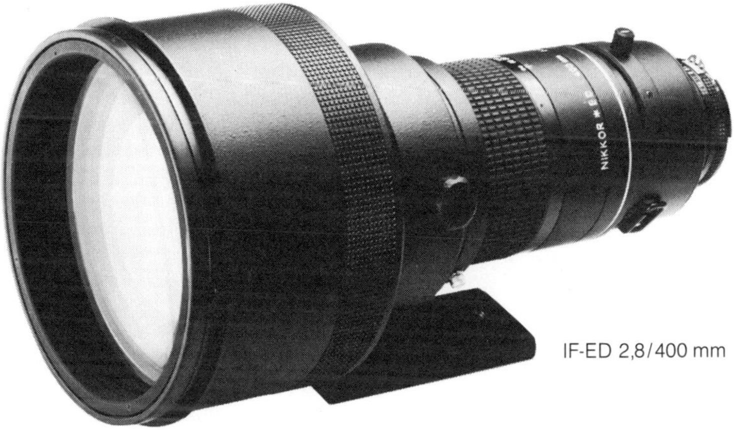

IF-ED 2,8/400 mm

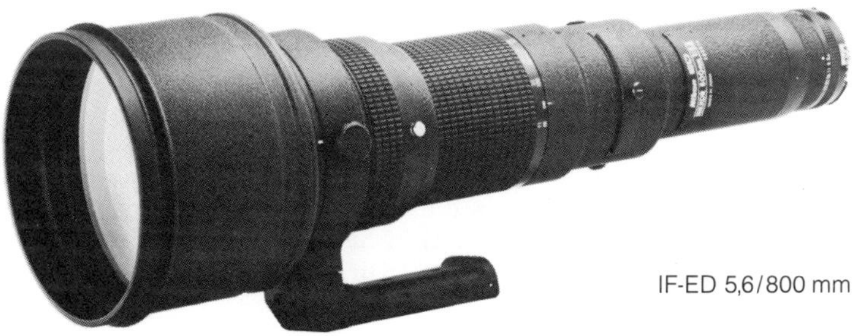

IF-ED 5,6/800 mm

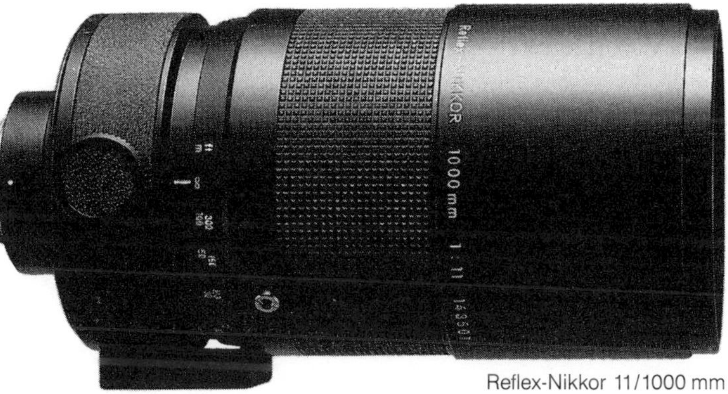

Reflex-Nikkor 11/1000 mm

Zoom Lenses

Wide-Angle zooms: two popular wide-angle zooms in the Nikon program, the 25-50mm, *f*4 and the 35-70mm, *f*3.5 have been discontinued and replaced by modern AF models. We would like to point out that the convenience of a zoom lens only really starts to show when it is used in autofocus mode. Nikon have vast experience in the design of zoom lenses and first introduced a Nikkor lens with a variable focal length in 1959. In 1967 engineers presented the first zoom lens in the world for 35mm cameras with a 6x zoom range, the 50-300mm, *f*4.5. Six years later they set another world record with the Zoom-Nikkor 28-45mm, *f*4.5, the first wide-angle zoom in the world.

Still available are the Zoom-Nikkors 28-85mm, *f*3.5-4.5, the 35-70mm, *f*3.3-4.5, the 35-105mm, *f*3.5-4.5, and the 35-135mm, *f*3.5-4.5 which are also all available in an AF version. The first two of the above-mentioned zooms are two-ring models with separate rings for focusing and zooming. The others have a single focusing/zooming ring allowing you to focus and zoom simultaneously.

The Zoom-Nikkor 35-200mm, *f*3.5-4.5 is only available in the manual focusing version. It is a very interesting model with an extreme zoom range from wide-angle to telephoto as well as being moderate in size and is therefore ideal for news and travel photography. It can replace a whole array of fixed focal lengths and so become your favorite travelling companion when every ounce of weight counts.

The 50-300mm, *f*4.5 ED is the oldest in the Nikon zoom lens program. It has been improved several times, including the utilization of ED glass, and was the first zoom of all to cover a 6x zoom range when

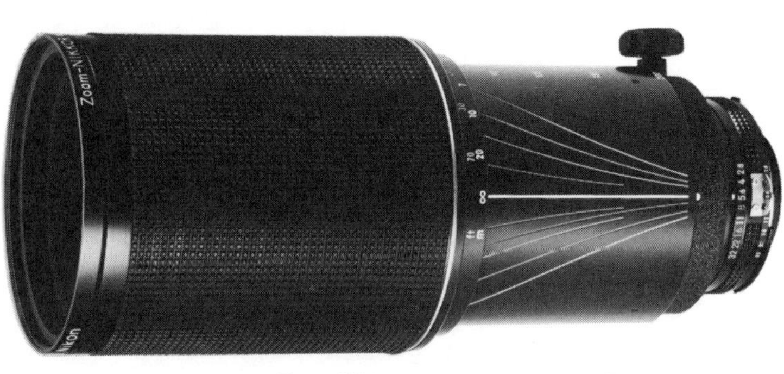

Zoom-Nikkor 2,8/80 ~ 200 mm ED

it was introduced. Focusing and zooming are done with two independent rings. It has been available in the zoom program longer than any other lens, together with the Zoom-Nikkor 80-200mm, *f*4, which has also been improved several times in the course of its existence. The latter has a single focusing/zooming ring, though. The E series Nikon zooms 75-150mm, *f*3.5 and 70-210mm, *f*4, which can be used on the F4 too, have been discontinued as well as the Zoom-Nikkor 50-135mm, *f*3.5. The first Zoom-Nikkor 80-200mm, *f*2.8 ED has been replaced by a more modern model. The Zoom-Nikkor 100-300mm, *f*5.6 is a fairly new model and the most moderate in price of all the Nikon non-AF telephoto zooms. It represents an ideal complement to one of the wide-angle zooms with a longest focal length of 85 to 105mm.

The super-telephoto Zoom-Nikkor 360-1200mm, *f*11 ED has been discontinued. This may seem regrettable to those who considered a zoom lens of this range ideal for wildlife photography. Probably only a few of these extremely expensive and unique lenses were ordered and so production could no longer be maintained. The Zoom-Nikkor 180-600mm, *f*8, which is still listed in some recent brochures and handbooks, could only be obtained on special order for quite some time before being discontinued a while ago.

The most extreme telephoto zoom still available today is the Zoom-Nikkor 200-400mm, *f*4 ED. This high-speed zoom is highly corrected against image defects by the use of ED glass. It has a remarkably consistent sharpness throughout the zoom range. The large maximum aperture provides an exceedingly bright viewfinder image and makes manual focusing very easy. The zoom is equipped with a tripod collar with three sockets for well-balanced operation, which can be rotated for horizontal as well as vertical format shooting. Focusing and zooming are done with a single ring.

Night Lens

Even though the Noct-Nikkor is not any faster than the fastest normal lens in the Nikon program, it is much more suitable for low-light shooting, thanks to its special correction. This was achieved by incorporating an aspherical front lens element ensuring an optimum correction for coma, particularly at the maximum aperture, thus making bright point sources of light, near the edges of the picture, appear as dots rather than comet-shaped blurs as often happens with conventional lenses. It produces surprisingly sharp and contrasty pictures even in very dim light. You should not expect this lens to meet the highest demands concerning flatness of field and vignetting as needed for reproduction, though. The Noct-Nikkor is a specialist trimmed to do best in low-light conditions and at night. It cannot do any better than conventional models in normal situations.

Macro Lenses

Nikon offers three manual-focusing lenses for close-up photography. Unlike the new AF, version none of them allows lifesize, that is a ratio of 1:1, reproduction without accessories. Nevertheless, experience shows that manual focusing is usually more convenient for macro-photography. The easiest way to focus is to preset the desired reproduction scale on the lens and then move to and from your subject with the camera until it appears in focus in the viewfinder or until the F4's electronic rangefinder signals the in-focus indicator LED to light up. Micro-Nikkors are available with focal lengths of 55mm, 105mm, and 200mm. The Micro-Nikkor 55mm, *f*2.8 is ideal for short focusing distances for reproductions whereas the Micro-Nikkor 105mm, *f*2.8 will allow the arrangement of appropriate illumination which will force the lens further away from the subject. The Micro-Nikkor 200mm, *f*4 IF is ideal for shooting small animals outdoors. It enables you to remain as far from the animals as is neccessary to be successful.

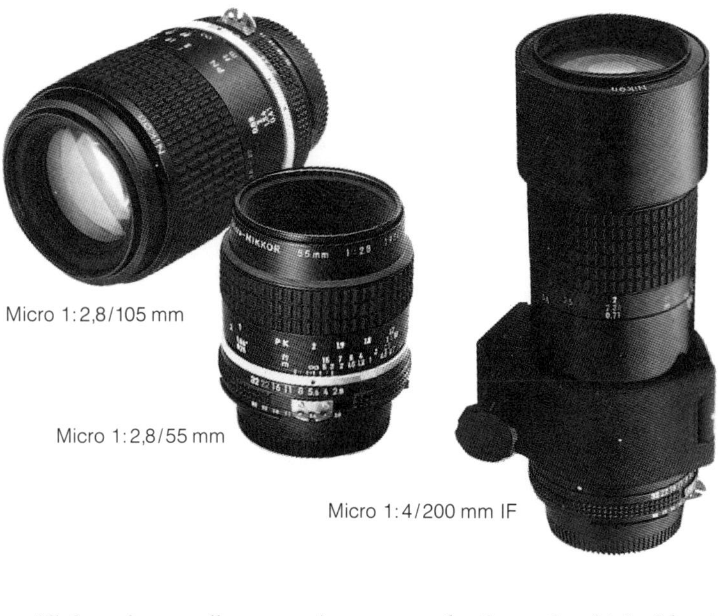

Micro 1:2,8/105 mm

Micro 1:2,8/55 mm

Micro 1:4/200 mm IF

All three lenses allow a maximum reproduction ratio of 1:2 without additional accessories. Lifesize reproductions call for the automatic extension rings PK-13 for the 55mm Micro-Nikkor, the PN-11 for the 105mm lens, and the teleconverter TC-301 in the case of the 200mm lens.

The effective aperture is reduced when you employ extension rings and teleconverters but this does not make any difference with the F4 since the automatic metering system registers these changes. The teleconverter TC-301 doubles the focal length of the Micro-Nikkor 200mm, *f*4 IF to 400mm, so you can either move even further away from your subject for the same reproduction ratios or stay as close as before for twice the ratio, but the effective maximum aperture is reduced to *f*8.

Perspective Control Lenses

Nikon offers two lenses especially for architecture and indoor photography, whose optical systems can be shifted up to 11mm off-axis and additionally be rotated a full 360° for perspective control. They are the PC-Nikkor 28mm, *f*3.5 and the PC-Nikkor 35mm, *f*2.8.

The possibility of controlling the perspective is especially useful in avoiding converging lines when you make pictures of buildings, but the shifting facility can also be employed to avoid obstructing elements

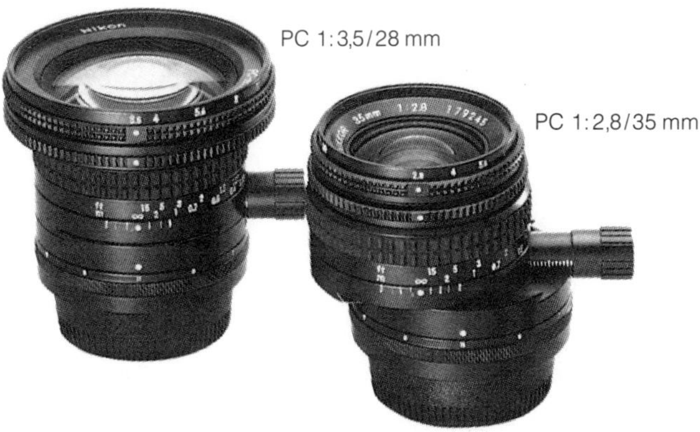

located at the edges of the frame, i.e. at both sides or at the top or bottom. The optical system's rotating mechanism allows shifting in any direction.

The two PC-Nikkors differ in speed and focal length. You can choose between a larger angle of view and a slightly smaller maximum aperture, or a smaller angle of view in connection with a larger maximum aperture. When you employ PC lenses on the Nikon F4 you will have to do the metering and focusing first and only after that the correction of the perspective. It is most convenient to start from the central position. Aim the camera at your subject, keeping the film and object planes parallel. Should the subject extend beyond the upper edge of the picture frame you can shift the front part of the PC-lens upwards with the knurled knob until your subject appears completely within the frame. If your subject extends beyond the left or right frame edges just rotate the system until the knob is on the opposite side. The E-type focusing screen will prove to be very helpful in controlling the changes in perspective. Its etched grid of horizontal and vertical lines is ideal for architecture when the camera/lens alignment is critical.

If, for example, cars or street lights interfere with your composition, all you have to do is to move the camera's position until they disappear and then rearrange the perspective which has then been changed with the position of the camera. The lens's image circle and the picture format limit the possible amount of perspective control by shifting. Together with the maximum permissible shift value scale on the rear ring of the lens barrel, the shift scale next to the knob tells you exactly how far the lens can be shifted in the various positions without leading to vignetting or a loss of sharpness. If the dimensions or location of your subject should force you to shift the lens beyond the recommended maximum permissible shift-value, try to see to it that the image defects appear in less prominent parts of your picture, such as the background or the sky. Of course, you can employ the shift mechanism for many other creative effects besides perspective control. You can easily produce panoramic pictures, blurring effects by shifting during the exposure, or so-called double images.

Medical-Nikkor 120mm, *f*4 IF

This is a special lens for close-up photography. Its built-in ringlight flash greatly simplifies the illumination of subjects at short range. It was presented in 1980, introduced into the market in 1982, replacing the previous Medical-Nikkor 200mm, *f*5.6. It is used mostly in scientific and medical photography but is also very popular with the many professionals and amateurs specialising on macro-photography. The lens allows stepless reproduction ratios from 1:11 to 1:1. The additional close-up lens, which extends the ratio to 2:1, is supplied with the lens. The IF mechanism makes focusing fast and easy since the lens barrel is not extended and its centre of gravity remains nearly the same throughout the focusing range. The automatic setting of the appropriate aperture according to the manual distance setting also simplifies the operation. The film speed being used must be set on the lens first, so the correct amount of flash illumination can be controlled by the automatic guide-number system. The ringlight flash located around the optical axis provides virtually shadowless illumination of your subject. The relatively long focal length allows larger distances from the subject, especially helpful in medical photography or when shooting subjects it's hard to get at. Focusing is possible from 1.6 to 0.35m without the close-up lens and from 0.33 to 0.26m with it.

The option of controlling the reproduction ratio in use in the viewfinder is very convenient, since the photographer can stay informed about the resulting scale while composing and focusing. If you wish, these data can also be imprinted on the film.

A built-in lamp can assist focusing. It is switched off automatically 16 sec. after being activated to conserve power and also immediately after firing the ringlight. As a power source for both the flash and the focusing lamp either the DC battery pack LD-2 taking 8 AA-size 1.5 volt batteries or the AC power unit LA-2 for operation directly from the mains can be utilized. The whole unit is relatively compact and light. This lens weighs only about 920g and is only 150mm long.

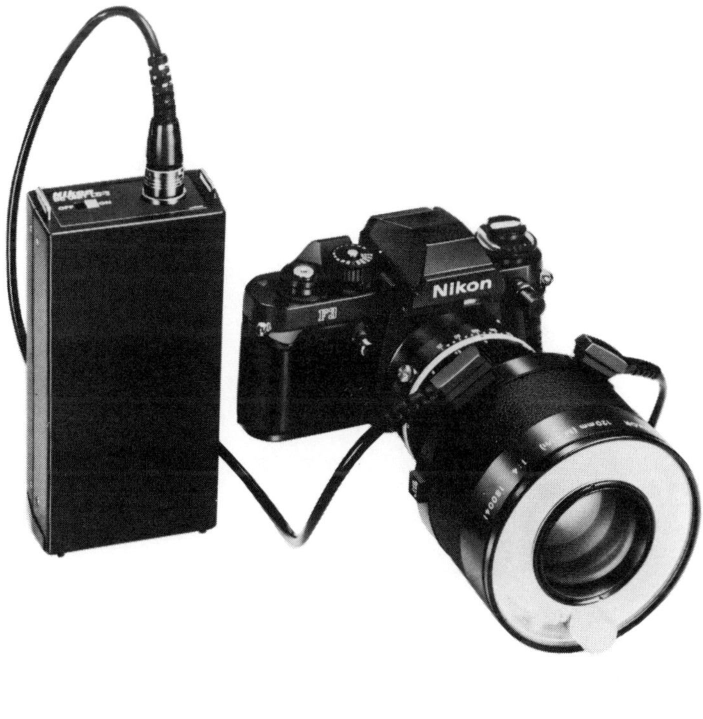

UV-Nikkor Lenses

Both the UV-Nikkors 50mm, *f*4.5 and 105mm, *f*4.5 lenses were designed especially for scientific and technical photography such as in forensic science. This new type of special lens produces the highest image quality without the need to refocus even in ultra-violet light. Therefore, information otherwise unaccessible to the human eye can be made visible and recorded with UV-light, which is employed in medical and forensic fields as well as in examining works of art and industrial products, and in production control.

The UV-Nikkors have a spectral range from 220nm to 900nm with 70% transmission. Aberration defects and distortions were virtually eliminated throughout the spectral range. Refocusing is unneccessary in the whole UV-range thanks to the fluorite and quartz glass used in the lens design.

Both UV-Nikkors allow a maximum reproduction ratio of 1:2 which can be read off a scale from 1:10 to 1:2. Special UV-filters and a gelatine filter holder, as well as a retro-ring allowing the lenses to be used in the retro-position on the camera or a bellows to achieve even greater ratios, are supplied with the lenses. When you use the lenses in the retro-position you must employ the stop-down metering method. In such cases focusing is not facilitated by the focusing ring on the lens, but by moving the whole equipment towards or away from the subject.

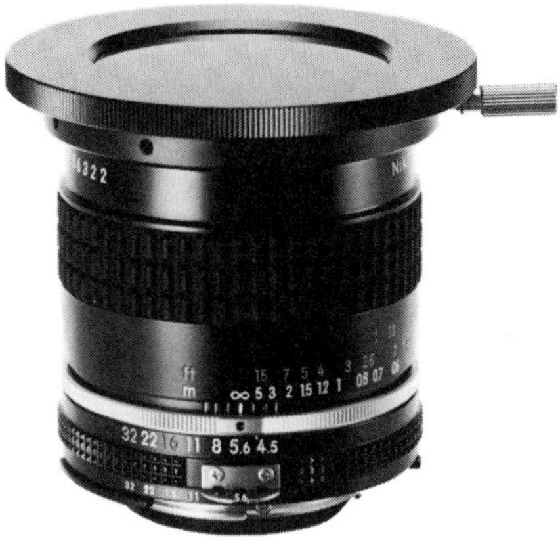

Teleconverters

Besides the AF Teleconverter TC-16A, with its 1.6x increase in focal length and possibility of using non-AF Nikkors in autofocus mode, Nikon offers another four teleconverters. They can be divided into two groups – one with a 1.4x increase and one with a 2x increase in focal length. The converters TC-14A (1.4x) and TC-201 (2x) are designed for use with lenses of up to 200mm focal length. Nikon recommends the converters TC-14B (1.4x) and TC-301 (2x) for lenses with focal lengths as 300mm. Because the converters represent the best possible combination with the respective lenses, their use will cause virtually no deterioration of image quality. They are manufactured according to the same stringent standards as all Nikon lenses. They are also applied with Nikon's integrated coating to enhance contrast and colour rendering. The use of a converter does lead to a reduction of the maximum aperture. Doubling the focal length costs two *f*-stops and the 1.4x converters lead to a loss of one *f*-stop. Buying a converter will not only save money but also keep your equipment within a reasonable volume. A photographer could turn his fast 300mm lens into a 420mm or a 600mm combination with a 1.4x or 2x converter, respectively. You can stow away a compact converter in your gadget-bag much easier than the corresponding long lens.

In addition, teleconverters are excellent accessories for close-ups since they extend the focal length of lenses without changing their shortest focusing distances. So they also increase the maximum reproduction ratio. As has been described above you can achieve a scale of 1:1 when you use the Micro-Nikkor 200mm, *f*4 IF with the TC-301.

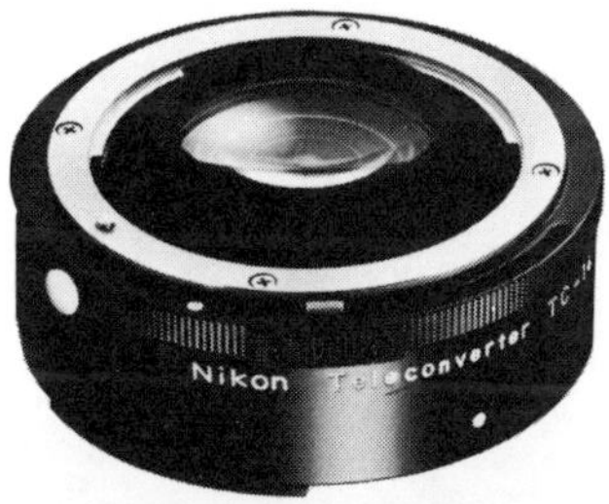

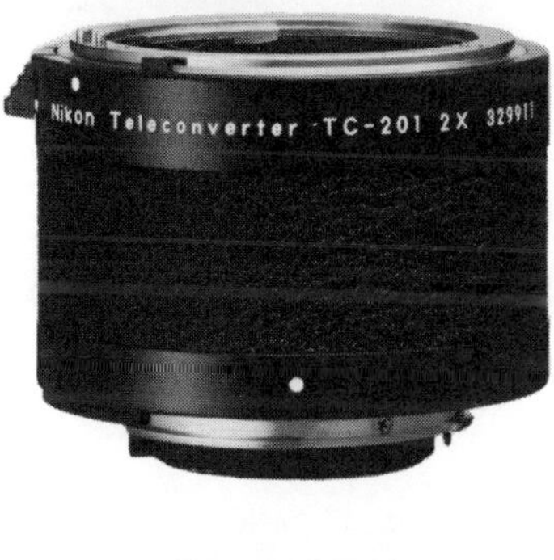

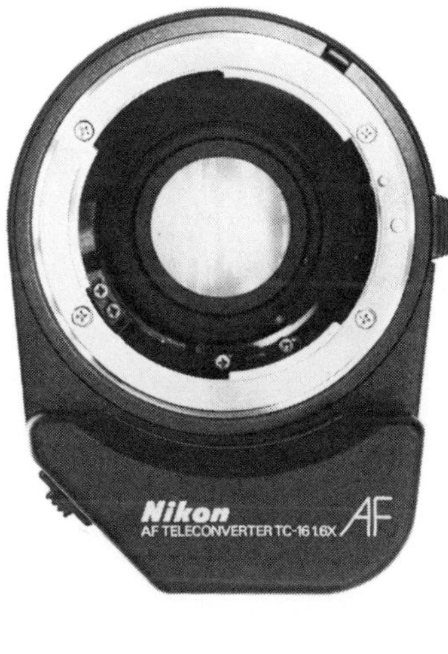

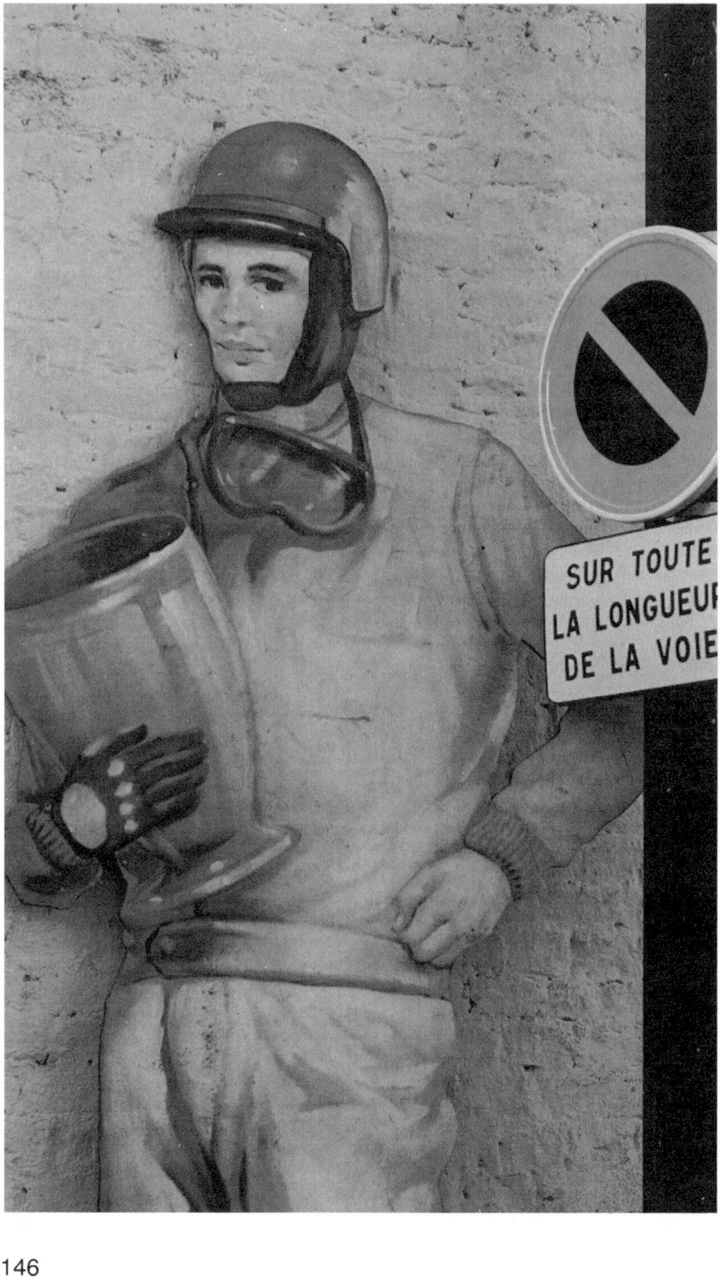
SUR TOUTE
LA LONGUEUR
DE LA VOIE

Viewfinders

The Nikon F4 offers the photographer just the view he requires in any shooting situation thanks to the possibility of changing the viewfinders. A total of four viewfinders are available, each one offering virtually 100% frame coverage so the photographer can determine the picture frame precisely. Not all metering modes are available with every finder.

Multi-Meter Finder DP-20

This is the F4's standard finder, and the only one which allows Matrix metering mode. The eyepiece is the same high-eyepoint type as in the F3HP and allows adjustment, for near- or far-sighted photographers, to within a range of –3 to +1 dioptres. In order to adjust two of the four metering systems in the viewfinder to the different brightness of the interchangeable screens, you can compensate exposure with a screw-like dial while controlling the setting in a window on the right-hand side of the viewfinder. The finder also has a metering mode selector dial and an eyepiece shutter to prevent stray light from entering when you use a cable release or remote control equipment. In addition, the viewfinder is equipped with an ISO-type hot shoe with three additional contacts for the control of Nikon AF-system Speedlites.

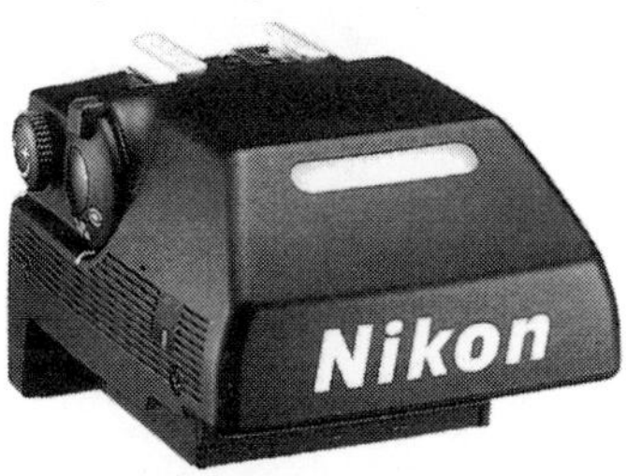

Accessories for the Multi-Meter Finder DP-20: a number of convenient accessories assist the use of the Multi-Meter Finder DP-20 as well as extending its possibilities. Most important for near- or far-sighted photographers are the Nikon eyepiece correction lenses which are the same as the ones available for the Nikon F3HP. You can choose from five lenses with –3, –2, 0, +1 and +2 dioptres. Together with the

Centre-weighted metering guarantees correctly exposed pictures when subjects are evenly illuminated without very much contrast.

correction system incorporated in the standard viewfinder of the F4, the combined adjustment range is extended from –5 to +4 dioptres.

The rubber eyecup DK-2 protects the eyepiece from stray light and thus improves the contrast of the viewfinder image which, in turn, makes composition and focusing easier.

The right-angle viewing attachment DR-3 provides an upright and unreversed image at a right-angle to the axis of the lens. It is also equipped with an individual dioptre adjustment system. It is perfect for reproduction and when it is neccessary either to view from above or from the front of a camera mounted on a copy-outfit.

The eyepiece adapter DK-7 is neccessary if you wnat to mount DR-3 on the Multi-Meter finder DP-20. The adapter is also necessary when using the eyepiece magnifier DG-2 which provides a 2x magnification of the central portion of the viewfinder image. DG-2 is also equipped with an incorporated dioptre correction mechanism.

AE Action Finder DA-20

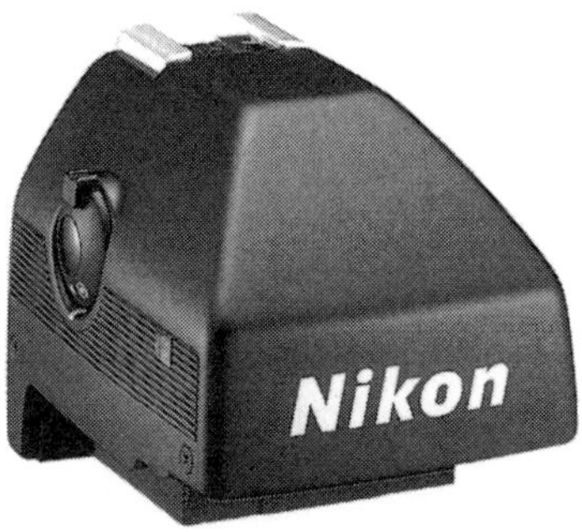

This viewfinder has been developed for situations which demand a greater viewing distance, such as when wearing a helmet or goggles. It is also helpful when the camera is encased in a special housing for underwater photography. A rubber hood and a rubber eyepiece cover are provided. The metering mode selector has positions for spot and centre-weighted modes. Matrix-metering is not available.

6x High-Magnification Finder DW-21

In macro-photography, especially with high reproduction ratios, pinpoint focusing is essential because of the minimal depth-of-field. The high-magnification finder provides a very clear view of the entire image frame at approx. 6x magnification. The finder's outstandingly corrected optical system also has a dioptre adjustment from –5 to +3 incorporated. A rubber eyecup to shield the eyepiece from stray light and an eyepiece

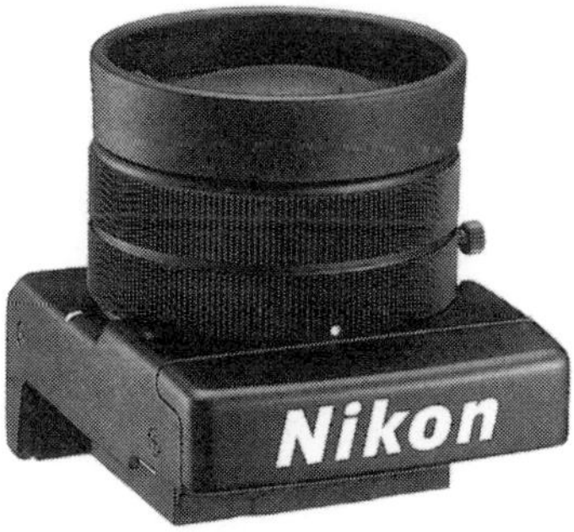

cover are provided. Consistant with its intended employment the high magnification finder only allows spot metering which is done with the sensor in the camera body as the finder has no metering system of its own.

Waist-Level Finder DW-20

This kind of finder, which is very convenient in many situations, is rarely available for other than medium-format cameras. Nikon's Waist-Level Finder DW-20 offers advantages in 35mm photography. It allows viewing from a comfortable position from above when the camera is positioned very near to the ground and can also be used to shoot with the camera held above the head in a crowd. Working with the camera mounted on a copy stand is much easier with the DW-20, as well. The built-in flip-up magnifier provides an approx. 5x larger image of the centre of the frame, for easier and more accurate manual focusing. The finder's design does not allow an integrated metering system so you will have to resort to the spot metering mode with the sensor incorporated in the camera body.

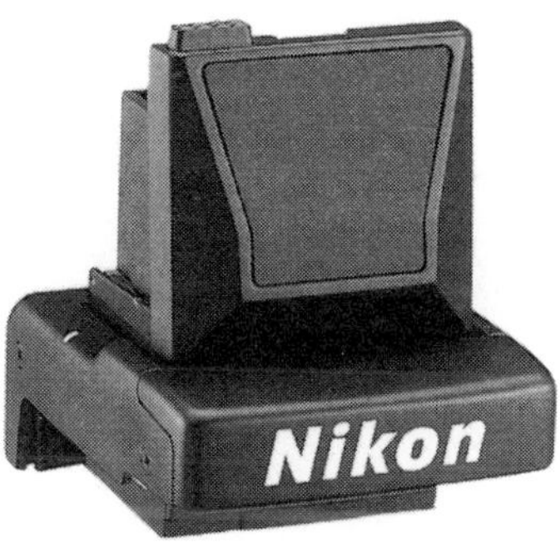

Interchangeable Focusing Screens

The Nikon F4 comes equipped with the standard new advanced Brite View screen type B, which is excellent for most photographic situations, but special situations may call for special screens. In order to adapt the F4 to any individual task, 13 different screens are available which can easily be changed by the photographer himself. All of them are made of Nikon ground glass.

In order to change the screens, first remove the finder then lift up the rear edge of the screen with your fingernail and remove it. To install a screen, simply insert the front edge under the central ridge and then push the rear edge down into place. The characteristics of the different screens are as follows:

Type B: Brite View screen as provided with the Nikon F4. Ideal for general photography with the Multi-Meter Finder DP-20; 5mm dia. and 12mm dia. reference circles for spot and centere-weighted metering modes as well as rectangular focusing brackets.

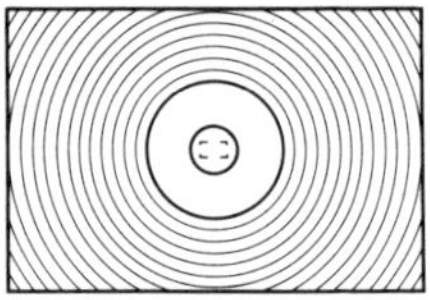

Type U: matte/fresnel field, reference circles for spot and centre-weighted metering, and the rectangular focusing brackets; suitable for telephoto lenses longer than 200mm.

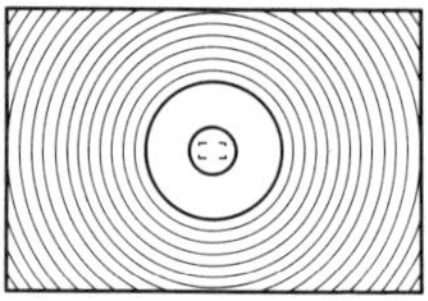

Type F: especially suitable for photography with mirror lenses. Has the reference circles for the metering modes and the rectangular focusing brackets.

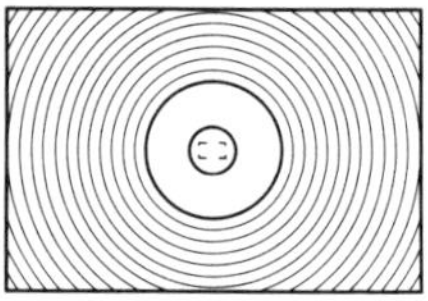

Type C: designed especially for micro photography, astro-photography, and other high-magnification applications. The fine-ground matte field has a 5 mm dia. clear spot and cross-hairs for parallax focusing on aerial images.

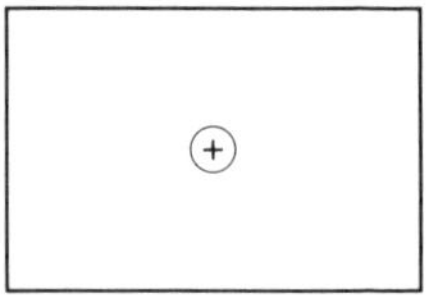

Type M: fine-ground matte/fresnel field with a 5mm dia. clear spot and cross-hairs for parallax focusing on aerial images, plus millimeter scales for the calculation of individual reproduction ratios or other measuring purposes. Provides a brilliant image even in dim light and is especially suitable for close-ups, micro photography, or other high-magnification applications.

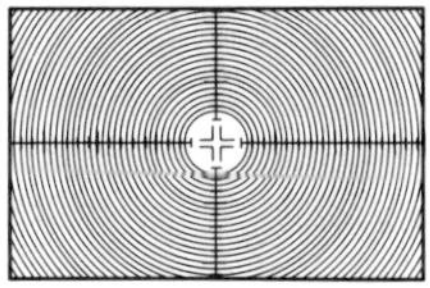

Type E: in addition to its matte/fresnel field, reference circles for spot and centre-weighted metering modes, and the focusing brackets, also has a grid of etched horizontal and vertical lines. Ideal for architectural photography and for working with PC-Nikkors. The gridlines are also useful when composing in general photography.

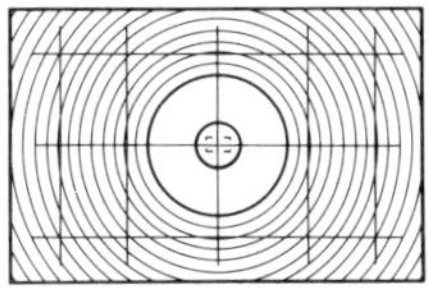

Type J: good for general photography and manual focusing with matte/fresnel field, microprism focusing spot, and reference circle for centre-weighted metering.

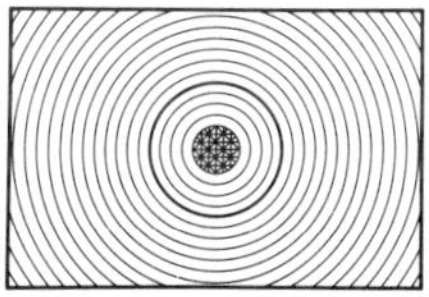

Type K: matte/fresnel field and its Brite-View split-image rangefinder spot, well suited for general photography. 3mm dia. split image spot surrounded by 1mm wide microprism ring which allows fast and accurate focusing for subjects with vertical lines or ill-defined contours.

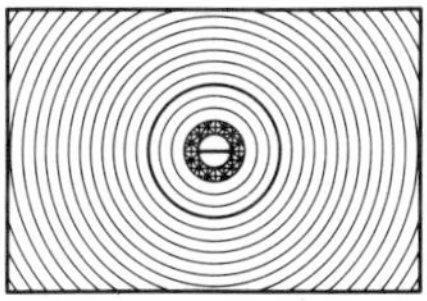

Type P: similar to type K but the Brite-View split-image rangefinder line is at a 45° angle. In addition, the screen has an etched horizontal and vertical line running through the centre to aid composition. Facilitates fast and easy focusing for subjects with horizontal or vertical lines or ill-defined contours.

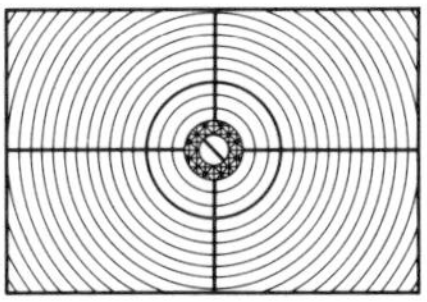

Type G: especially suitable for focusing manually on fast moving subjects in dim light, thanks to its extra bright 12mm dia. microprism focusing spot. Depth of field preview is not possible. Four versions available (G1-G4) specially adapted to different focal lengths.

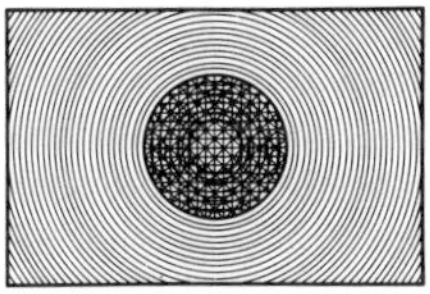

Speedlites for the F4

At present the Nikon Speedlite program consists of four dedicated flash units with incorporated AF illuminators to support autofocus operation in dim light or even total darkness. The various automatic functions in flash photography have already been described. The differences between the units, not only in their guide numbers but also in their features, will be described in the following pages.

Nikon Speedlite SB-24

The SB-24 is the most powerful flash unit with an integrated AF illuminator in the Nikon program. If you intend to employ the autofocus mode in dim light, the F4's focus mode selector must be set to Single Servo mode **S**. Combined autofocus/flash operation is not possible in Continuous Servo mode **C**. As soon as you lightly press the shutter release button – after having switched on the Speedlite – the AF illuminator will automatically project a patterned beam of light onto the subject to support the autofocus operation whenever conditions are dim or totally dark. The in-focus indicator in the viewfinder will confirm a correct focus setting.

The following exposure modes are available; Fill-in Flash mode with either Matrix or Centre-Weighted metering, TTL automatic flash control or automatic computer-controlled non-TTL flash, as well as automatic flash output control when the camera is operated manually. All the information that is important for flash exposure control like film speed, angle of view, or the focus setting is processed automatically and taken into account by the camera computer.

The flash head is automatically adjusted to the focal length of the lens being used, within the range of 24 to 85mm. This includes the focal length setting of zoom lenses which ensures a perfect illumination with the least possible power consumption. The SB-24's guide number changes depending on the flash head's position. With an ISO 100 film you will have GN 50 (in metres) at the 85mm position, 42 at 50mm, and 30 at 24mm. You can also change the flash head manually with the Zoom button on the back of the unit to position 24mm, 28mm, 35mm, 50mm, 70mm, and 85mm. This possibility offers many creative techniques culminating in an effective spotlight.

The flash head can be tilted upwards in four click-stop positions – 45°, 60°, 75°, and 90° – after the release lever has been unlocked and rotated 90° to the right in three click-stop positions and 180° to the left in six fixed positions. The flash head's normal position is locked to prevent accidental missetting and it can also be set to a 7° downward direction or any intermediate position between the indexed ones.

The possibility of employing the rear-blind sync flash technique is another one of the SB-24's specialities. In order to do this, set the sync mode selector on the back of the unit to the **REAR** position. Normally, the flash is synchronised to the exact time the first shutter blind has completely cleared the frame. When using a slower shutter speed after the flash's short burst of light, light sources from moving subjects cause traces on the film, running in the same direction, for as long as the shutter remains open. They come to lie in front of the subject which has

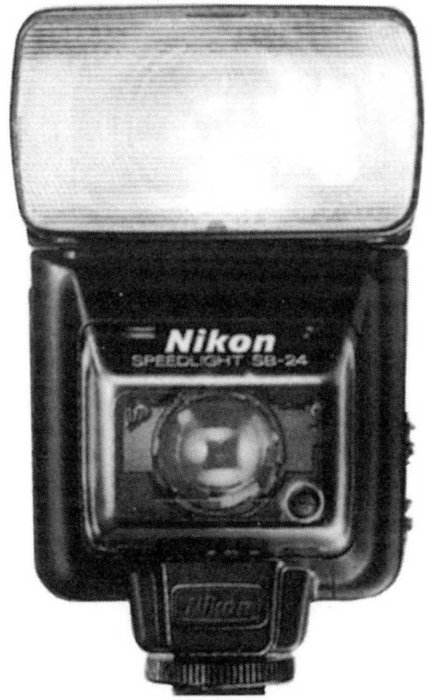

The speedlite SB-24 is the most powerful AF flash in the Nikon system. It allows a number of professional flash techniques.

only been illuminated by the flash in the beginning of the exposure and frozen in that position. In rear-blind flash sync photography the F4 synchronises the flash to the instant just before the second shutter blind begins to move. Therefore the light traces will appear behind the subject in this mode making the picture look a lot more natural. When you employ the aperture priority or program exposure modes you will have to set the SB-24 to the **REAR** position if you wish to compensate differently bright backgrounds with slower shutter speeds than 1/60th sec. You should be careful with these slower speeds, though, because very fast-moving subjects may have left the frame before the output of the flash! Aiming the camera in the direction of the subject's movement may help in such cases but the complete background will appear blurred then. You should use a tripod if you want to avoid blurring and camera shake.

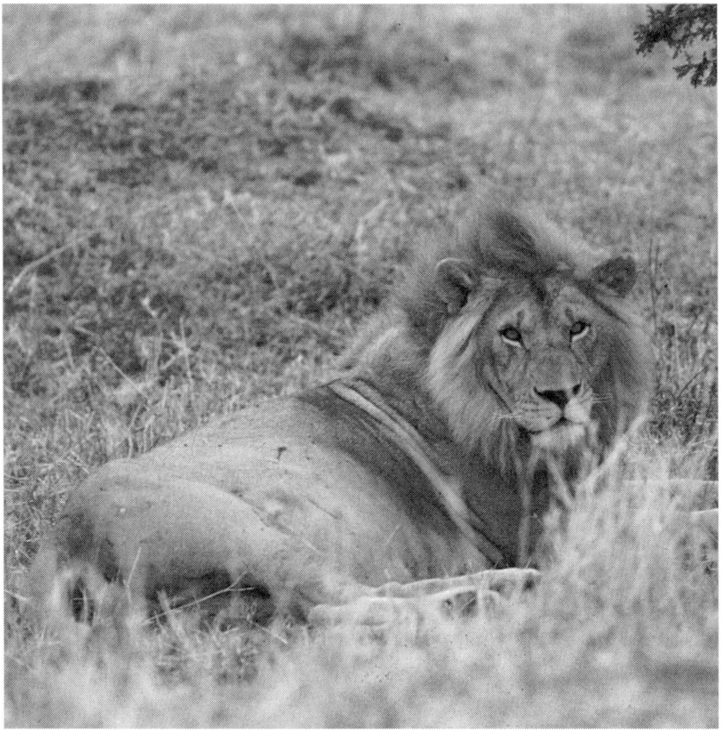

Fast telephoto lenses are a necessity for photographing wildlife in its natural habitat. Besides the need to span larger distances, poor lighting conditions can also cause a problem.

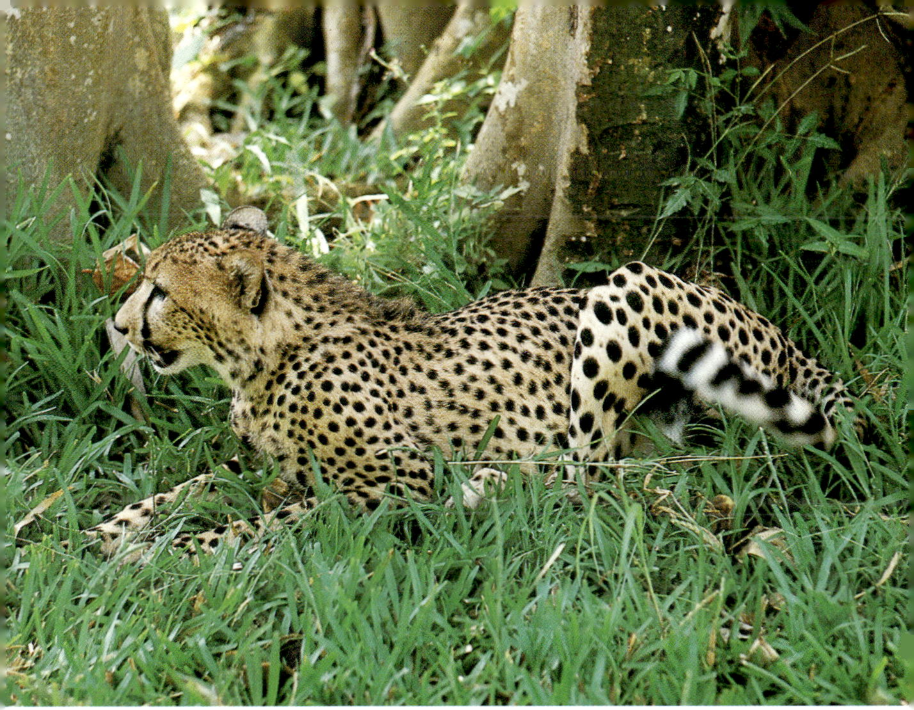

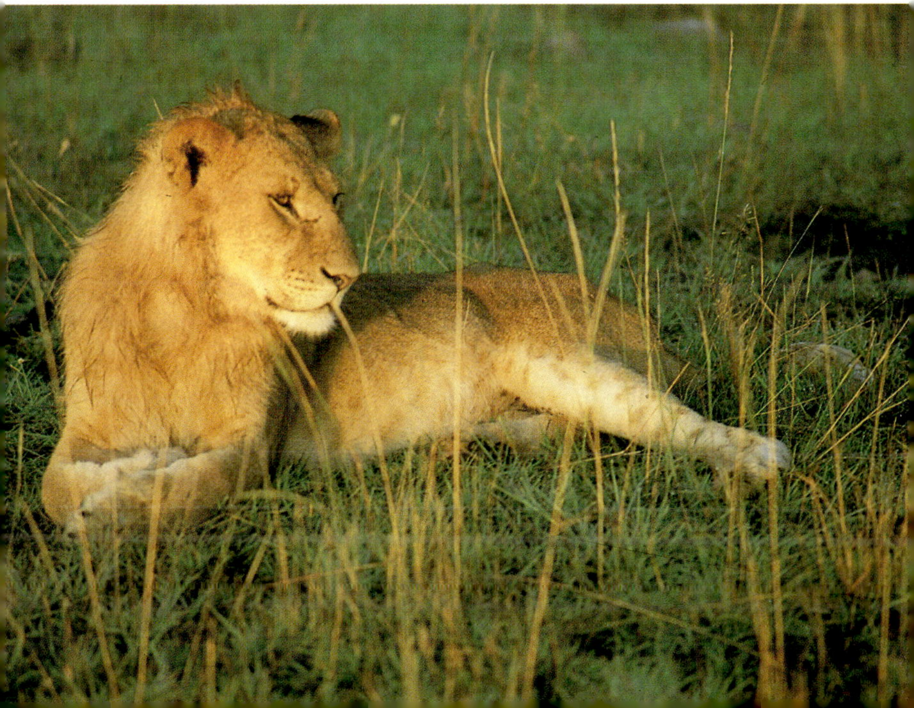

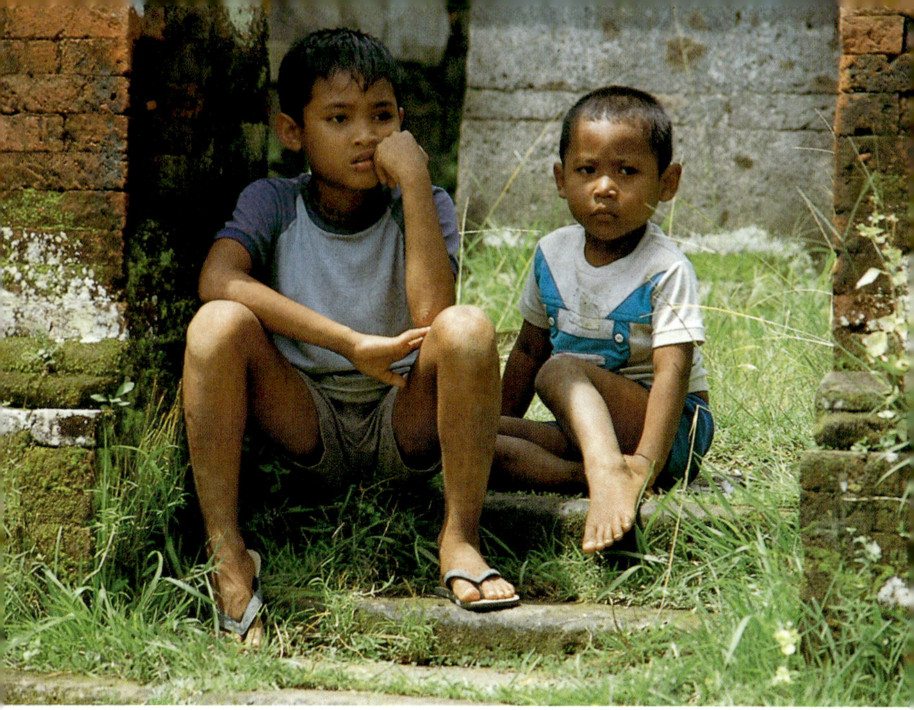

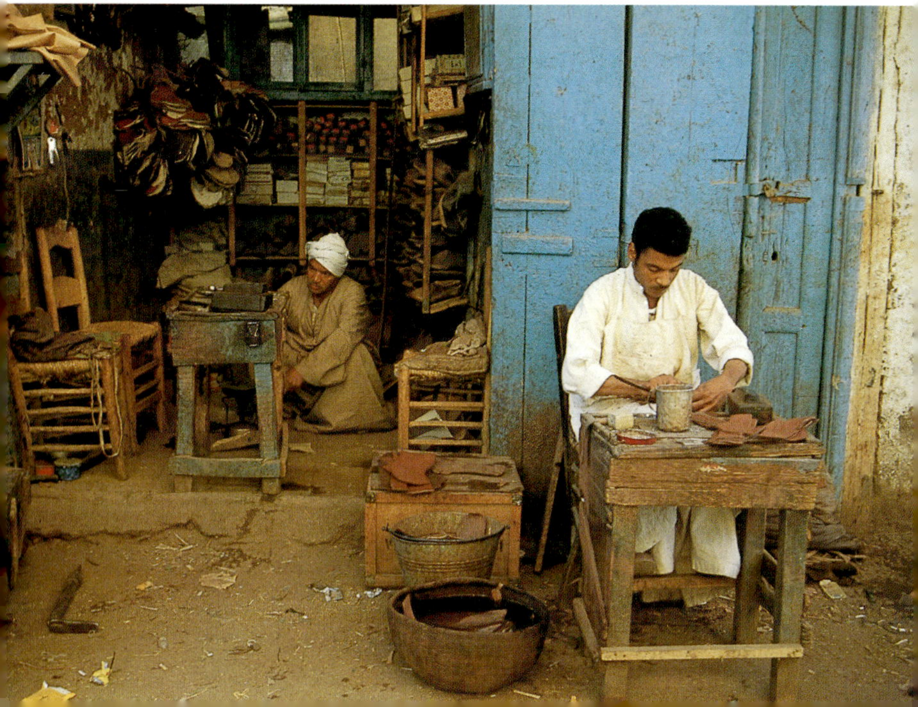

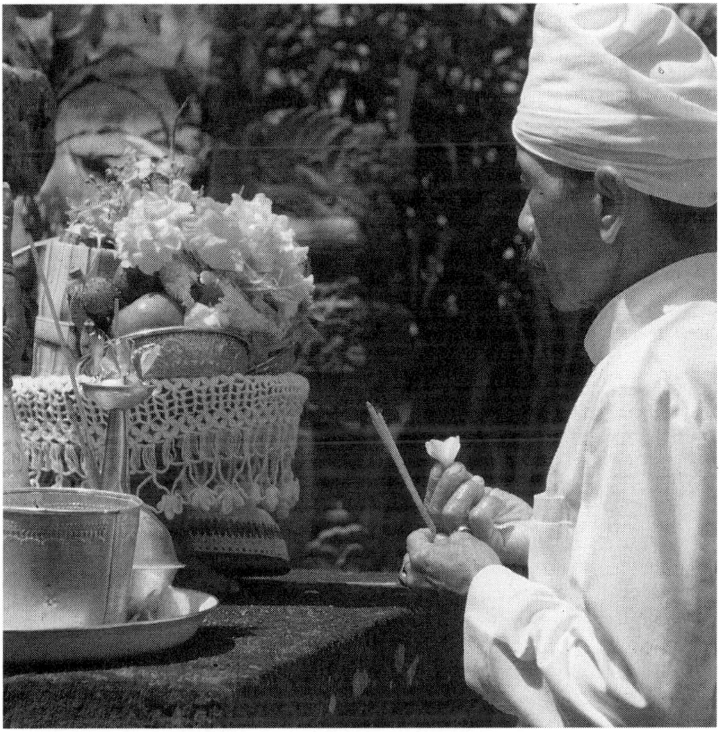

Zoom lenses are essential for quick snapshots while travelling. They permit fast and precise control of the frame. Together with matrix metering and autofocus operation they allow speedy and incospicuous shooting.

Metering system	Exposure mode (Speedlight setting →)	SB-24 at TTL	SB-23/22/20/18/16B/15 at TTL	SB-24 at TTL
Matrix Metering	PH/P/S/A	Matrix Balanced Fill-Flash	Matrix Balanced Fill-Flash	Matrix TTL Flash
	M	Matrix Balanced Fill-Flash	Matrix TTL Flash	Matrix TTL Flash
Center-Weighted Metering	PH/P/S/A	Center-Weighted Fill-Flash	Center-Weighted Fill-Flash	Center-Weighted TTL-Flash
	M	Center-Weighted Fill-Flash	Center-Weighted TTL-Flash	Center-Weighted TTL-Flash
Spot Metering		Spot TTL Flash		

The Nikon SB-24 Speedlight lets you take advantage of rear-blind synch flash

The SB-24 allows normal non-TTL automatic computer and manual flash output as well as automatic TTL balanced fill-in flash control with either the matrix or centre-weighted metering modes and the normal TTL automatic mode. It is possible to synchronise the SB-24 to the rear shutter blind in all these cases but not if it is used as a secondary unit in multi-flash operation.

Repeating flash photography is yet another one of the SB-24's features which allows one object to be depicted several times on one frame. The SB-24 lets the photographer choose both the number of flashes and their frequency and power according to the individual set-up. In order to utilize this function the flash mode selector on the back of the unit must be set to the repeating flash position and the camera's exposure mode selector set to manual. The shutter speed should be set to B for any desired length of exposure or to a speed slower than the complete duration of the repeating flash operation. If you accidentally determine a faster shutter speed not all of the flash bursts may be recorded in the exposure. After that the aperture set on the lens must also be set on the flash, and power output must be set to 1/8th or 1/16th with the **M** button on the back of the unit. You can choose the number of flash bursts and their frequency with the two buttons marked with triangles. Up to 8 bursts at 10 Hz are possible with fresh batteries. The optional DC-unit for external battery supply allows even more flash bursts. As in manual flash control you can check the possible flash distance and the neccessary aperture in the LCD in repeating flash mode. You can calculate the aperture with the equation:

$$\text{aperture} = \frac{\text{guide number}}{\text{flash-to-subject distance.}}$$

The guide number depends on the film speed being used and the position of the flash head, which can be taken from the appropriate chart.

Guide number:

m(ft) at ISO 100

Zoom setting / Flash output	24mm	28mm	35mm	50mm	70mm	85mm
1/1	30(98)	32(105)	36(118)	42(138)	47(154)	50(164)
1/2	21(69)	22(72)	25(82)	30(98)	33(108)	36(118)
1/4	15(49)	16(52)	18(59)	21(69)	23(75)	25(82)
1/8	10.5(34)	11(36)	12.5(41)	15(49)	16.5(54)	18(59)
1/16	7.5(25)	8(26)	9(29)	10.5(34)	11.5(38)	12.5(41)

Flash angle:

Zoom-setting	Horizontal	Vertical
24mm	78°	60°
28mm	70°	53°
35mm	60°	45°
50mm	46°	34°
70mm	36°	26°
85mm	31°	23°

Number of flashes and recycling time with manual control and full output:

Battery type	Number of flashes (approx)*	Recycling time (approx)
Alkali Type AA	100	7 sec
NiCd Type AA	40	5 sec
Alkali Type C in battery holder SD-7**	up to 200 up to 300 up to 400	6 sec 10 sec 30 sec

* Use of the AF-illuminator for autofocus reduces the number of flashes obtainable from a set of batteries.
** With 4AA alkali batteries in SB24

It is also possible to employ the SB-24 together with several other units to achieve a studio-like illumination with all of the automatic controls. In multiple flash photography the units must be linked to the F4 with Nikon Multiflash TTL Connection Cords. The sensor integrated into the camera body will control the output of all the attached flash units and switch them off as soon as the necessary illumination has been achieved. Up to five of the following Nikon Speedlites can be employed in this mode: SB-24, SB-23, SB-22, SB-21B, SB-20, SB-18, SB-16B and SB-15. The Speedlites SB-17 and SB-16A can be used as secondary units. TTL multi-flash cables of 1.5m and 3m are available to connect the flash units with each other via their TTL multi-flash sockets. The TTL Multi-Flash Adapter AS-10 is necessary to connect the Speedlites SB-22, SB-21B, SB-20, SB-18, and SB-15 when they are used as secondary units. The secondary units' power switch must not be set to **STBY** but to the **ON** position, because otherwise they would not be activated. The SB-23 cannot be used as a secondary unit. The SB-24 has a built-in TTL multi-flash socket for a connection to another Speedlite and a conventional sync terminal.

When several Nikon Speedlites are employed for multi-flash photography the electric current in the synchro circuit may exceed a certain level and you may not be able to release a second shot after the first. Either disconnect the master Speedlite from the camera in such a case or switch each of the units off and on once. In order to avoid such complicated additional operations, you should see to it that the combined total of the coefficients (see below) for all of the Speedlites used at any one time does not exceed 20 at 20°C. In case of higher temperatures such as 40°C the coefficient should not exceed 13.

The Numbers in the Parenthesis Indicate the Speedlite's Coefficients for Multi-Flash Operation:

SB-24 (1)	SB-23 (4)	SB-22 (6)
SB-21 (4)	SB-20 (9)	SB-19 (2)
SB-18 (16)	SB-17 (4)	SB-16 (4)
SB-15 (4)	SB-14 (1)	SB-12 (1)
	SB-11 (1).	

In spite of the many integrated features and its high guide number the Nikon Speedlite SB-24 weighs only about 450g without the batteries. It takes four AA-size 1.5v batteries or NiCd batteries of the same size. The large LCD on the back of the unit can be illuminated in order to set the different operating modes and to read the information in darkness or dim light.

Wide-angle lenses seem to extend space. Their perspective emphasises subjects in the foreground and makes the background dwindle into the distance.

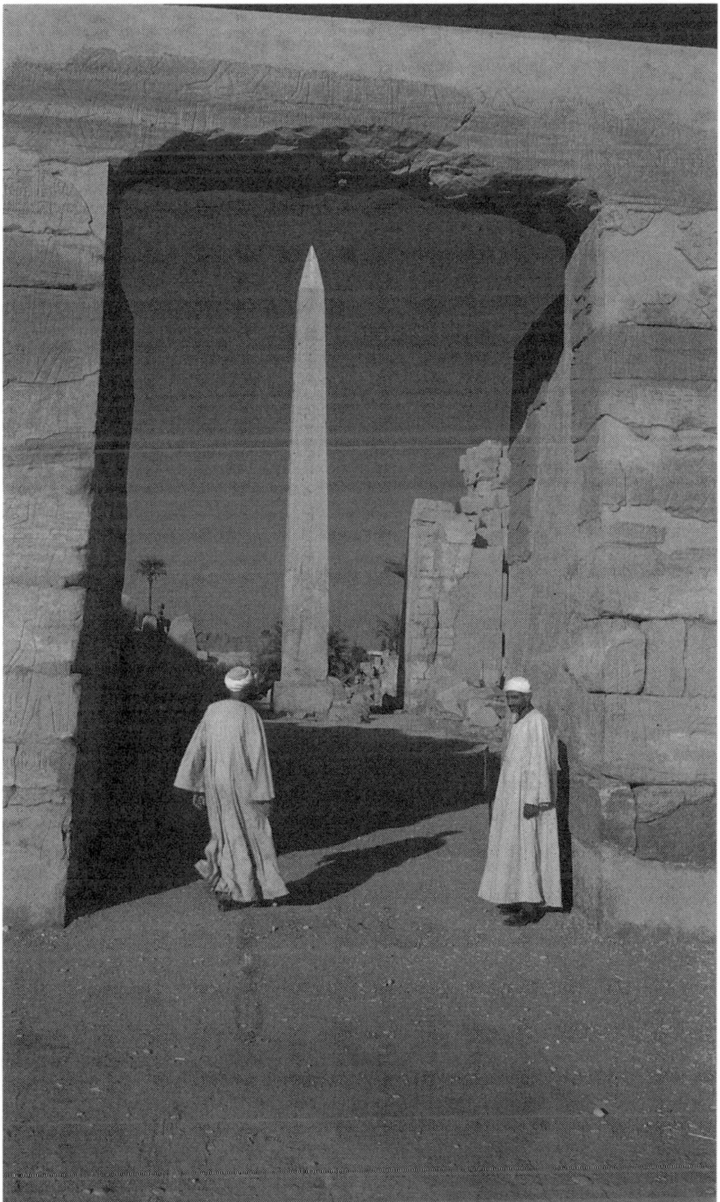

Accessories

TTL Remote Cord SC-17: this coiled cord is employed to connect the camera with a remote flash and facilitates automatic synchronisation and the flash-ready signal in the viewfinder, just as if the SB-24 were mounted directly in the Nikon F4's hot-shoe. It is equipped with two TTL multi-flash sockets besides the hot-shoe with the appropriate contacts. A threaded socket is set in the base in order to mount the terminal on a tripod.

TTL Multi-Flash Connecting Cords SC-18 and SC-19: both of these cords allow the linking of Speedlites with integrated TTL multi-flash sockets. They differ only in length; the SC-18 is about 1.5m and the SC-19 about 3m in length. Thanks to their threaded mounts they can be secured against unintentional disconnection.

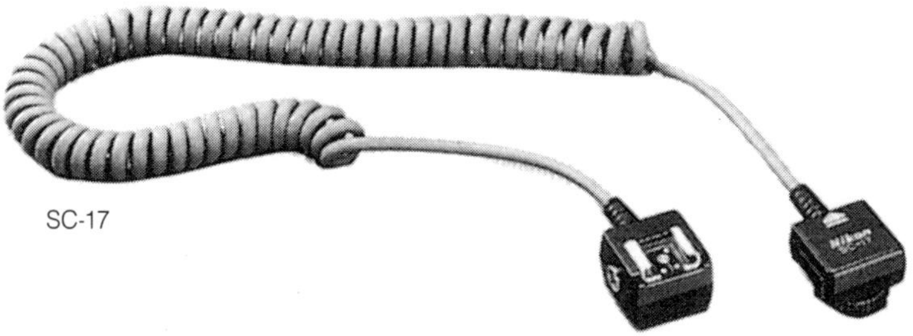

SC-17

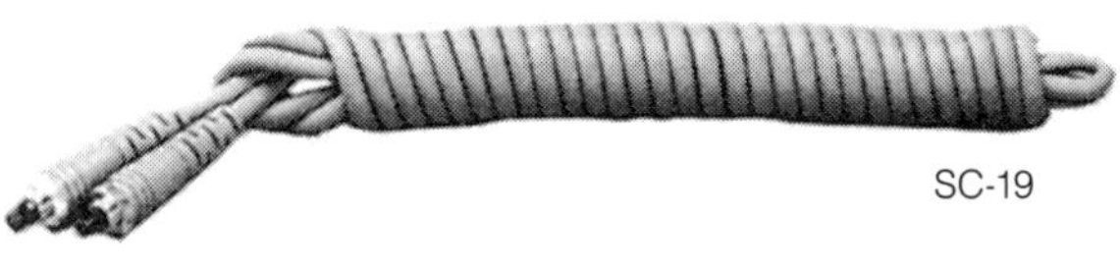

SC-19

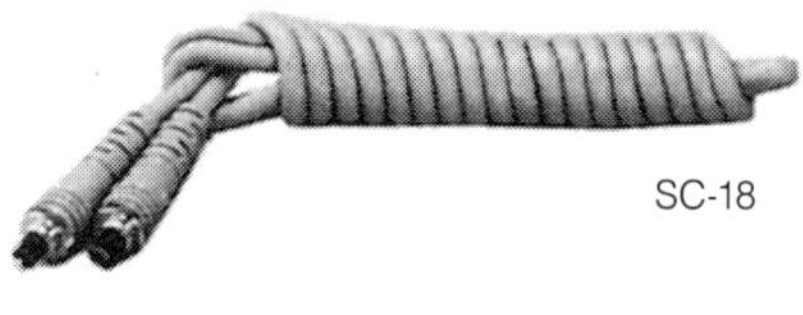

SC-18

TTL Multi-Flash Adapter AS-10: when you intend to use up to five Speedlites in connection with the SB-24 in multi-flash operation you will need this adapter. It has three TTL multi-flash sockets and a hot-shoe and also a threaded socket for tripod mounting.

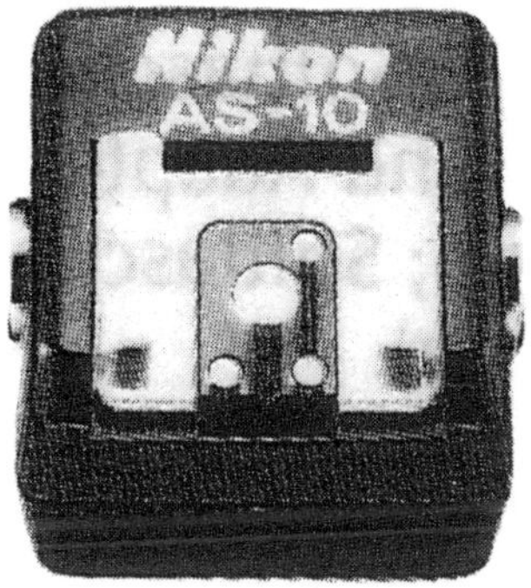

Up to five flash units can be connected to the Nikon F4 for automatic output control with the TTL Multiflash Adaptor AS-10.

DC Battery Unit SD-7: this battery pack can be employed as an optional external power source. It is connected to the external power terminal on the front of the SB-24 with the Power Cord SC-16. The SB-24 still requires its four batteries when the SD-7 is being used. The SD-7 offers a higher number of flashes, a faster recycling time, and more flash bursts in repeating flash mode.

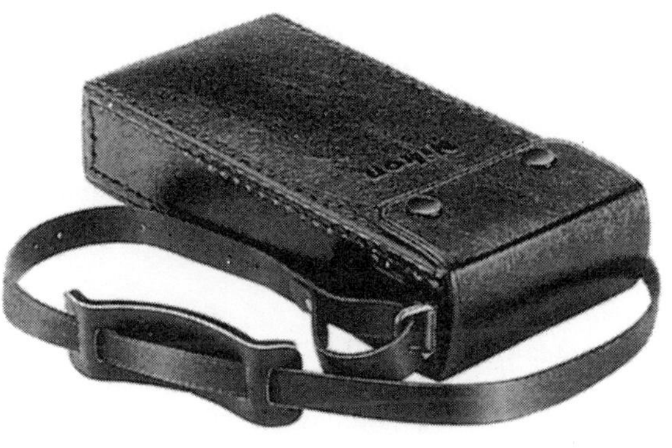

Nikon Speedlite SB-23

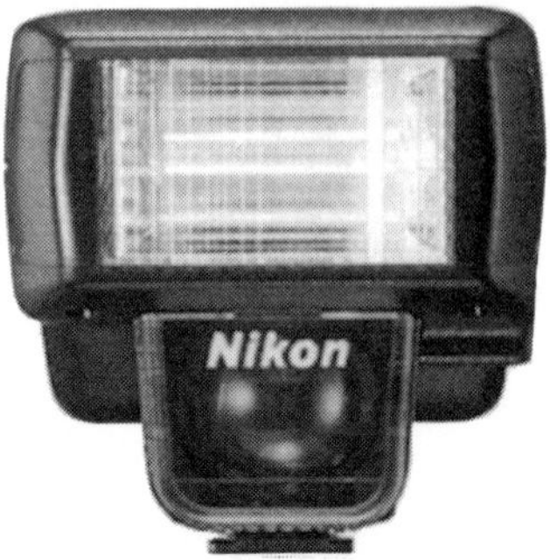

This, the smallest of the Nikon Speedlites with built-in AF-illuminators, weighs only 140g. In spite of its compact size it still has a guide number of 20 (in metres) at ISO 100. The fixed flash head has a coverage sufficient for lenses with 35mm focal length or longer. It takes four AA-size 1.5v batteries as its power source. Up to 400 flashes can be fired with one set of fresh batteries and the unit's recycling time is surprisingly short; two seconds. Non-TTL computer controlled automatic operation is not possible. This compact and light-weight unit is especially ideal for automatic daylight fill-flash photography. A flash-ready light indicates when the capacitator is completely loaded. Of course, this signal and the confirmation of a correct flash exposure can also be seen in the viewfinder. In order to conserve battery power the SB-23 has a stand-by circuitry that switches off the flash automatically whenever the shutter release button has not been activated for a length of time.

Nikon Speedlite SB-22

This Nikon AF flash unit has a guide number of 25 (in metres) at ISO 100 and is also equipped with an integrated AF illuminator that automatically projects a patterned beam of light to support the autofocus system whenever lighting conditions are poorer than –1 EV and the F4 has been set to S for Single Servo Autofocus. It also has a motor-drive mode which allows up to five flash bursts per second. The flash head exactly covers the angle of view of a 35mm lens. Together with an additional diffusor screen it can be adjusted to use 28mm lenses. The flash head can be tilted 90° upward for bounce-flash operation and 7° downward for parallax compensation in close-up photography.

An incorporated sensor allows non-TTL computer flash output control as well as TTL automatic flash operation. Within the manual mode flash output can set to 1/1, 1/2, 1/4, 1/8, and 1/16. Recharging time is about four seconds. Four AA-size 1.5v batteries or the equivalent NiCd batteries are neccessary for power supply. The film speed range is from ISO 25 to 1600. The flash unit weighs only about 250g without batteries. A switch on the back of the unit is utilized for film speed setting and the indication of the flash ranges in the two non-TTL computer controlled automatic settings. Next to this switch you will find a button for test-firing a flash, a flash-ready light, and an indicator for a tilted flash head. The unit also has a TTL multi-flash socket.

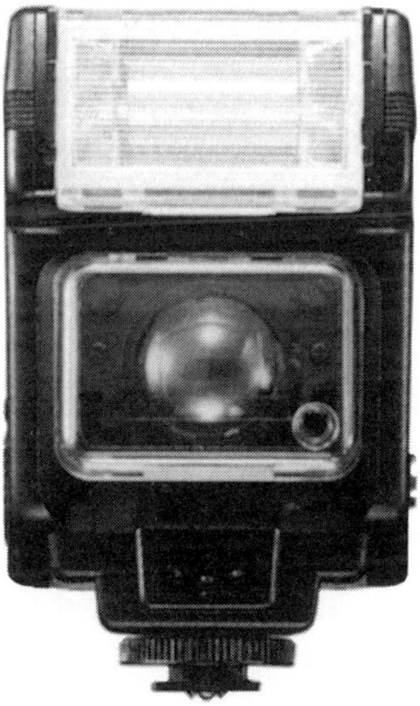

Nikon Speedlite SB-20

This AF-flash unit is the second-most powerful in the Nikon program. It is suited both for TTL automatic, as well as non-TTL computer controlled automatic flash operation. You can switch the modes with the selector on the back of the unit. Every aperture from *f*2 to *f*22 is available in TTL-mode. Of course, programmed cybernetic sync flash is also possible. Depending on the chosen film speed, five aperture settings for automatic flash control are available, in the non-TTL computer mode, which are selected with a switch and must be set manually on the lens. In manual mode flash output can be reduced to 1/2, 1/4, 1/8, or 1/16.

The illumination angle can be matched to correspond to the angle of view of lenses with 28mm, 35mm, or 85mm focal length. The flash head can be tilted upward in indexed positions of 45°, 60°, 75°, and 90°. The SB-20 also has a TTL multi-flash socket for the use of another flash unit. It is quite compact, in spite of its high guide number it weighs only 260g without the necessary four AA-size 1.5v batteries.

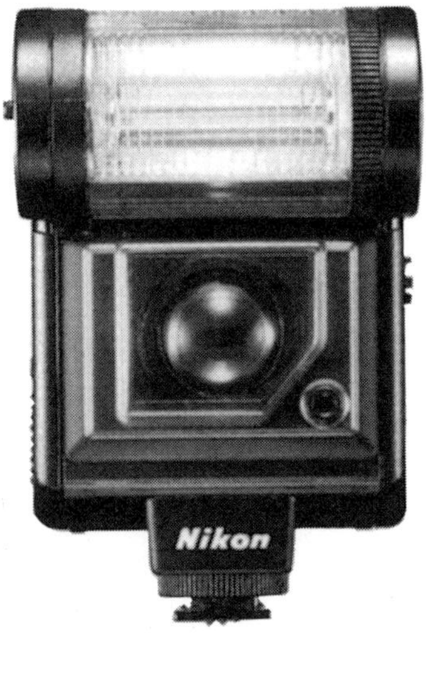

Using the Nikon Speedlite SB-24 will automatically lead to correctly exposed flash pictures.

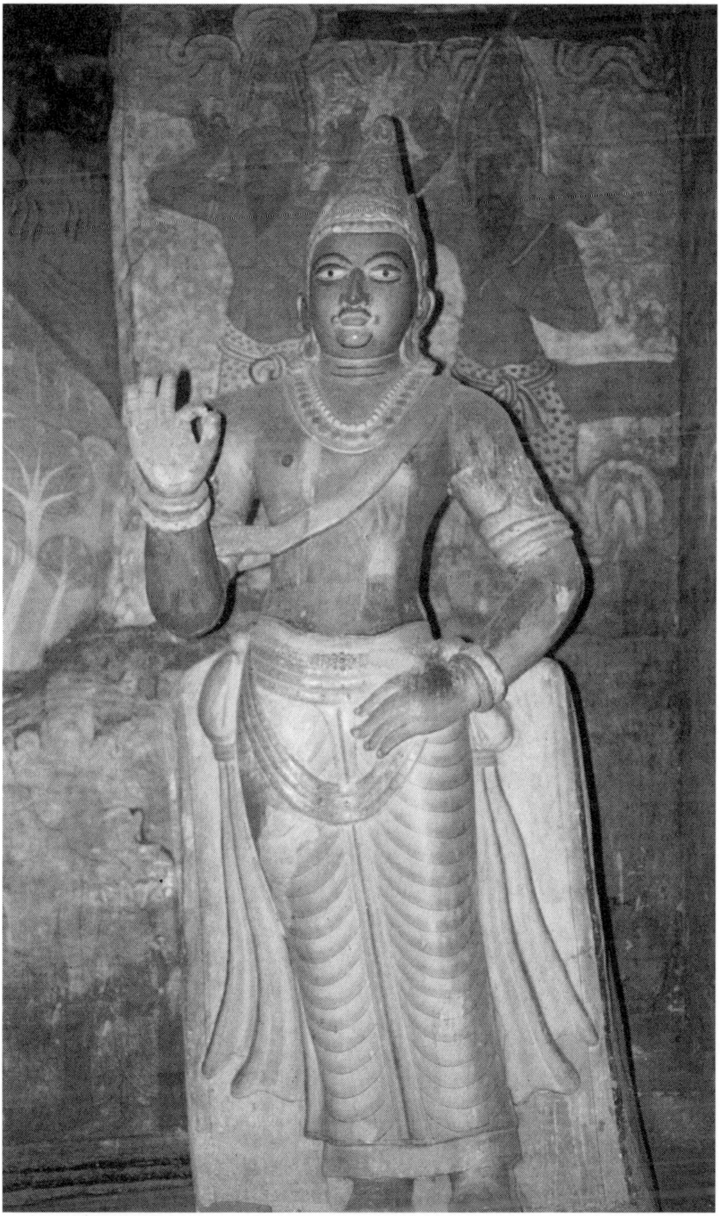

Close-Up Photography

There are three ways for a photographer to achieve real close-ups. In order to depict small and tiny objects in frame-filling natural, or even enlarged, size he must either further the extension of the lens, use close-up lens attachments, or employ macro-lenses. Of course, a combination of all three accessories is possible, too. Normal lenses designed for general photography usually have a restricted extension capability due to their construction, limiting their shortest focusing distance to about ten times their focal length. This, in turn, allows no higher reproduction ratios than about 1:10. Some zoom lenses have additional macro positions which also allow close-ups with scales up to 1:3 or 1:4. But that is the final limit. In order to achieve greater magnifications you will have to resort to the proper accessories.

The Nikon program of close-up accessories offers an array of equipment for all three methods of macro-photography, such as retro-rings to mount the lens in the opposite position, a copy stand to facilitate first-class reproduction, a macro ring light for perfect illumination, a slide copying unit, and a focusing stage for the exact alignment of the whole reproduction unit.

Reproduction Ratio and Depth-of Field

A reproduction ratio is a proportional factor indicating how much larger or smaller an object is recorded on the film. A value of 1:1 indicates a life-size reproduction. Whenever the first number is larger than 1 the object is being reproduced much larger, as the number indicates. If the second number is larger the reproduction is smaller by that factor. In general photography it will probably not be very important to know the exact reproduction ratio but in technical and scientific applications precise data may be crucial to determine the original size of the photographed object.

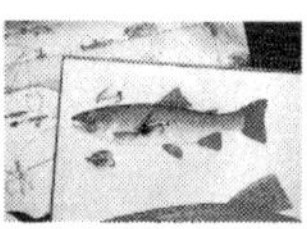

1/8X

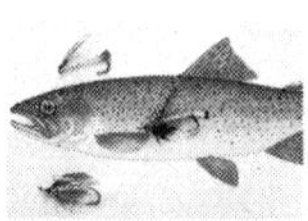

1/4X

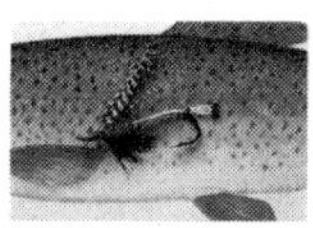

1/2X

Before TTL-flash metering was available the exact reproduction ratio used to be necessary to calculate the correct *f*-stop. A change in the reproduction ratio is achieved by furthering the optical system's extension, which in turn, makes a different effective *f*-stop necessary. The longer the extension, the greater the loss of light. The Nikon F4's TTL flash control registers such changes automatically.

Regardless of the extension accessories being used, be they bellows, extension rings or teleconverters, loss of light is always the result. This is a big problem for macro-photography since increasing the reproduction ratio not only causes an increasing loss of light but also a reduction in the depth of field. So, if important subject details are not supposed to disappear in the unsharp zones the appropriate aperture must be chosen.

The easiest way out of this dilemma, which is to select slower shutter speeds, often proves unacceptable because of the danger of blurring moving subjects. The second-best solution, the use of a faster speed is also not recommended because close-ups especially call for pin-point sharpness and the highest possible resolution. The increasing graininess of faster films usually rules this possibility out. The only thing left when shooting static subjects is the use of a sturdy macro copy stand, a tripod with a focusing stage, or the use of an electronic flash.

Nikon close-up attachment lenses are very simple accessories and allow macro photography to a limited degree. They are screwed into the lens and shorten its focal length resulting in a shorter focusing distance, which, in turn allows greater reproduction ratios.

Nikon Close-Up Lenses

These kind of attachments, that shorten the focal length of the lens optically and thus facilitate greater reproduction ratios from the shorter camera-to-subject distances, are the most convenient and cheapest accessories for close-ups. They take up little space and are screwed onto the lens like a filter. They do not affect the lens's aperture but you do have to stop-down more than usual for the best possible results.

A combination of several close-up lenses will allow even greater

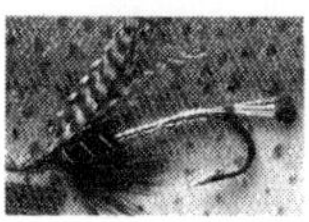
1X

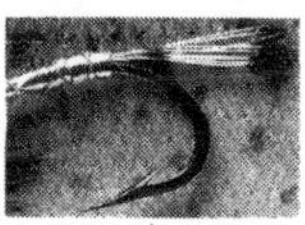
2X

4X
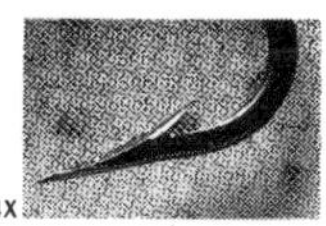

8X
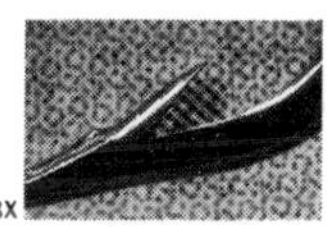

reproduction ratios. But, since the image quality deteriorates in such cases it is not recommended to use more than two close-up lenses at a time. The stronger lens should always be mounted first. Nikon close-up lenses are available with filter threads of 52mm and 62mm. There are versions designed for shorter and for longer focal length lenses. They are available with 0.7, 1.5, and 3.0 dioptres for shorter lenses. The achromats consisting of two elements are made for telephoto lenses in 1.5 and 2.9 dioptres. The latter are also available for lenses with 62mm filter threads.

In order to calculate the approximate camera-to-subject distance when the lens is set to infinity, divide the number 100 by the total dioptre number. The result is the distance in cm.

Automatic Nikon Extension Rings

Extension rings allow considerably greater reproduction ratios than is possible with close-up lenses. They are mounted between the camera body and the lens and most of the latter's functions, such as full-aperture metering, are not affected. Thanks to this the picture frame can be viewed and composed with a rather bright viewfinder image. Critical focusing in macro-photography becomes much faster and more definite due to this feature. The Nikon program offers extension rings with lengths of 8mm (PK-11A), 14mm (PK-12), 27.5mm (PK-13), and 52.5mm (PN-11). The Micro-Nikkor 55mm, *f*2.8 with PK-13 allows life-size shooting. Extension ring PN-11 also allows a 1:1 reproduction ratio when used with the Micro-Nikkor 105mm, *f*2.8.

Extension rings can be combined to achieve even greater lengths. The shorter the focal length of the lens in use, the shorter the focusing distance and, in turn, the greater the reproduction ratio achieved will be. The compact dimensions of extension rings, and the convenient working

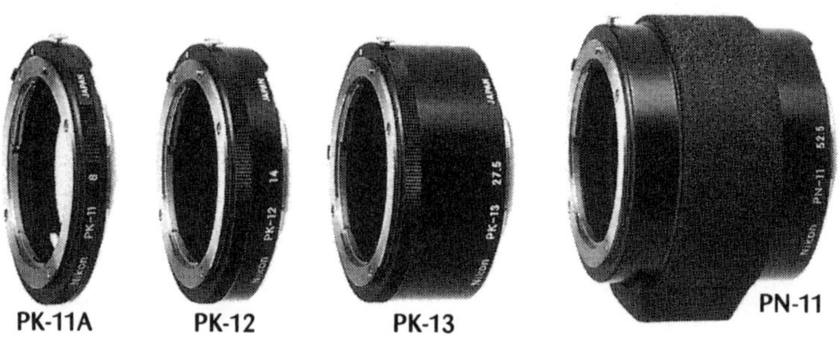

PK-11A PK-12 PK-13 PN-11

conditions they secure, by retaining full-aperture metering and automatic aperture control, make them very popular accessories for close-ups.

Nikon Retro-Rings

In order to achieve a better image quality in close-ups, photographers often use normal and wide-angle lenses in the so-called retro-position. This means mounting the lens, with its front facing the camera body, on the latter's bayonet by an adapter-ring which is screwed into the filter thread of the lens. Nikon offers the retro-ring BR-2A for the F4 which allows lenses with 52mm threads to be mounted on the camera. In addition, the adapter ring BR-5 is available in order to mount lenses with a 62mm filter thread on the retro-ring BR-2A. By employing lenses in a position opposite to that for which they were designed, i.e. by turning around their ratio between the subject-to-lens and the lens-to-film plane distances, their image quality for close-ups can be improved.

This configuration, meant to increase the reproduction ratio, has only one drawback; the loss of full aperture metering. The stopdown metering mode must be utilized. As generally recommended in macro-photography, focusing should not be attempted with the lens ring but by moving towards or away from the subject with the complete equipment until the viewfinder image appears sharp.

Nikon Bellows Attachment PB-6

Unlike extension rings, the Nikon bellows attachment PB-6 allows extensions necessary for certain reproduction ratios to be set continuously. The PB-6 is also mounted between a macro-lens and the camera, which can be rotated for vertical or horizontal format shooting. Reproduction ratios of 1:1 to 4:1 are possible with a 50mm lens . Lenses can be mounted in the retro-position to avoid aberrations in the extreme close-up range. The PB-6 has a double focusing stage rail; one is used to fix the reproduction ratio and the other for precise focusing. The maximum extension is 208mm but it can be increased to 438mm with the Extension Bellows PB-6E. If you utilize the complete possible extension with a 50mm lens you can achieve a maximum reproduction ratio of 8.5:1.

A number of useful accessories increase the possibilities of the bellows even further. You can produce duplicates and trimmed negative areas of 35mm slides with the Slide Copying Adapter PS-6, which takes slide mounts of up to 4mm thickness as well as complete film rolls. You can employ either the mechanical double cable release AR-7 or the mechanical/electrical double cable release AR-10. The AR-7 is screwed into the release terminal on the back of the camera and bellow's lens frame. The AR-10 is plugged into the remote terminal of the High-Speed

The Nikon Bellows attachment PB-6, the extension PB-6E, and the slide copying unit PS-6 allow reproduction ratios of 1:1 and more. In addition they allow precision framing. Bellows represent the most professional approach to close-up photography.

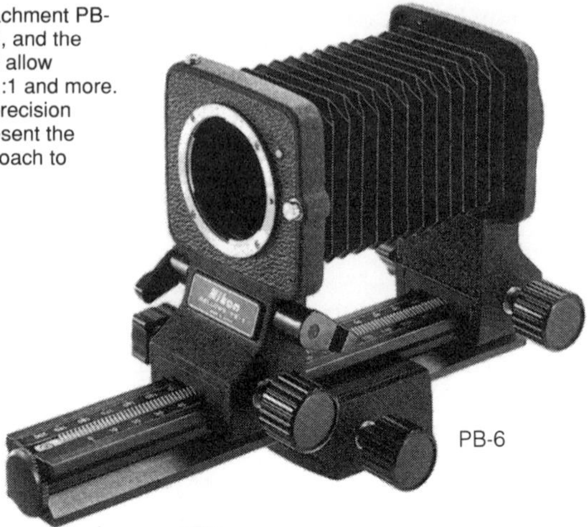

PB-6

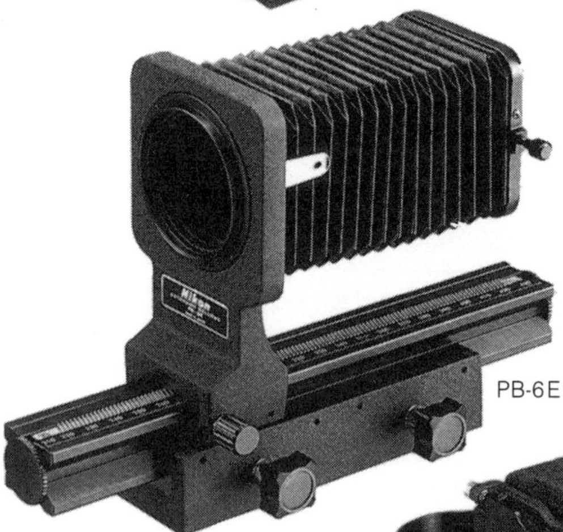

PB-6E

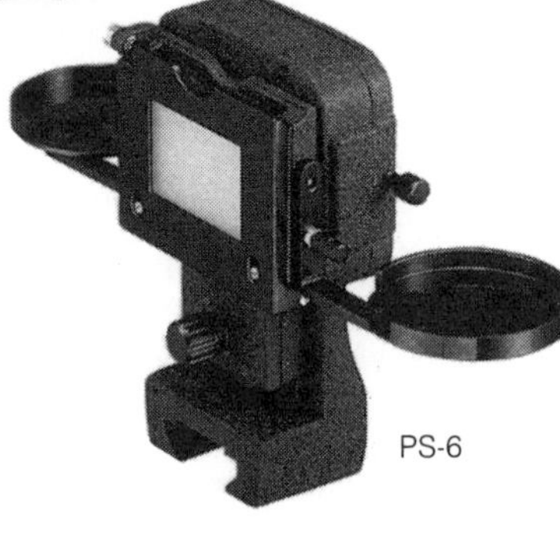

PS-6

Battery Pack MB-21 or the External Power Regulator MB-22. The double cable releases maintain the automatic aperture control of the lens so that composition and metering can be done at full aperture. When either cable release is partly depressed the lens is stopped down to the preset aperture and the shutter is released only when they are fully depressed. They can be locked for long time-exposures.

The possibility of reversing the front frame is very convenient since lenses can thus be employed in the retro-position without the need for additional adapters. Thanks to the integrated threaded socket the bellows can be mounted on a tripod.

The Macro Copy Stand PB-6M: makes photographs of tiny objects easy when used with the bellows. It is equipped with clamps for a specimen-holder and can be illuminated from below. The Focusing stage PG-2 facilitates convenient focusing by shifting the complete equipment. It also has a tripod mount socket and can be attached to the bellows either vertically or horizontally.

Nikon Repro Copy Outfit PF-4

The combination of the F4 with this convenient copy stand PF-4 meets professional demands. In order to mount the F4 complete with the High-Speed Battery Pack MB-21, the camera holder adapter PA-4 is available. The sturdy rectangular column of the outfit with the camera holder is connected firmly to the base-board. Height adjustments are easy thanks to an incorporated counter-weight. A separate micrometer adjusting knob is available for focusing. The camera can be turned to the left and to the right by 45 or 90° on the stand to photograph large objects. The PF-4 can be used without the base-board with the help of the table-clamp PC-3.

Nikon TTL Macro-Ringlight SB-21

This electronic flash unit was developed especially for individual illumination arrangements in close-up photography which it greatly simplifies. Complicated calculations involving extension factors when using bellows is unnecessary thanks to the F4's TTL flash output control in connection with the SB-21.

This consists of a power unit for the energy supply and a flash head with its two separate flash tubes which can be activated individually. When you use both flash tubes the result will be a shadowless and flat illumination. When you only use one, an object's three dimensions can be depicted much more vividly by intentional selective illumination and well-placed shadows. In addition to TTL control, manual mode is also possible with either 1/4 or 1/16th power output. A special diffusor for flash-to-subject distances of less than 40mm is available which ensures a soft and even illumination. The flash head is mounted onto the lens with the help of one of the two adapter-rings, of 52mm and 62mm filter thread, provided with the flash. A integrated pilot lamp assists with focusing and composing.

The Macro Ring-Light SB-21 uses four AA-size 1.5v batteries or the equivalent NiCd batteries. The usable film speed range for TTL control is from ISO 25 to 1000. The guide number is 13 (in metres). It can also be used with the Battery Unit LD-2, which takes eight AA-size batteries, or with power from the mains via the AC Power Pack LA-2. The complete SB-21B is surprisingly light. The flash head weighs only about 145g and the power unit is AS-14 256g.

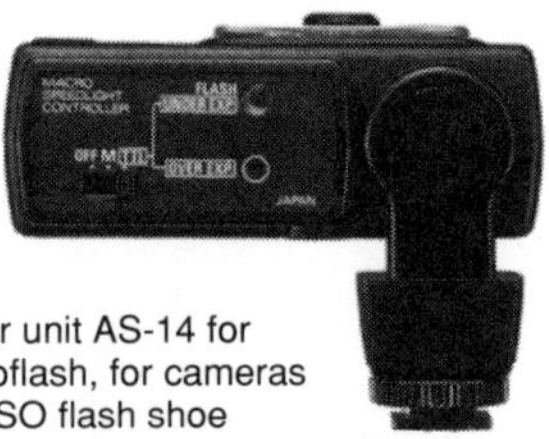

Power unit AS-14 for Macroflash, for cameras with ISO flash shoe

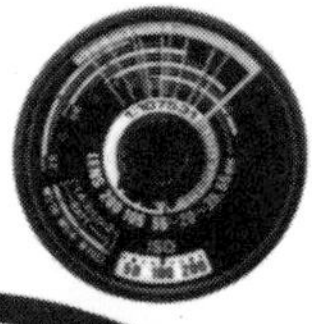

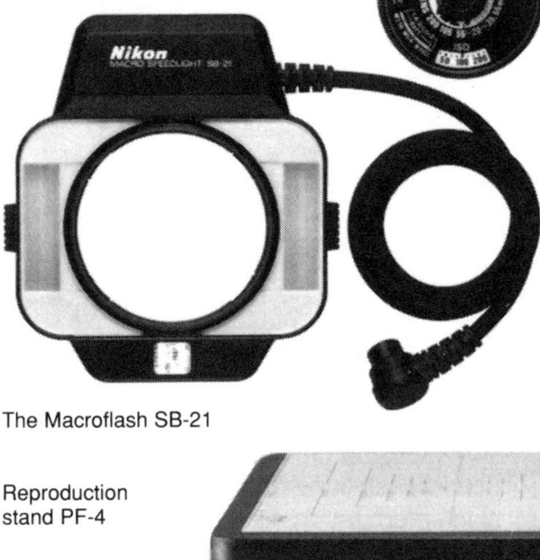

The Macroflash SB-21

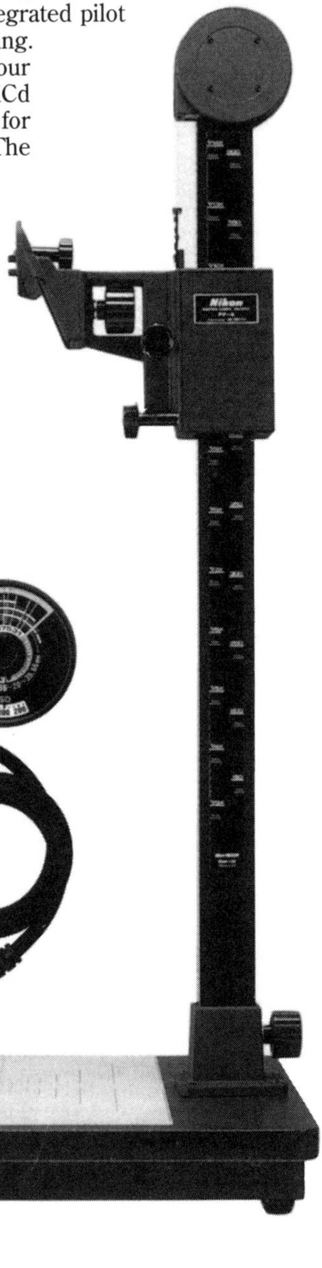

Reproduction stand PF-4

Other Accessories

The F4's three interchangeable backs further extend the camera's numerous possibilities. Imprinting data is the most insignificant of the many modes. The multi-control backs allow a number of additional functions.

The Data-Back MF-22: this data-back is designed to imprint data on the frame. You can have the data imprinted in the following ways – year/month/day, month/day/year, month/year/day, or day/hour/minute. The integrated clock counts in the 24 hour-mode. Usable film speeds are from ISO 32 to ISO 3200. Imprinting can be switched off if you prefer. A long-life lithium battery type CR-2025 supplies the necessary energy. The data back weighs 100 grams without the battery.

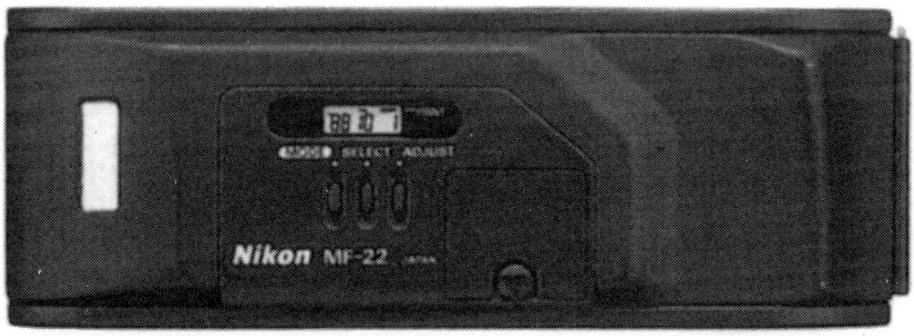

The Multi-Control Back MF-23: the MF-23 does not have very much to do with conventional data-backs anymore. Whereas the latter usually imprint the data in the lower right-hand corner of the frame, this data-back gives the photographer the possibility to utilize the space between the frames for the data. This makes it possible to record the data without interfering with the picture. Next to the date and time in different order you can also have the frame number, a serial upcount number or a fixed number as well as shutter speed and aperture data imprinted. Exposure compensation values can also be imprinted. In addition to these imprinting functions the MF-23 also allows the photographer to employ further operation modes with the F4. Together with the multi-control back you can make use of the automatic interval timer. In this case you can determine the starting time, the time between the intervals, and the total number of intervals as well as the number of frames in one interval. An exposure delay function allows you to determine any amount of delay between pressing the shutter release button and the exposure. The multi-control back can also be programmed to let the camera expose for any length of time up to 999 hours, 999 minutes and 999 seconds. Automatic bracketing allows you to let the camera make up to 19 continuous exposures with differences between each exposure that can be set in increments of 1/3 EV and 1/2 EV.

The "Freeze-Focus" function extends the possibilities of autofocus. The camera will automatically release the shutter as soon as a moving object reaches a preset focus setting in this mode. The Nikon F4 can even be used as an alarm-clock or as a reminder of a certain date. If you wish, the back will indicate a preset time daily with an acoustic signal. Or you can program it to sound when the film roll is finished or after a preset amount of shots. This last function is convenient for reporters who may not be able to pay attention to the film counter in the hottest action but do want to be reminded to check the number of frames left in order to decide if they have to load a new film or if the remaining number of shots suffice for the next assignment. The F4's possibilities are also greatly increased by the multi-control back's option to combine some of its functions. In spite of the many additional functions the MF-23 weighs only 20 grams more than the MF-22, both without batteries, but it does need two of the lithium batteries CR-2025. Film speeds from ISO 25 to ISO 3200 can be used.

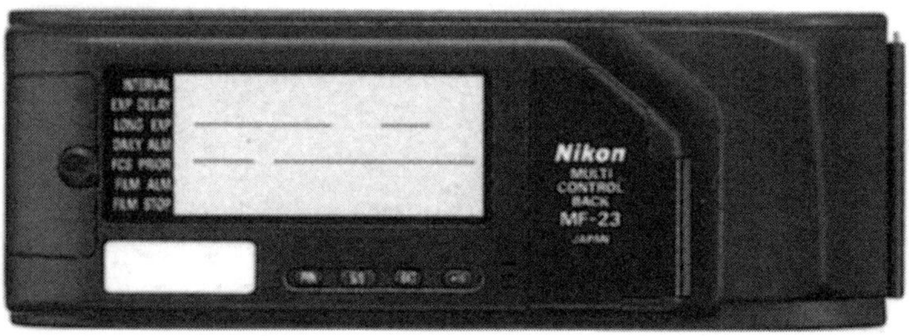

The Nikon Multi-Control Back for 250 Exposures MF-24: this back for the use of bulk film was developed for scientific and sports documenting applications. The back is equipped with two film magazines for up to 10 metres of film for about 250 frames. Its energy is supplied either by the High-Speed Battery Pack MB-21 or the External Power Regulator MB-22. The connection is made with the cable that fits into the socket on the bottom-sections. The transformer in the MB-22 reduces the voltage delivered by the AC/DC Converter MA-4 from 15 to 8.2 volts. The connecting cord MC-11 is neccessary to link the converter MA-4 to the MB-22. Thanks to its threaded plug it can be screwed securely into place without the risk of slipping off accidentally. The imprinting and the other functions are identical to those of the MF-23.

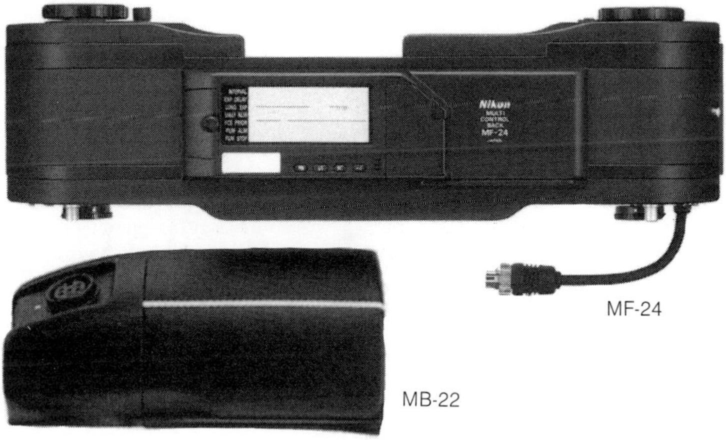

The Remote Control Accessories

The photographer will not be able to operate the Nikon F4 directly in every shooting situation. In some cases even the slightest touch could lead to the danger of blurred pictures because of camera shake. In other situations the camera and the photographer are located at different positions so it must be possible to operate the equipment from a long distance. Nikon's accessory program for the F4 is a rich source for such assignments and has a solution for every problem.

The Nikon Cable Release AR-3: in order to avoid camera shake when shooting with long telephoto lenses from a tripod or at extremely close range Nikon offers cable releases for the F4. The AR-3 and the double cable release AR-7 for the use with the bellows PB-6 are completely mechanical types and can only be connected to the release terminal on the back of the camera. They cannot be connected to the Nikon High-Speed Battery Pack MB21's or the External Power Regulator MB-22's remote terminal. The double cable release AR-10 is available for those cases.

The Remote Cord MC-12A: this remote cord of three metres length is fitted with a handgrip with a two-step shutter release button. When you partly depress the latter the camera's metering and AF-system are activated. When the button is fully depressed the shutter will be released. The button can be locked for convenient long time-exposures. The cord is screwed into a remote terminal.

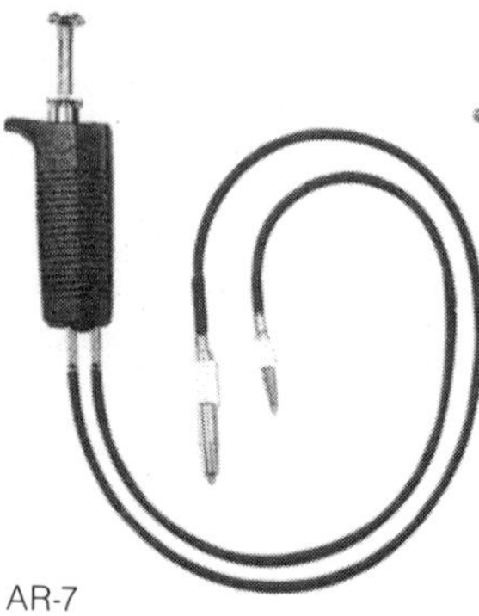

AR-7

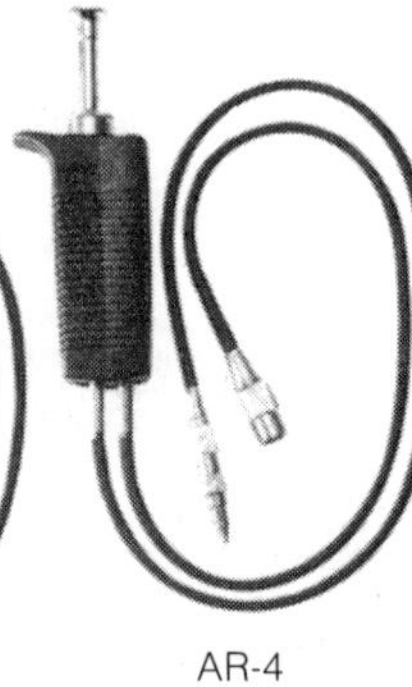

AR-4

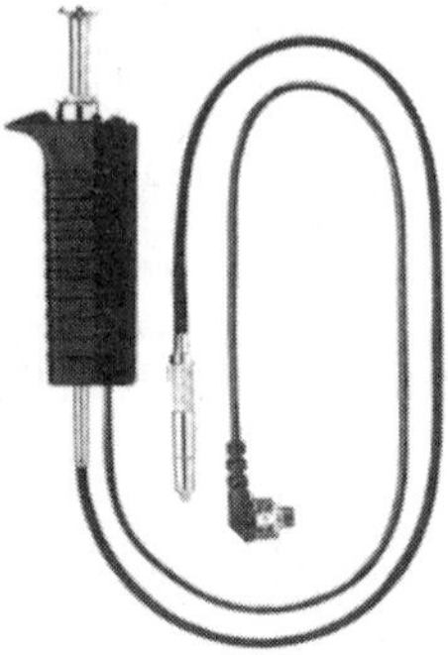

AR-10

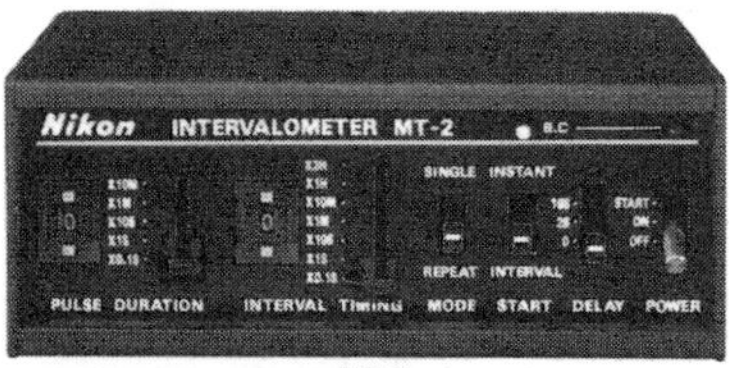

MT-2

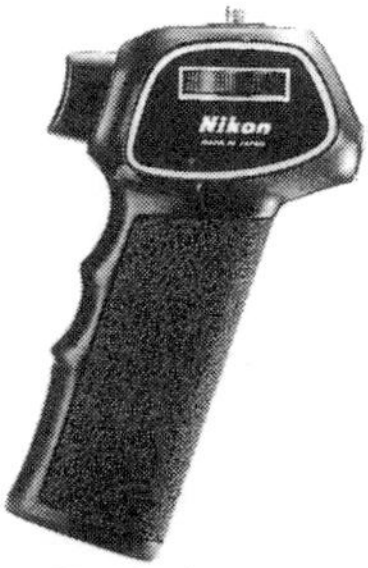

Pistol grip

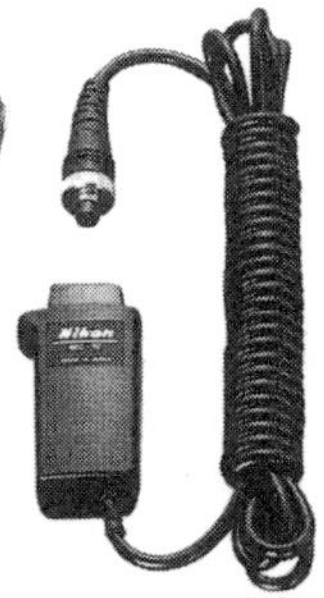

MC-10

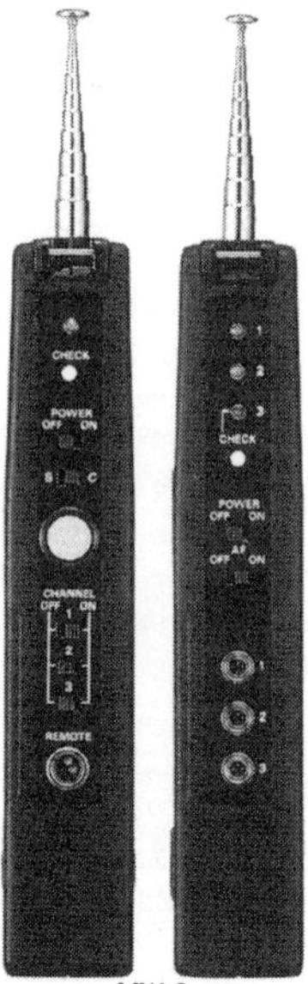

MW-2

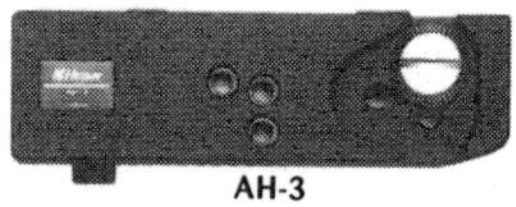

AH-3

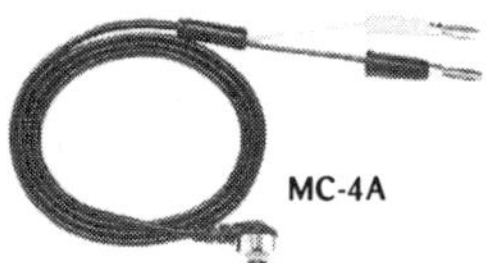

MC-4A

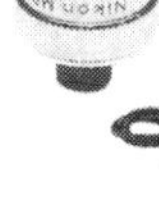

MR-3

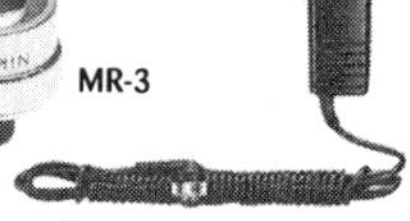

MC-12A

The Nikon Remote Cord MC-4A: this cord was developed to fire several F4 cameras simultaneously. It is linked to the remote terminals of the MB-21 or the external power regulator. The other end has plus and minus banana-type plugs.

The Nikon Remote Control Set MW-2: this set, consisting of a transmitter and a receiver, allows remote radio control up to 700 meters. Three separate channels allow three cameras to be operated independently.

The Nikon Intervalometer MT-2: this unit enables you to do time-lapse photography as well as to program irregular remote-controlled operation. The quartz-controlled MT-2 allows either a 2 sec. or a 16 sec. shutter release delay, so that sufficient time for focus corrections or for flash recycling remains. The intervalometer can be combined with other remote-control accessories.

The Nikon Pistol Grip Mod. 2 and the Connecting Cord MC-3A: this convenient pistol-grip can be screwed into either the camera's tripod socket or the tripod mounting collar of a super-telephoto lens. It enables you to have a more stable hold the complete equipment for telephoto shots and close-ups. The pistol grip's release button is linked to the High-Speed Battery Pack MB-21's or the External Power Regulator MB-22's remote terminal with the MC-3A connecting cord so the camera can be released through the grip.

The Nikon Connecting Cords MC-17 and MC-17S: both of these cords are utilized to fire two cameras almost simultaneously. They differ in length – the MC-17 is three metres – and the MC-17S only 40 cm long. If you employ the Multi-Control Data Back MF-24 for 250 exposures on the F4 this camera will have to be the master unit.

The TV Remote Control Video Viewfinder: this finder which was presented as a working prototype at the 1988 Photokina and is not available yet allows total remote control of the Nikon F4 including visual control with the help of a monitor. It is simply mounted instead of a normal viewfinder and allows you to control all of the camera's functions, except the self-timer, from anywhere away from the unit as well as to see the viewfinder image on a monitor. The maximum usable distance is 100 meters. The viewfinder consists of a pentaprism, a second rectangular prism, the recording optics, the CCDs, and the necessary electronic circuitry.

The recording sensor for a black and white reproduction is a 2/3" CCD Chip with 250,000 effective pixels. The integrated optics make up a lens *f*2/20 mm with automatic aperture control and a built-in infrared

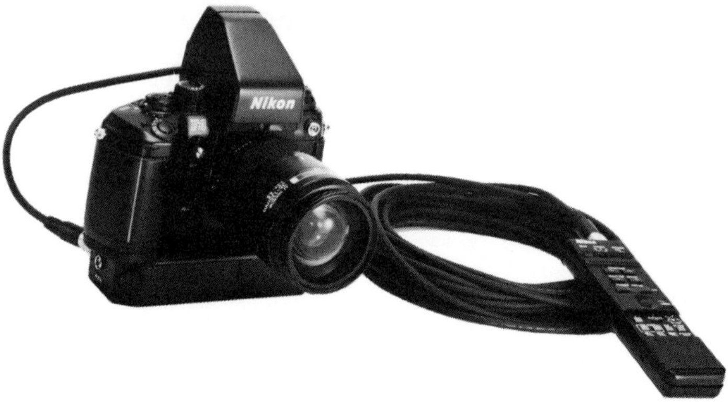

filter. It transmits about 90% of the frame horizontally and 100% vertically which leads to a frame ratio of about 4:3. The TV-finder needs a minimal brightness level of 100 Lux together with a lens speed of *f*1.4.

Power is supplied by a 9.6 volt battery-pack or a 12 volt mains converter. Energy consumption is below 3 watts. The finder part itself weighs about 300 grams, the power unit 190 grams, and the remote control unit only about 140 grams. Applications for the TV-finder can be in the technical and scientific areas, in medical photography, for example in the operating room, in wildlife photography and observations.

Filters for Better Pictures

Filters for Nikon lenses are either screwed onto the front of the lenses or into special filter-holders, which are slipped into the barrel of the lens, or have a screw or bayonet fitting onto the back of a few lenses. In all four cases the effect is the same: certain portions of the visible as well as the invisible spectrum of the light raysgoing through the lens are absorbed. Selective use of filters can improve image quality and color rendition in both colour and black and white photography. But they can also be employed creatively to emphasize certain effects or even to supress subjects.

Nikon filters are made of high-quality optical glass meeting the same high quality standards as Nikkor lenses. They are precision-ground for flatness and polished to assure that both sides are exactly parallel. Remarkably thin filter rings allow them to be used even on wideangle lenses without causing vignetting. Nikon filters are available with threads from 39 mm to 122 mm. Not all types are available in the extreme sizes. Polarising filters are only available in the sizes 52 mm, 62 mm, and 72 mm, which also goes for the soft-focus-types.

Filters for Black and White Photography

Since the human eye has a spectral sensitivity differing from that of black-and-white films you can influence the colour rendition of these films very effectively by using filters. Contrast can be improved, too. For example, blue skies often look too flat on black-and-white prints because the film is more sensitive to blue and ultraviolet light than to other colours. When you use a filter that absorbs these colours you can achieve an increase in contrast. Clouds are rendered brighter and the sky darker. Nikon offers a total of seven types of filters for black-and-white photography.

Yellow: yellow filters absorb both the blue and the ultraviolet light. They let the sky appear darker on the print. Since they also remove some of the haze from distant subjects they are good for landscapes and telephoto shots. Nikon offers three different yellow filters, the very light Y44, the medium Y48, and the dark Y52.

Orange: the effect of the orange filter O56 is even stronger than that of the yellow ones. In addition to blue and ultraviolet it also absorbs green light. It leads to a pronounced emphasis of the sky, and green of plants is also darkened. It is used preferably for super-telephoto shots because it greatly enhances a landscape's contrast. Orange filters interfere with autofocus operation so you will have to focus manually with them.

Red; the R60 filter has the strongest effect of all in black-and-white photography. It absorbs all the colours of the spectrum except red. As a result a blue sky is rendered almost black. Clouds are dramatically emphasized and, for example, green foliage contrasts strongly to red blossoms. A red filter is also often used to create special effects in infrared photography. Red filters interfere with autofocus operation, so manual focusing becomes necessary.

Green: green filters absorb both red and blue light, while allowing yellow and green light to pass through relatively freely. Nikon offers two different green filters. The XO absorbes less red light than the X1 but both absorb the some amount of blue, so the XO's effect is slightly less, creating a spectral emphasis similar to that of the human eye. It is ideal for general photography. The X1 renders human skin better – thanks to its stronger effect and is popular in portraiture because of this.

Filters for Colour Photography

Nikon offers five different kinds of filters for colour photography with different colours and effects. They are mainly intended to balance the different light temperatures with the different types of film.

Amber: these filters screen out blue with their reddish colours and thus prevent a blueish cast in daylight shots. Two types of these color-correction filters are available. The weaker A2 will warm up "cold" light in heavily overcast weather or in the shade and the stronger A12 is employed with tungsten film when shooting under daylight illumination.

Blue: Nikon blue filters are available in three strengths. They filter out the red part of the light and lead to a colder rendering. The B2 blue filter has the weakest effect and is often used to "cool down" the warm look whenever the sun is standing very low. If you should use clear flashbulbs the B8 filter is needed to neutralize the red tint. By suppressing the red part of the light produced by incandescent bulbs the B12 neutralizes their colour casti on daylight-type film.

Filters for Black and White and Colour Photography

Ultraviolet Filters: UV-filters substantially absorb the ultraviolet light invisible to the human eye, and so lead to sharper and clearer black and white pictures. Thanks to its multilayer coating the L37C renders a higher transmission rate than the L39. The latter is recommended for black-and-white photography in the mountains and on the beach. Both filters can be left on the lens as a protection since they do not effect the colour rendering.

Skylight Filter L1BC: this filter also absorbs UV-light. It has a multilayer coating and renders warmer colours by preventing the bluish cast caused by invisible ultraviolet light. It can also be left on the lens as a protection.

Neutral Density Filters: ND-filters absorb all colours equally and so reduce the amount of light that reaches the film. They have no effect on the colour balance. Their varying densities can help achieve a slower shutter speed or a larger aperture. Nikon offers four different ND-filters. They can be used to control the exposure in connection with lenses with fixed apertures, for example, or when the exposure meter's working range is exceeded.

Soft-Focus Filters: these filters are only available with a 52 mm thread. Their softening effect is especially ideal for portraiture or pictures of blossoms. Nikon soft-focus filters come in two strengths. The filter No. 2 will allow you to create a "foggy" effect in your landscape photographs. Both filters allow autofocus operation.

Polarizing Filters: in order to prevent focusing errors or difficulties the Nikon F4 should only be used with circular polarizing filters, as linear polarizing filters may interfere with the operation of the AF-system . Both filters can reduce reflections from non-metallic surfaces and can thus increase colour saturation. Reflections from glass windows or water surfaces can be suppressed. The filtering effect can be increased or reduced and controlled in the viewfinder by rotating them in their mounts. Nikon offers both linear and circular polarizing filters. The former are cheaper.

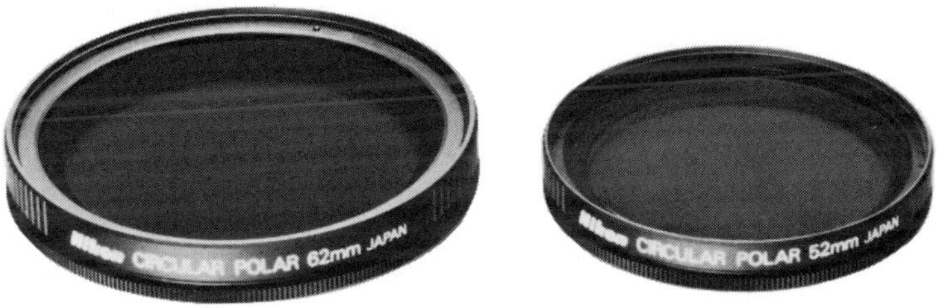

Gelatine Filter Holders: in order to employ Kodak Wratten gelatine filters with the F4, Nikon offers the filter holders AF-1 and AF-2. The AF-1 can be screwed onto lenses with a 52 mm filter thread, whereas the AF-2 is meant for lenses with 72 mm threads. The adapter-ring 72-62 UR-1 allows the use of the AF-2 on lenses with 62 mm filter threads.

Filter Cases: up to six filters with 52 mm threads fit into the convenient filter case CA-1, especially handy outdoors. The filter case CA-2 is meant for 39 mm filters, which are mainly used in the slip-in filter holders in telephoto lenses.

Care and Servicing

The Nikon F4 is a very strong construction since it is a camera designed through and through for tough everyday professional use. But, at the same time, it is also an ultramodern high-tech product which will not allow any servicing at the hands of the photographer. So, in case of any malfunctioning it is absolutely necessary to take it to a Nikon service centre. If the camera is employed professionally, putting it to special strains and demands, a regular maintenance is recommended.

Coping with the Cold: fresh batteries are essential when you have to work in the cold. The F4 works perfect down to temperatures of –20° C. Carry the camera underneath your coat to keep it warm and thus ensure flawless operation. The camera should only be exposed to such environmental conditions when you actually work with it. Many photographers have a so-called "pocket oven" in their gadget bag in order to keep their equipment at a normal temperature. Whenever the equipment is suddenly exposed to much lower temperatures the viewfinder and the lens may cloud up temporarily.

Tropical Conditions: heat and humidity can damage your equipment. The best protection in tropical conditions is to store it in an air-tight case. Put some silica-gel bags in the case, too, in order to absorb the existing humidity. Every once and a while this silica-gel should be dried in an oven in order to preserve its effect.

Heat: you shoud never expose the Nikon F4 to extreme heat. Keep in mind, that the temperatures inside a car can reach far more than 50° C very quickly. This could lead to a temporary "black out" of the LCDs in the viewfinder and also effect your film material. So, never leave your equipment standing in the blazing sun, regardless of whether it is in your gadget-bag or your car.

Dust and Sand: even though all the buttons, dials and levers of the F4 are O-ringed, in dusty areas or in wind-blown sand such as on the beach, in a desert, or on a safari you should only take the camera from its case when you really intend to shoot.

Handling Heavy Telephoto Lenses: the Nikon F4's bayonet is subjected to extreme strain whenever you mount a heave telephoto lens. The bayonet is made of a special high-quality alloy, manufactured extremely accurately, and adjusted to be perfectly parallel to the film plane. Strong levering forces or bumps caused especially by long and heavylenses can lead to the bayonet surface becoming misaligned. That is why you should never carry your equipment by the camera alone but always support the lens too if possible. Most of the longer telephoto lenses have a collar to mount the combination on a tripod. They also have eyelets to fasten a neck-strap.

Some Things to Keep in Mind

The ultra-thin shutter curtains are especially vulnerable to mechanical damage. They should never be touched, not with your fingers and not with the film leader. The reflex-mirror, the focusing-screen and the DX-contacts should also not be touched. Dust is best removed with a blower-brush. In case of any malfunction, check the batteries first; are they OK or exhausted, and are they inserted properly? You can clean the eyepiece with a piece of soft cotton cloth that has been washed several times. Do not use alcohol.

We recommend a cotton bud that has been moistened with alcohol to remove smudges from the surface of a lens. Carefully wipe the surface in widening spirals from the centre to the edges. Be careful not to leave traces.

Be extremly careful when you use spray gun-type blowers as they can damage the glass surface, especially when ED-glass is used for a front lens element. Keep the blower at least 30 cm from the lens and do not concentrate on one spot.

Never lubricate the camera with any kind of oil or grease. Remove the batteries if you intend to leave the camera unused for a longer period of time. Leaking batteries can damage your camera. If this has happened take the camera to an authorized service station to clean the battery compartments. Never attempt to repair anything yourself.

The best way to store your camera is inside a plastic bag together with a couple of packets of silica-gel in a cool and dry place. The camera should not be stored in a leather case as the leather can deteriorate in a closed bag. Whenever you send your camera to be repaired include as complete as possible description of how and when the defect occured. This makes it very much easier for the technicians to find the flaw and helps keep the costs down. In case of faulty exposures include the lens used, since it may be the automatic aperture at fault. If your equipment is still under warranty be sure to enclose the guarantee cards. Defects caused by misuse are not within the warranty. Defects should be repaired as soon as possible after they occur. Keep the original packaging for the lenses and camera as they are ideal for shipment purposes. But pack them in another outer package for protection during transit. You should also insure the valuable contents against loss or damage in the mail.

Nikon AF lenses						
Lens	Groups/ elements	Angle of view	Filter thread (mm)	Lens hood	Weight (g)	Diam x length (mm)
Zoom						
3,3 – 4,5/ 24 – 50 mm	9/9	84 – 46°	62	HB-3	375	70,5 × 73,5
3,5 – 4,5/ 28 – 85 mm	11/15	74 – 28°	62	HB-1	540	71 × 89
2,8/ 35 – 70 mm	12/15	62 – 34°	62	HB-1	665	72 × 95
3,3 – 4,5/ 35 – 70mm	7/8	62 – 34°	52	HN-2	275	70,5 × 61
3,5 – 4,5/ 35 – 105 mm	12/16	62 – 32°	52	HB-2	460	69 × 87
3,5 – 4,5/ 35 – 135 mm	12/15	62 – 18°	62	HB-1	630	72 × 109
4,0 – 5,6/ 70 – 210 mm	12/9	34 – 11°	62	HN-24	590	73,5 × 108
ED 2,8/ 80 – 200 mm	11/16	30 – 12°	77	HN-28	1200	85,5 × 176,5
Wide-angle						
2,8/24 mm	9/9	84°	52	HN-1	260	65 × 46
2,8/28 mm	5/5	74°	52	HN-2	195	65 × 39
Telephoto						
1,8/85 mm	6/6	28° 30'	62	HN-23	415	71 × 58,5
2,8/180 mm IF-ED	6/8	13° 40'	72	integrated	750	78,5 × 144
2,8/300 mm IF-ED	6/8	8° 10'	39	integrated	2700	133 × 255
4/300 mm IF-ED	6/8	8° 10'	39	integrated	1330	89 × 211
Standard						
1,4/50 mm	6/7	46°	52	HR-2	255	65 × 42
1,8/50 mm	5/6	46°	52	HR-2	210	65 × 39
Special						
Micro 2,8/55 mm	5/6	43°	62	—	420	74 × 74
AF Tele-converter TC-16A	5/5	—	—	—	150	69 × 30

Notes

Conventional Nikon lenses and their compatibility for AF function with the F4								
Lens	**Focusing**		**Exposure mode**				**metering method**	
	AF	M/E	P	S	A	M	MM	MI
Zoom lenses								
3,5–4,5/28–85 mm		●			●	●		●
3,3–4,5/35–70 mm		●			●	●		●
3,5/35–70 mm		●			●	●		●
3,5–4,5/35–105 mm		●			●	●		●
3,5–4,5/35–135 mm		●			●	●		●
3,5–4,5/35–200 mm		●			●	●		●
4/80–200 mm		●			●	●		●
4,5/50–300 mm ED		●			●	●		●
5,6/100–300 mm		●			●	●		●
4/200 – 400 mm ED		●			●	●		●
8/180 – 600 mm ED					●	●		●
Wide-angle lenses								
5,6/13 mm		●			●	●		●
3,5/15 mm	①	●			●	●		●
3,5/18 mm	①	●			●	●		●
2,8/20 mm	①	●			●	●		●
2/24 mm	①	●			●	●		●
2,8/24 mm	①	●			●	●		●
2/28 mm	①	●			●	●		●
2,8/28 mm	①	●			●	●		●
1,4/35 mm	①	●			●	●		●
2/35 mm	①	●			●	●		●
2,8/35 mm	①	●			●	●		●
Standard lenses								
1,2/50 mm	①	●			●	●		●
1,4/50 mm	①	●			●	●		●
1,8/50 mm	①	●			●	●		●
Telephoto lenses								
AF 2,8/80 mm	①	●			●	●		●
1,4/85 mm	①	●			●	●		●
2/85 mm	①	●			●	●		●
1,8/105 mm	①	●			●	●		●
2,5/105 mm	①	●			●	●		●
2/135 mm	①	●			●	●		●
2,8/135 mm	①	●			●	●		●
2,8/180 mm ED	①	●			●	●		●
2/200 mm IF-ED	①	●			●	●		●
AF 3,5/200 mm IF-ED	①	●			●	●		●
4/200 mm		●			●	●		●
2/300 mm IF-ED	①	●			●	●		●
2,8/300 mm IF-ED	①	●			●	●		●

Conventional Nikon lenses and their compatibility for AF function with the F4

Lens	Focusing		Exposure mode				metering method	
	AF	M/E	P	S	A	M	MM	MI
4,5/300 mm		●			●	●		●
4,5/300 mm IF-ED		●			●	●		●
2,8/400 mm IF-ED		●			●	●		●
3,5/400 mm IF-ED		●			●	●		●
5,6/400 mm IF-ED		●			●	●		●
4/500 mm IF-ED P		●	●	●	●	●	●	●
4/600 mm IF-ED		●			●	●		●
5,6/600 mm IF-ED		●			●	●		●
5,6/800 mm IF-ED		●			●	●		●
8/800 mm IF-ED					●	●		●
11/1200 mm IF-ED					●	●		●
Mirror lenses								
8/500 mm					②	②		●
11/1000 mm					②	②		●
11/2000 mm					②	②		●
Fisheye lenses								
2,8/6 mm	①	●			●	●		●
2,8/8 mm	①	●			●	●		●
2,8/16 mm	①	●			●	●		●
Special lenses								
PC 3,5/28 mm		③			④	④		●
PC 2,8/35 mm		③			④	④		●
Micro 2,8/55 mm	①	●			●	●		●
Noct 1,2/58 mm	①	●			●	●		●
Micro 2,8/105 mm	①	●			●	●		●
Micro 4/200 mm IF		●			●	●		●
Medical 4/120 mm		●				⑤		●
UV 4,5/105 mm		●			●	●		●
Series E lenses								
2,8/28 mm	①	●			●	●		●
2,8/135 mm	①	●			●	●		●

Key:

AF	Autofocus
M/E	Manual/electronic focus-assist
P	Program mode
S	Shutter speed priority
A	Aperture priority
M	Manual
MM	Matrix metering system
MI	Centre-weighted integral metering

① with AF Teleconverter TC-16A
② Aperture cannot be preselected
③ unless the PC Nikkor lenses are shifted from the optical axis
④ Exposure is determined by preselection of aperture
⑤ with shutter speed preselection of 1/125 or longer, flash required.

Nomenclature of the F4

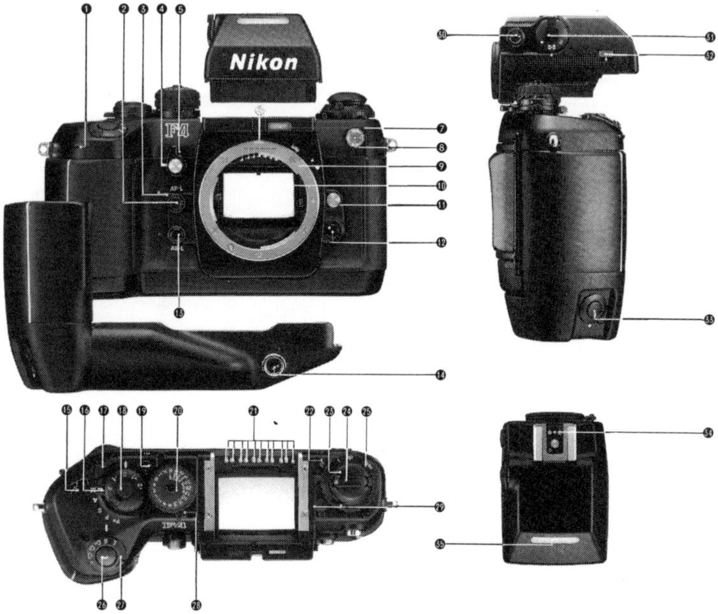

1 Self-timer indicator LED
2 AF-L button
3 AF-L/AE-L simultaneous lock lever
4 Depth-of-field preview button
5 Mirror lockup lever
6 CPU contacts
7 LCD illumination window (body side)
8 Sync terminal
9 Meter coupling lever
10 Reflex mirror
11 Lens release button
12 Focus mode selector
13 AE-L button
14 Remote terminal
15 Frame counter
16 Exposure mode selector
17 Multiple exposure button
18 Exposure compensation dial
19 Film rewind lever (R1)
20 Shutter speed dial
21 Finder contacts
22 Alert LED
23 Film rewind knob
24 Film rewind crank
25 Film speed dial
26 Shutter release button
27 Film advance mode selector
28 Viewfinder illuminator switch
29 Finder release lever
30 Dioptre adjustment knob
31 Metering system selector
32 Compensation value scale window
33 MB-21's shutter release button

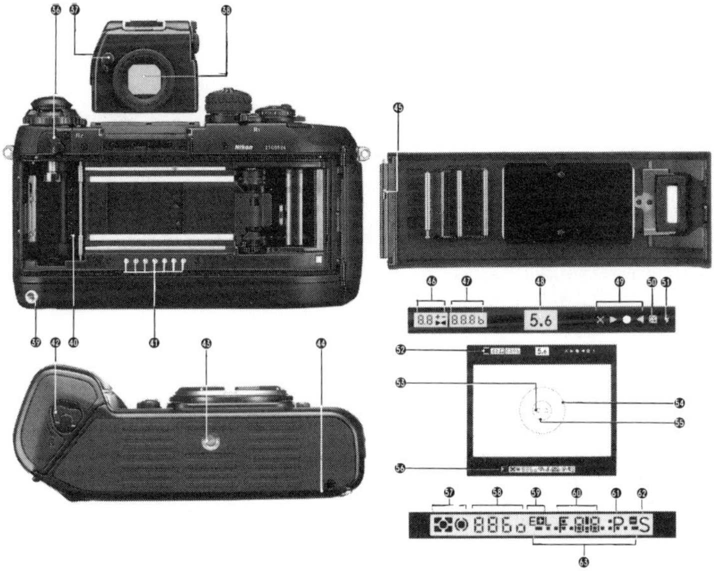

34 Accessory shoe
35 LCD illumination window (finder side)
36 Film rewind lever (R2)
37 Eyepiece shutter lever
38 Viewfinder eyepiece
39 Release terminal
40 DX contacts
41 Data back contacts
42 Release lever
43 Tripod socket
44 Guide hole
45 Camera back release
46 Exposure compensation value
47 Frame counter
48 ADR (aperture direct readout)
49 Focus indicators
50 Exposure compensation signal
51 Flash ready-light signal
52 Body side display
53 Focus brackets
54 12mm Ø reference circle
55 5mm Ø reference circle
56 Finder side display
57 Metering system
58 Shutter speed
59 AE-lock indicator
60 Aperture (P/S)
A (A)
No indication (M)
61 P (P)
No indication (S/A/M/)
62 S (S)
No indication (P/A/M)
65 Electronic analog display (M)
No indication (P/S/A)

Index